'A vitally important, powerful, and painful family story . . . I was gripped as *Inge's War* revealed secrets within secrets, and exposed the dark realities of ordinary people's wartime lives to the light'
– Suzannah Lipscomb

'O'Donnell beautifully weaves together her family history with themes of love, guilt and betrayal'
– Jack Fairweather, bestselling author of Costa-prize winning *The Volunteer*

'Fabulous'
– John Crace

'I can't recommend this book highly enough ... a beautifully told story of tragedy and hope'
– Ed Balls

'A superbly nuanced reclamation of history and family secrets ... a timely reminder that a nation's politics and people are not one and the same ... and that women, across ages and cultures, have silently borne the brunt of war in ways we are only beginning to reckon with'
– Brian Van Reet, author of *Spoils*

'A saga filled with love and betrayal and secrets … O'Donnell has recorded this story so meticulously and beautifully that it will remain forever in our consciousness'
– David Grann, *New York Times* bestselling author of *Killers of the Flower Moon* and *The Lost City of Z*

'This exceptional account transforms a private tragedy into a universal story of war and survival'
– *Publisher's Weekly* Starred Review

'This compelling testimonial details the deprivations German citizens faced during the war and reveals a dark part of Danish history. The perspective is enlightening and the accounts of sexual abuse are timely to the continuing Me Too discourse. This memoir deserves a wide audience'
– *Booklist* Starred Review

'With *Inge's War*, O'Donnell has created a story that reads like a novel filled with fascinating history and excellent detective work'
– *BookPage*

'A stunning read that offers a rare insight into what it was like to be an ordinary German citizen during the war'
– Natasha Harding, *Sun*

'First love betrayed, chaos and flight, and sexual violence, shame and despair. … It is a moving story, sensitively told'
– Guy Chazan, *Financial Times*

INGE'S WAR

A Story of Family, Secrets and Survival Under Hitler

Svenja O'Donnell

EBURY
PRESS

1

Ebury Press, an imprint of Ebury Publishing
20 Vauxhall Bridge Road
London SW1V 2SA

Ebury Press is part of the Penguin Random House Group of companies whose
addresses can be found at global.penguinrandomhouse.com

Penguin
Random House
UK

First published by Ebury Press in 2020
This edition published by Ebury Press in 2021

Maps © Emily Faccini 2020

Lines from *Einem Alten Architekten in Rom* by Josef Brodsky appear in
the author's own translation

www.penguin.co.uk

A CIP catalogue record for this book is available from the British Library

ISBN 9781529105476

Typeset in 12/16.75 pt Garamond Classico
by Integra Software Services Pvt. Ltd, Pondicherry

Printed and bound in Italy by Grafica Veneta S.p.A.

The authorised representative in the EEA is Penguin Random House Ireland,
Morrison Chambers, 32 Nassau Street, Dublin D02 YH68

To my mother, Beatrice. This is also her story.

And why shouldn't a bird be called
a Caucasus, a Rome, a Königsberg?
When all around us there are only bricks
and broken stones; no objects, only words.
And yet – no lips. Only the sound of twittering.

Joseph Brodsky, *Einem Alten Architekten in Rom*

CONTENTS

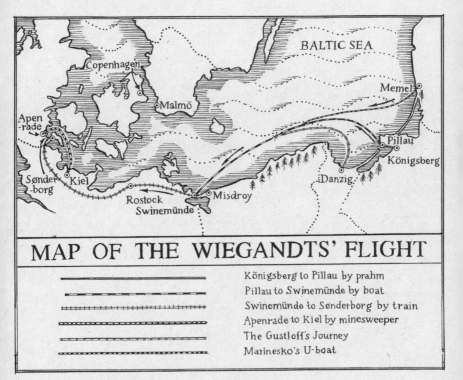

MAP OF THE WIEGANDTS' FLIGHT

Königsberg to Pillau by prahm
Pillau to Swinemünde by boat
Swinemünde to Sønderborg by train
Apenrade to Kiel by minesweeper
The Gustloff's Journey
Marinesko's U-boat

LIST OF ILLUSTRATIONS

Königsberg, June 1932

Albert Wiegandt folded his newspaper in half, obscuring the front-page headline: SEVEN INJURED IN KÖNIGSBERG STREET FIGHTS. Stacking it into a neat pile with his papers, he locked everything in his desk. Every Friday without fail, he left the office early, at 3.30 p.m., to take his daughter, Inge, for a hot chocolate at the Cafe Berlin. The small, blue-fronted establishment near Königsberg's Paradeplatz, busy with tourists in summer and students from the nearby Albertina University the rest of the year, was rather unprepossessing at first glance. It had simple wooden chairs and tables, and none of the plush leather upholstery of the old town's most fashionable restaurants. The cafe's success lay in its reputation for serving the best hot chocolate in the old town. It was so thick your spoon would almost stand up on its own when you tried to stir it, and was served in large white porcelain cups that smelt of cinnamon and cocoa, topped with rich whipped cream, with a pot of milk to thin it on the side.

Those Friday afternoons were a favourite ritual of theirs. Albert had first taken Inge to the cafe when she was five, as a special treat, to allow his wife Frieda an hour's undisturbed practice at the piano; a grateful Frieda, whose playing had suffered a little from the demands of motherhood, had encouraged the habit ever since. He and Inge would sit together and he would tell her about the latest happenings in the wine and spirits trade, which restaurant had placed the biggest order and who was making the best schnapps.

Inge would tell him about her week at school, which lessons she'd enjoyed the most, which girls were in trouble with the teacher and which tricks they had played on each other; he would laugh heartily over every scrape and commiserate over the small trials of a schoolgirl's life.

Inge was born in July 1924, two years after her parents' marriage, and had come to them almost as a miracle, as Albert and Frieda had met and fallen in love late in life. Albert was forty-five and Frieda thirty-nine at the time of Inge's birth. She was now eight years old, a pretty, blue-eyed girl with thick, dark curls, a quick smile and a vivacious manner. She was an only child and, though charming, could be demanding too. Her parents, and sometimes even the other inhabitants of their block of flats, indulged her more than they ought.

Albert took off his jacket as he made his way to the Altstadt where they lived, in Königsberg's very centre, to collect his daughter. It was a warm afternoon, presaging the intense heat that often descended on the city at the height of summer. A farmer's son from Grünwalde, some 150 kilometres east of Königsberg, as a young man Albert had turned his back on a life spent working the land, with its harsh winters and isolation, to make his name as a merchant. He loved the city with the zeal of a convert; it held the refinement, the bustle and the success he had been denied in childhood, which he relished. With his attractive, cultured, musical wife and his little daughter, he had achieved everything he'd ever wanted, but he had been somewhat troubled of late.

As he walked, he thought again about the article that he had read that morning in Königsberg's liberal newspaper, the *Königsberger Allgemeine Zeitung*, about the clashes between local communists and the Sturmabteilung, the paramilitary group led by the NSDAP, the new Nazi Party which was growing in popularity all over

Germany. It had reported terrible beatings: a young man of twenty-three lay close to death. It was the latest in a series of incidents that had plagued Königsberg in recent months.

Albert had previously dismissed clashes between Nazis and communists as something that happened in the distant capital, Berlin. But their increasing frequency in Königsberg was starting to bring the violence and agitation of Germany's new political era uncomfortably close to home. Politically, Albert was a centrist, a soft conservative with liberal leanings, who disliked violence and only bothered about politics if they affected his business as an importer of fine wines and spirits, or his more recent venture, a schnapps factory. He had joined the trade after returning wounded from service as a soldier in the First World War, before a legacy from his father helped him set up on his own. Business had been tough to start with; the aftermath of the war had brought great poverty, and it was some time before luxury goods such as wine and fine spirits flourished as they had before the war. Germans who had endured wartime starvation found they fared little better in peacetime, as punitive reparations crippled Germany's economy, bringing persistent food shortages and hyper-inflation.

In spite of all these difficulties, Albert had persisted, and his hard work had paid off. His business provided him with a comfortable income, and he dearly loved his family. But things were changing; his social circle included a number of Jewish friends, and he was not blind to the Nazi Party's violent anti-Semitism, the attacks of its Brownshirt gangs, or its alarmingly populist rhetoric. His wife's uncle, a professor of botany at Albertina University, whose judgement he respected, had convinced him early on that the Nazis were criminals and thugs. Anti-Semitism had been on the rise throughout the 1920s, fuelled by the harsh economic climate, but the waves of attacks on the Jewish community always eventually subsided.

3

Albert did not know that only a few weeks later Nazi gangs would turn Königsberg's streets into a bloodbath, in a series of murders and attacks they styled as a revolt against 'communist terror'. The federal elections of 31 July 1932 would unleash a wave of terror in which Nazi activists killed twenty-five people, including the editor-in-chief of the socialist newspaper *Königsberger Volkszeitung*.

Even after that violent summer, Albert told himself that the Nazi gangs' violence against Jewish businesses, and their rising popularity, was just a temporary blip. He did not go as far as some of his acquaintances, who held the view that giving the Nazis a brief taste of power might help restore order by quieting the threat from Polish nationalism in the west, and Communism in the east. He simply hoped that the popularity of this new and violent party would die down and his life could carry on undisturbed.

Thomas Mann, writing for the *Berliner Tageblatt* newspaper in early August 1932 from his holiday home in Nidden, a hundred kilometres northeast of Königsberg, hoped the violence that hit the city in the first week of that month would finally open the eyes of its intelligentsia.

Will the bloody days of pillage in Königsberg make the adorers of this emotional movement that calls itself National Socialism – even the pastors, professors, lecturers, and literary figures who follow it while chattering – finally open their eyes to the true nature of this national disease, this jumble of hysteria and musty romanticism, and its mega-phone-Germandom, which is the caricature and degradation of everything that is German?[1]

Mann would ultimately be disappointed. Königsberg's middle class, Albert included, chose apathy over protest, a decision that would have devastating consequences.

But all this was yet to come, and as he walked home to pick up his daughter on that hot June afternoon, Albert tried to put all thoughts of politics out of his mind. At five minutes to four, punctual as ever, he reached the front door of his building, a tall, five-storey residential block of white stone built in the early nineteenth century to accommodate Königsberg's growing middle class. He rang the doorbell and waited. Inge was a little slower to come down than usual. When she finally appeared a few minutes later, it was no laughing child that greeted him at the front door, but a dejected little girl whose eyes were red from crying. She was silent as she took his hand and walked with him to the Cafe Berlin. She sat at the table, eyes downcast, barely touching her cup of chocolate. Neither the extra whipped cream he had asked for, nor the suggestion they go and buy marzipan from the bakery to take on their picnic in the woods the next afternoon, succeeded in lifting her spirits.

Albert hated to see his daughter upset and he grew concerned, for he knew how much Inge loved these country outings. The Wiegandts would drive to his brother's farm once a month. In the winter, they took long sleigh rides over the snowy fields, snuggled together in the back seat and wrapped in furs to guard against the sharp cold; in the autumn, they picked wild mushrooms and berries, rambling for hours in the vast woods nearby. But it was their summer picnics, when the woods and meadows were full of wild flowers, that his daughter loved the most. Albert had expected the mention of the next day's outing, accompanied by the promise of marzipan, which Frieda only allowed her occasionally, to bring her out of what he had at first thought must be a sulk.

'What is troubling you, Ingechen?' he asked.

*

The calamity that had robbed Inge of all enjoyment of her Friday treat had taken place shortly after Frieda had walked her to school that morning. Her best friend Lotte had been waiting for her at the gate, and whispered in her ear a name that promised trouble: 'Greta.' Blonde where Inge was dark, with large brown eyes to Inge's slanted blue ones, Greta was, apart from Inge herself, the most popular girl in school, and her nemesis. The rivalry between Inge Wiegandt and Greta Schwartz was played out through small acts of attrition in the schoolgirls' daily lives. One week, Greta would walk through the school gates with her long plaits swinging, wearing a new frock with a French lace collar. The next, Inge, shaking her loose curls in defiance, would come tripping into class in a pair of new buttoned soft leather boots from Prague.

For the past few days, talk in the small girl's school had focused on the annual party to be held the coming Monday. The girls were to bring in a bouquet of their favourite flowers to mark the last week of the summer term, a festive gesture that soon turned into a popularity contest. Inge knew all eyes would be on her and Greta and that, despite the new dress her mother had bought her, her success would rest on the bouquet. She had planned hers weeks ahead. Albert had taken her to the florist near the Oberteich gardens, which was one of the best and most expensive in town. They had ordered a bunch of pink roses and sweet peas framed with ferns. The shop had promised to make it up with the freshest flowers and deliver it to the Wiegandts' home first thing on Monday morning, in time for the start of the school day.

But that morning, Lotte whispered in her ear: 'Greta said her parents had a special crown of flowers made for her, and she's going to wear it.'

By the mid-morning break, the news was all over the school. Greta would upstage Inge, and her triumph was assured.

Inge sobbed as she related this to Albert that afternoon. He listened, his expression grave, though his eyes twinkled with amusement. He waited until Inge finished her story, glanced at his watch, and stood up to beckon the waiter over. The anxiety caused by this morning's newspaper report was all but forgotten; this crisis, he could resolve.

'We must do something, and quickly,' he said, throwing down some coins beside his half-full cup and grabbing his daughter by the hand. 'If we hurry, we will get to the florist just before it closes.' Together, they almost ran in the direction of the Oberteich gardens.

It was a triumphant Inge who walked into school on Monday morning, accompanied by Frieda and Albert, a crown of pink roses and white hot-house hydrangeas on her head. Lotte came to stand beside her and the whole class watched, holding their breath as Greta made her entrance, her crown of white roses and pink lupins visibly the smaller of the two. She stopped beside Inge and stared, before plucking a fat hydrangea from Inge's crown and crushing it under her toe. Within seconds, the little girls had set upon each other, cheered on by a delighted mob of schoolgirls. When their horrified parents and teachers finally prised them apart, broken stems and wrenched-off petals were all that was left of the two flower crowns.

Years later, on board the ship that was taking him away from his homeland for ever, Albert remembered the sight of the crushed flowers, the ugly, senseless destruction of something beautiful.

London, August 2019

A secret lay at my family's heart, unspoken, undisturbed, unsuspected, for decades. I never set out purposefully to unearth it; I was in the middle of my journey before I knew it had even begun. It was a search for the truth that would take me across Europe, through past and through present, leading me to question the facts I had grown up with and that made me who I was. It started innocently enough, one afternoon in April 2006, with a simple phone call.

I had taken a trip to Kaliningrad on a bit of a whim, just a few months into my posting as a correspondent in Russia. Keen to explore the country and having only ever seen Moscow and St Petersburg, the city of my mother's birth had seemed a good place to start. I was the first of my family to return to Kaliningrad since my grandmother had left it more than sixty years before, when it was known as Königsberg. I had learnt a few things about my family's life there, and how they came to leave it, at intervals throughout my childhood. My grandmother had fled Königbserg to escape the Russian advance at the end of the war, her elderly parents in tow and my toddler mother in her arms. The details of the story, as related by my mother, who had been too young to remember events first-hand, were sketchy. She told us her family was East Prussian, but I had little understanding of what that actually meant. It was a place that no longer existed, a name unfamiliar to my generation, even to those friends who had grown up in Germany. As collective memories of the past go, this one had been all but lost; within the greater tragedy of the Second World War and the horrors of the Holocaust, there had been no room for stories of the hardships of those Germans not singled out by the Nazis for persecution. Of their life in Königsberg, I knew very little, save that my family had been given two hours to leave, had lost everything they owned, and had never returned. I was told of a ship they had fled on, with very few details of how they had got there, or when. It became part of our family mythology, an escape steeped in mystery, of which my grandmother never spoke.

Viewed on a map, Kaliningrad is an anomaly, a small patch of land facing the Baltic Sea, sandwiched between the vastnesses of Lithuania and Poland. In technical terms, it is an exclave, since it shares no land border with Russia and is fronted by the sea; in geographic terms, you could say it is to Russia as Alaska is to the US. For several centuries, it was a part of Germany, until it was captured by Soviet forces in 1945 and formally annexed to the USSR through the Potsdam Agreement that summer. The few articles I had found about it focused on the period that followed the fall of the Iron Curtain. The subsequent decades brought heavy job losses and, after the fall of Communism, Kaliningrad became a hub of drugs and human trafficking, with a rampant heroin problem and the highest rate of HIV in Europe. In the years just prior to my arrival, the early 2000s, it benefited from an economic boom, but it still felt like a place in flux, headed for an uncertain future.

I had set out from Moscow with vague expectations. My colleagues had tried to warn me. Kaliningrad, they told me, was an ex-Soviet military outpost. No one, absolutely no one, they claimed, ever went there for a holiday. I dismissed these warnings as typical Russian cynicism. I pictured old buildings of faded prettiness, the kind that gently fell apart at the seams, with perhaps a glimpse of forests in the background. I had been to St Petersburg two weeks before and imagined Kaliningrad to be a smaller version; another city built on a river, on the banks of which buildings of classical proportions faced each other. I imagined broad avenues with rows of plane trees and ancient oaks. I had read somewhere that in early spring, the region, once called East Prussia, was full of nesting storks.

The train station was a nineteenth-century German red-brick building with a large archway, which had survived the city's tumultuous past and had been given a revamp a couple of years before. The shiny floors and large brass chandelier of the main entrance were typical of the Gothic grandeur of Russian public buildings, of which I had grown rather fond. The style rather suited the old columned window the entrance had retained, stretching almost from floor to ceiling, reflecting the light of the morning in the brass and the glow of the chandelier's electric candles.

Curiosity and anticipation formed a knot in my stomach, which tightened as I made my way towards the exit. Sight of the street was hidden by a portico and as I opened the glass door a gust of wind whipped across my face, the cold cutting through me like a knife. I blinked as I adjusted to the harsh light, expecting the avenues I had seen in my mind, but instead finding myself looking at a sea of concrete. There were no trees, nor even a street, just an expanse of tarmac that stretched out into a car park, before merging into a busy four-lane road. Tall concrete apartment blocks dominated the skyline, small windows dotting the facades. The din of traffic in the morning rush hour was deafening, and everything – the road, the walls, the sky, even the light – was grey. The air was filled with the smell of car fumes and the sound of their horns beat a deafening drumroll as I walked towards the river, where my slim and somewhat unprepossessing guidebook told me the old city lay.

If the guidebook was any indication, Kaliningrad's attractions were sparse. It focused almost exclusively on the tomb of Immanuel Kant, an unremarkable red stone mausoleum, and the neighbouring cathedral, which had been a burnt-out shell until its reconstruction in the 1990s. I started walking along a road as wide and busy as a motorway, feeling my hands go numb as I held the strap of my bag across my shoulder. I had forgotten my gloves.

I stopped when I reached Kaliningrad's historical centre, along the Pregolya River, known in German days as the Pregel, past a waterfront fringed by construction sites. It was a misty day, and every minute the cold and damp reminded me that early spring in Eastern Europe still felt very much like winter. The riverbank before me held all the charm one could expect of a former Soviet nuclear base. Needless to say, this was not the scenic pilgrimage that I had hoped for.

Little was left of the thriving German university town once known as Königsberg, birthplace of Kant and capital of East Prussia, a kingdom founded by the Teutonic Knights in the thirteenth century that would later become a part of Germany. East Prussia, taking the brunt of retribution for Nazism's crimes, suffered the most tragic fate of Germany's eastern territories. All its German inhabitants, the region's vast majority, fled, died or were deported. East Prussia's population, which had stood at 2.2 million in 1940 was reduced to 193,000 at the end of May 1945.[2] Those who survived were used largely as slave labour, before being deported to Soviet-controlled East Germany in 1947, part of a wider expulsion of Germans from Europe's East which saw 14 million people displaced. Under Soviet rule, Königsberg was stripped of what was left of its German identity. In 1946, East Prussia was divided between Lithuania, Poland and Russia, and Königsberg was renamed Kaliningrad in honour of Soviet leader Mikhail Kalinin. Purged of its German population and largely destroyed, the city's 700 years of German culture were consigned to oblivion.

Underwhelmed and disappointed by a city that I felt ought to have moved me, I had called my grandmother to mark the occasion. We had never been close, and were not given to long conversations, let alone confidences. We saw each other once or twice a year at most on her visits to our family home in south-west France, or my occasional trips to the northern German city of Kiel, where she lived with her husband. An aloof, somewhat self-ish woman, quick in her criticisms, she had never embraced the traditional grandmother role. Her visits were always tense, reducing my usually even-tempered mother to a nervous wreck. Whenever she came, grievances followed: the cakes, which were always fresh and home-baked, were never quite as good as those she bought in Germany. She liked her tea served weak, requiring a separate teapot. She always, even in the height of summer, com-plained of the cold.

Our phone calls were usually reserved for birthdays and fol-lowed a set pattern, lasting ten minutes at most. We would discuss the weather in Kiel, which she always, come rain or shine, described as unseasonal. She would tell me who had come to her birthday party, and often did not ask about my life at all. After further small talk, laced with an implied criticism of our failure to visit her more often, she would be the first to hang up.

But that day, standing by the river in this strange place my family had come from, staring at a crane lifting large slabs of con-crete on the construction site on the opposite bank and shivering with cold, I was struck by a sense of occasion. My fingers were clumsy with cold as I dialled her number, and waited for her to answer.

'I just wanted to say hello,' I said, a little awkwardly. 'I'm in Kaliningrad.'

I waited for my grandmother to speak. She was not a sentimen-tal woman, but the dead silence with which she met my greeting took me by surprise.

I'd never known her lost for words. The silence at the other end of the line dragged on. I studied my hands; they were tinged with blue. I waited for her to say something as I stared at the opaque surface of the river, worrying that the pay-as-you-go card on my phone was about to run out.

Her voice, when she finally spoke, was unsteady.

'The circle is closing,' she said.

I realised that, for the first time since I had known her, she was crying.

This foreign and intimidating city, thousands of miles from home, had brought us closer than we'd ever been before. I didn't know how to comfort her; I had never heard her sound so vulnerable. I can't remember who resumed the conversation first, only that when she spoke again, she mentioned the names of places, old names long since forgotten: Königsberg, Rauschen, Insterburg, Cranz. I taught her the new: Kaliningrad, Svetlogorsk, Chernyakhovsk, Zelenogradsk. I wondered what in this landscape of her past, which spoke so little to my present, had triggered so much emotion in her. This brief excursion, undertaken so lightly, had left me with nothing but questions.

There were other facts about my grandmother that were hazy and never spoken about. Her husband was not my mother's biological father, though he had raised her for most of her childhood. My mother had told me this when I was thirteen; I had never suspected it until then. She told me that my grandmother had met my mother's real father when they were both very young, during the war. He was from a proud and aristocratic family; my grandmother had met his sister at finishing school and their romance had caused a huge family row. It had been a teenage love affair, ended by war. As for how and why it ended, even my mother said she wasn't entirely sure.

Ours was an open family, where no topic of conversation was discouraged; only when it came to my mother's family did a certain reticence set in. The reticence was not hers, but one I had unconsciously developed. I was a half-German, half-Irish child growing up in Paris, attending a French school. Part of the second generation to grow up in a Europe at peace, my understanding of history was shaped through classroom tales of villains and heroes. I had never really thought about the people in between. The lessons about the Second World War at school set out the horrors of Nazism and glossed over some of the shadier aspects of France under the Vichy regime – namely the collaboration – focusing instead on the French Resistance and General de Gaulle's heroism. For a long time, I only thought of Germany in the Second World War as a land of evil. My mother was of a generation that worked hard to understand the crimes perpetrated in her parents' time, and she did her best to ensure we understood the evils of anti-Semitism, that we learnt that all men and women, all religions and races, were equal. She told us, whenever my brother and I asked, that her family had not liked the Nazis. But my sense of Germanness, as a child, was never free from that taint.

On a school trip to a Second World War museum in Normandy at the age of nine, I had felt the eyes of my schoolmates on me as we entered the room dedicated to Holocaust victims. I was the only half-German child in the class: it was the first time I had felt shame because of it. In that moment, I had clung to my mother's statement, and used it to imagine my grandparents as heroic objectors. Perhaps it was the fear that what my mother had told me about her parents' antipathy to Nazism might not be true that made me reluctant to ask her for more details.

But in Kaliningrad, these questions surged up again. I wondered who that part of my family had been, what my links were to this strange and unwelcoming land. I wanted to know it all: their lives, their habits, their beliefs, their war, their flight. And, almost as if she had read my mind, my grandmother, for the first time, invited me into her past.

'I have so much to tell you,' she said.

Her comment, though brief, marked the start of a decade of discoveries. They came about through hours of conversation in which she slowly revealed herself to me. After her death in 2017, it led me across Europe's east and west, retracing old footsteps, delving through archives and family letters, finding lost relatives to help me piece together the story she had kept secret for so long. My knowledge of it remains in some parts imperfect, for memory is subjective and fragile. Sometimes I have filled in the gaps using old letters and photographs, historical facts and accounts of those who remember, but I am satisfied that I have found its truth, and will tell it as best I can. At its heart is a story of love and family, of a girl from a vanished land who lived through a time when Europe, and its humanity, collapsed.

PART I

Chapter One

A LITTLE BLACK ALBUM

There is a photograph of my grandmother, taken when she was twenty-five, which my mother first showed me when I was still a child. Dark curls tied back by a silk scarf, eyes set in a round face with high Slavic cheekbones, she was beautiful, and she knew it. Hers was a delicate prettiness that she retained throughout her life, but this picture showed something that I couldn't quite define. Though her mouth was laughing, her eyes suggested defiance, and the wariness of a woman older than her years. By then she was already a mother, had loved, lost, and fled her home and rebuilt her world from scratch. She was in search of a new beginning, an ordinary life, free of the upheavals and the trauma of the one she'd left behind. Looking at it again, knowing what I do now, I think of how the future must have seemed to her back then, still so young, having already lived through so much.

My grandmother and her husband lived in Kiel, on Germany's Baltic coast, where my mother and her sister, Conny, were raised. Since we lived in Paris, my brother and I saw them only a couple of times a year. We spoke German to them and they knew no other language. Everyone referred to them as Mutti and Vati, the German for Mum and Dad. For all the motherliness of her nickname, my grandmother kept her grandchildren at a distance. She was a woman to whom criticism came more easily than praise. My mother and she weren't particularly close. Aged eighteen, my mother had packed up her car and driven to Paris, where she had stayed for good. Kiel, she told me, was a city she had never belonged to, and whose people made her feel like a changeling. It was only much later, once I had started my search, that her words started to make sense.

I didn't see my grandmother until a few months after my trip to Kaliningrad. I had returned to Moscow full of curiosity about her emotional reaction, and what it was she wanted to tell me, but the demands of a busy journalist's life soon put it to the back of my mind. It was only when I returned home for a holiday, and decided to spend a few days visiting my grandparents in Kiel, that I remembered the strangeness of the moment we had shared, the questions it had raised. I wanted to find the answers.

I arrived at their home, a small but comfortable flat in a modern block, in time for the daily ritual of afternoon coffee. Vati, a giant of a man, greeted me with an all-enveloping hug, while my grandmother, more reticent, kissed me on the cheek in greeting. They ushered me out to the garden and into their new pride and joy, a *Gartenhaus*, a glorified shed containing a small table and four overstuffed chairs, a concession to al fresco dining in a city where the wind from the Baltic usually made it too cold to sit outdoors for very long. It stood at the bottom of a neat lawn that they shared with a neighbour, bereft of plants save for a single neatly trimmed shrub. The wood of the *Gartenhaus* was new and smelt of pine sap and fresh varnish, the blinds on its windows were painted forest green. We sat – elbows tucked in, for space was tight – and I noticed that the fabric of the chair covers, a green stripe, matched the colour of the coffee cups.

Everything about the scene was neat and predictable; nothing in it explained the emotion my grandmother had betrayed, just a few months before, when I had called her from Kaliningrad. But something between us had changed. I felt it in the squeeze of her hand when I arrived, in her delight at the Russian shawl I'd brought her: our new, indefinable, shared sense of place. A door had been opened, if only by a crack, into a past she had hitherto kept silent. Instinct told me to tread carefully, so I bided my time, and waited.

They went to bed early, leaving me alone in their living room. I unfolded the sofa bed and looked around me at the photograph albums and framed portraits, the ordinary signs of a long, shared family life: my mother and her sister on their wedding days; my brother and I receiving our university diplomas; Vati on a sailing holiday, at the helm of a boat. There were very few knick-knacks; every three years or so, my grandmother had the urge to throw things out and start anew.

I looked through the bookshelves for something to read, eventually taking up a glossy, coffee-table volume about German castles. I soon grew a little cold and, seeing the Russian shawl I had bought draped over an armchair, went to pick it up. A small black leather photograph album fell from its folds. It contained twenty pages at most and had an envelope tucked in the front. Inside was a card with a black border, an order of service from the funeral of my great-grandmother Frieda, who'd died in 1968, and a crumpled cutting from a German newspaper, dated 1995. I laid it out flat and read the headline: A NIGHT OF DEATH ON THE BALTIC SEA.

It was a commemorative piece to mark the fiftieth anniversary of the sinking of the *Wilhelm Gustloff*, a transport ship that had been torpedoed by the Red Army in January 1945. The journalist set out the facts with meticulous bleakness: the ship had carried a few soldiers, but of its 10,000 passengers most had been civilians, women and children fleeing the Soviet advance on East Prussia. It had sunk in the Baltic Sea, at the height of winter; only a few hundred survived. I had heard of this tragedy before, and knew my mother, grandmother and her parents had also fled Königsberg by sea, on another ship. Had whoever compiled the album put the article next to the notice of Frieda's death, as a reminder of her luck in having survived? I put the envelope and its contents aside and turned to the album.

INGE'S CONFIRMATION.

Its opening page was blank apart for a single inscription in green ink, '*Unsere Omi*', 'Our grandmother', written in a hand I recognised as my mother's. The first photograph took up an entire page: a portrait of a group in formal attire with an adolescent girl in a white dress, whom I recognised as my grandmother, sitting front and centre. But it was the caption that made my heart jump: 'Königsberg, April 1939', five months before the start of the war. I flicked through the rest of the photographs. There weren't many from those years, six perhaps, in black and white, much-faded snapshots of ordinary life, and a large, old-fashioned business card reading 'Alfred Wiegandt, Königsberg Pr. Spirits, Wines, Wholesale, Liquor manufacturer'. A group walking in an unfamiliar landscape of dunes, somewhere by the sea, the caption beneath identifying the place by its old Prussian name of 'Rauschen', the men in summer suits, the women in cotton dresses. Five people sitting round a dining-room table draped in tablecloths and decorated with a vase of flowers, one of whom I recognised as Frieda, smiling, in a leather armchair in the corner opposite. A picture of an old gentleman with a Kaiser Wilhelm moustache, captioned '*Onkelchen*' – Uncle. I turned another page; the date written beneath had jumped forwards to 1962.

I turned back to that first group picture. It was too formal a picture to have been a birthday; the hot-house flowers and ornaments on a display trolley, carefully framing the party, had an air of solemnity. Two young men stood at the back, looking slightly bored; another in the uniform of the Luftwaffe, the German air force, was standing next to a girl in white satin with a corsage of artificial flowers, staring into the camera. The older people looked a little drawn, my great-grandparents on either side of their daughter, Frieda in a dark dress with a ruffled white collar, Albert in white tie; I noticed that his moustache was clipped into the style made infamous by Hitler. Inge's hair was styled in heavy, old-fashioned plaits wound round her head that made her look older than her fourteen years, and she wore a dress of white gauze embroidered at the neckline. She had the gawky stance of the adolescent, her shoulders hunched, trapped in a body that was not quite a woman's, nor still a girl's. I recognised her expression from the memory of my own teenage years, one of mutinous boredom.

ALBERT WIEGANDT

Königsberg Pr.

Spirituosen - Weine - Großhandlung
Likörfabrik

ALBERT'S BUSINESS CARD.

The next morning at breakfast, my grandmother noticed the album on the coffee table. She smiled and went to sit on the sofa, picking it up, opening it at the first page, and bid me sit beside her. And she started to tell me the stories of her lost world.

It was April 1939. They had planned the party weeks in advance, but Inge already wished it was over, and there was still dinner to endure. Her mother and the dressmaker had made such a fuss over every detail of her confirmation outfit, from selecting the best white silk organdie, to picking the embroidery at the collar, but Inge thought the result old-fashioned and dowdy. She had seen the dress she really wanted in one of the fashion magazines she and her friend Lotte poured over for hours, after Lotte's older sister had finished with them. It had been part of a feature on the looks

ALBERT AND FRIEDA AT HOME.

favoured by film stars, a long, elegant design of peach satin with a sweetheart neckline, the sleeves barely covering the shoulders, the skirt draped at the hip and finishing in a long fishtail. She had cut the picture out carefully and shown it with reverential awe to Frieda, who burst out laughing.

'*Liebchen*, you are far too young for a dress like this! Besides, your confirmation is a serious occasion, not a film party.'

She'd heard the peals of laughter through the sitting-room door as Frieda recounted the incident later to her friends.

Her cheeks still burned at the memory of that laughter as she stood in church that morning, waiting for the service to end. Only the pastor made her smile, when he told her how pretty she looked.

'Not long now until you get your first ballgown!' he said, with a wink. He was a large man, whose imposing physique was tempered by a friendly and jovial manner. Her parents always spoke of him with affection and respect. Recently, though, she'd heard her father tell Frieda in hushed tones at home that the pastor would have to start being more careful. She wondered what her father had meant, but guessed it must be because of the way he had started saying his prayers during the Sunday service every week.

The Wiegandts were Lutherans, the majority faith in Königsberg, an undemanding, sober denomination that required little of them save attending church on Sundays. Unlike many others of his cloth at the time, their pastor was not shy of openly adhering to his robust Christian principles. He saw clearly through Nazism's xenophobic rhetoric and the hundreds of decrees which had restricted the public and private lives of Jewish citizens in the six years since the Nazis had been in government. He could not ignore the burning of synagogues, the smashing of Jewish businesses, the persecution of any groups singled out for not falling in with their creed. From the day Hitler gained power, the pastor's sermons had changed. He extolled the virtues of peace and tolerance as never before, his oratory becoming more impassioned as the months went by. Every service would end with him leading the congregation in the Lord's Prayer, adapting its closing line. The Wiegandts would wait for it, eyes closed, not daring to look up or at each other as the full force of the pastor's voice was directed towards any Nazi official present. He'd done it again in her confirmation service that morning, when he'd spotted her mother's second cousin in his Luftwaffe uniform, his fashionable wife on his arm.

'And deliver us from *this* evil.'

Albert's brow had furrowed when he first saw the young man. Frieda had tried to calm him down as he raised his voice, hearing him say, 'These young men think war is just a game.' Inge knew her father had fought in the last one. He still limped from a piece of shrapnel that had wounded him in the knee and caused him bouts of rheumatism. Her mother, she knew, had been a nurse on the Eastern Front, but she couldn't imagine either of them in war. The romance of it did not fit with her staid, middle-aged, respectable parents. They spoke of it very little and with horror, but to Inge the thought of war was at least an exciting one, compared with the dullness of their world. She thought her cousin looked very handsome in his pilot's uniform, and his blonde wife, in her white satin dress, just like the women she admired in magazines.

Her uncle Max, she thought, would have been able to make her father feel better by telling a joke. She felt a pang, remembering that Uncle Max was no longer there. He was not really a relation but her father's best friend, and she'd called him 'uncle' ever since she was a little girl. He ran a fashionable club in the centre of town, where Königsberg's smartest people went to drink, have dinner and dance. Every other Tuesday, Max, Albert and two other old friends would meet in a private room there to play chess and talk politics, far from eavesdroppers, late into the night. She'd asked her mother what they talked about for so long, and why Albert would often come back looking worried and agitated. 'Politics,' Frieda had said. 'They're best left alone.' Inge knew her parents did not much like Hitler, though they were very careful when they spoke of him to others; her mother had explained to her that it was dangerous to tell people, even friends, what they believed. But Max refused to keep a low profile. 'I'm not going to make that ape-like salute they tell us to do,' he said.

A year ago, her father had come home early from the club one night, his face full of worry, to tell Frieda that Max had been taken away. He sat on the sofa, with tears in his eyes and Frieda's arm round his shoulders, as he told her what the old barman had said.

The previous Saturday evening, a senior Nazi official had dined at the restaurant. He and two other men had walked up to Max and greeted him with a 'Heil Hitler!', snapping up their arms in the Nazi salute; the barman thought they'd done so deliberately – Max's opinions about the Nazis were well known.

'Herr Max, he just raised his hat, as he always did, Herr Wiegandt,' the barman said, 'and returned their greeting by saying, "Good evening, gentlemen." Nothing would have made him *Sieg Heil*, Herr Wiegandt, but you know, it's just a hand gesture, and it might have saved him!'

Early on Tuesday evening, before Albert's arrival at the club, police had come to take Max away.

'You must go to Max's wife,' Frieda said.

'Yes,' Albert had replied. 'But we must be very careful now.'

Chapter Two

A TIME OF DARKNESS

Those first glimpses into my grandmother's past piqued my curiosity. I wanted to know more about the Wiegandts, about life between the wars, and I became hungry for books about the period. I ploughed through a turgid volume on the Weimar Republic, and another on the economy of the interwar years. In a second-hand shop in Hamburg, I found a stack of women's magazines from the late 1920s. I looked through the recipes, the advice columns, the fashion advertisements.

I thought often about my grandmother's confirmation photograph. The life it portrayed reminded me of a series of books I had loved as a child, *Nesthäkchen*, by Else Ury. They tell, over ten volumes, the story of another, typically middle-class German girl, Annemarie Braun, a doctor's daughter from Berlin, from her childhood just before the First World War to an imagined future. The first book was published in 1918 and has not been out of print since 1952. I dug out my old copies, which had been stored in the attic of our family home in France, and flicked through them. I realised that I had never read volume four, set during the First World War. After a little research I found a short biography of Ury that revealed why: Ury had been a fierce patriot and her description of war in that volume was deemed too nationalistic for modern German publishers. But it was the last line, stating the place and time of her death, that made me catch my breath: Auschwitz, 1943.

It was a stark reminder that the faces that stared from the little black album had all lived through these years. What had been their thoughts, their fears, their secrets? And did I really want to know?

Inge, or Ingeborg Gertrud Wiegandt as she had been christened, was an eight-year-old schoolgirl when Adolf Hitler seized absolute power in March 1933. Only nine months had passed since her playground fight over the floral crowns, but in East Prussia, as in the rest of Germany, much had changed. The previous July, the Nazis had become the largest party in the Reichstag in federal elections that sparked a wave of terror, leaving scores of people dead. In January, President Paul von Hindenburg appointed Hitler Chancellor of Germany. By the end of March, after another election that saw his party further increase its majority, the constitution was amended to name him the country's dictator.

The speed of Hitler's ascent was astonishing, and nowhere more so than in East Prussia, where in the space of five short years the vote share of the Nazi Party rose from less than 1 per cent to the highest in the whole of the Reich, as the German state was often referred to at the time. Nothing in East Prussia's voting history could have presaged this transformation. For decades, Königsberg had been a left-leaning city; even when, after 1920, the majority of voters switched to the right-wing National People's Party (DNVP), the left-wing Social Democrats still attracted substantial support, with Nazism's populist rhetoric failing to gain significant traction. It fared no better in rural East Prussia, a land of old estates run by the so-called *Junker* families, where voters favoured conservative or traditionally nationalist parties. All this changed in 1928, with the appointment of Erich Koch, a man of fanatical zeal and ruthless political ambition, as East Prussia's Nazi *Gauleiter*, or regional party head.[1]

The rapidity with which Nazism came to dominate East Prussia's political landscape serves as a lesson in how quickly fascist ideologies become entrenched if allowed to run unchecked. It is a textbook example of how the movement seduced all of Germany. Like most extreme ideologies, Nazism preyed on weakness and fear, traits which Koch, an agile political campaigner, quickly identified in East Prussia, and learnt to use with devastating effect. The region was the most easterly of the German territories, which had long given it a special status among nationalists, who saw it as an embattled borderland. Königsberg was a melting pot of cultures, all of which were rooted in the East; Latvian, Lithuanian, Polish and Yiddish were frequently spoken in the city's streets. At the outbreak of the Second World War, 300,000 Poles were living in southern East Prussia and 50,000 Lithuanians resided in the region's east. East Prussian families like the Wiegandts tended to define their identity around very eastern markers, in Frieda and Albert's case Königsberg and the Baltic coast. Berlin was a whole day's travel away – twice as far away as Warsaw. Albert's suits were made in Prague, and he chose to import Czech wines over West German ones. Both Albert and Frieda's families had been in East Prussia for generations; they never imagined that Inge or her children would live anywhere else. Frieda's sister Gertrud had moved to Berlin after her marriage, but had died young, severing the Wiegandts' only connection to the rest of their country. For their holidays, they chose the beauty and convenience of the Baltic coast, usually in Rauschen, though Albert had once taken Frieda and Inge to Nidden, on the Lithuanian side, a couple of hours' journey farther east.

The Treaty of Versailles, the agreement by which the First World War's victors redrew the lines and debts of Europe in 1919, intensified East Prussia's isolation, by handing over the strip of land between East Prussia and western Germany to a newly independent Poland. The decision was taken largely on ethnicity grounds, as the majority of the population was Polish, and was only a small part of a treaty designed to make Germany shoulder the blame for a conflict that had brought Europe to its knees.* But it added to the region's remoteness, and brought economic problems of its own. Practically, this made journeys to the west much more difficult: German nationals travelling to and from East Prussia by road now required a transit visa, and the curtains of train carriages were drawn while crossing Poland to discourage passengers from looking out. For trade, it meant goods that had previously travelled overland now had to go by sea, pushing up both import and export costs. East Prussia was completely cut off, and this piece of land, which became known as the Danzig or Polish Corridor became both a symbol and a symptom of East Prussia's isolation.

While rural East Prussia was traditionally supportive of conservative and nationalist parties, until the immediate aftermath of the First World War Königsberg had remained an enclave of the liberal left. Things started changing in the 1920s when years of economic depression, exacerbated by East Prussia's geographical isolation, made the region a ripe target for the politics of protest. The Nazi Party initially struggled to find a strong foothold in the region. It first found favour in the rural heartlands by promising to ban farm foreclosures and to increase agricultural funding. Then, gradually, its popularity spread to Königsberg. By portraying the region as a bastion of Germanness surrounded by enemies, the Nazis proffered

---

* For nationalists advocating a return to a strong Germany, the Danzig Corridor, as this strip of land became known, gained near mythic status and its recovery became their *raison d'être*. They inflated tales of mistreatment of ethnic Germans in the newly enfranchised Poland and fanned hatred of ethnic Poles. By 1923, more than half a million Germans had left the Polish-controlled corridor.

an electoral solution to workers with nationalist leanings, for whom the traditional right-wing parties were too bourgeois. Even the middle classes started to see Nazism as a way to protest against the economic hardships that had blighted them for a decade. To born propagandists like Koch, this was a political gift.

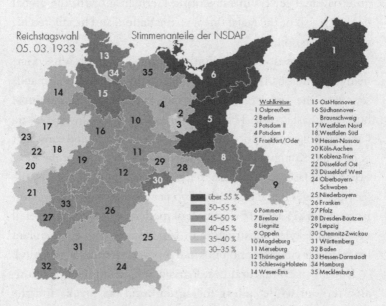

Reichstagswahl 05.03.1933

Stimmenanteile der NSDAP

über 55 %
50–55 %
45–50 %
40–45 %
35–40 %
30–35 %

Wahlkreise:
1 Ostpreußen
2 Berlin
3 Potsdam II
4 Potsdam I
5 Frankfurt/Oder
6 Pommern
7 Breslau
8 Liegnitz
9 Oppeln
10 Magdeburg
11 Merseburg
12 Thüringen
13 Schleswig-Holstein
14 Weser-Ems
15 Ost-Hannover
16 Südhannover-Braunschweig
17 Westfalen Nord
18 Westfalen Süd
19 Hessen-Nassau
20 Köln-Aachen
21 Koblenz-Trier
22 Düsseldorf Ost
23 Düsseldorf West
24 Oberbayern-Schwaben
25 Niederbayern
26 Franken
27 Pfalz
28 Dresden-Bautzen
29 Leipzig
30 Chemnitz-Zwickau
31 Württemberg
32 Baden
33 Hessen-Darmstadt
34 Hamburg
35 Mecklenburg

SHARE OF VOTES FOR THE NATIONAL SOCIALIST
GERMAN WORKER'S PARTY, MARCH 1933.

The son of a factory worker, Koch was born in Elberfeld, in Germany's Western Ruhr region in 1896. He turned to anti-communist ultra-nationalism while still a young man, after a brief flirtation with revolutionary socialism while serving as a soldier in the First World War. A fervent Nazi, he was one of National Socialism's earliest converts; he liked to boast he had been the party's ninetieth member when he joined in 1922. Upon his appointment as regional party chief, he convinced the Nazi leadership to allow him to tailor his speeches so they played on specifically East Prussian concerns. Koch surmised, correctly, that anti-Polish and anti-Bolshevik rhetoric would resonate more with the local population than generic Nazi tropes such as the role of 'international Jewry' in preventing German growth, the global banking crisis or the racial threat to the nation, and he tailored his speeches accordingly.

He also played on the region's economic fragility. While Germany as a whole had been greatly weakened by the financial demands set out by the Treaty of Versailles, import costs were an additional burden in East Prussia. The transit difficulties created by the Danzig Corridor inflated the price of raw materials, industrial and consumer goods, and Königsberg in particular soon became one of the most expensive places to live in the Reich. This was compounded by the fact that wages in the region were 70 per cent lower than the country's average. Deterred by the cost of modernisation and hampered by a feudal-style infrastructure of large estates with a dependent tenantry, agricultural conditions and practices were decades behind.

Koch focused on rural East Prussia first, whipping up nationalist fervour while calling for agricultural tax breaks and the scrapping of farm foreclosures. His strategy worked, and voters who had traditionally thrown their support behind the xenophobic, nationalist but more mainstream DNVP soon switched to the Nazis. As National Socialism's popularity surged, even a number of the *Junkers*, who had initially seen Hitler as a threat, convinced themselves he could be a useful foil to guard the region against the excesses of the Left, a position many would later come bitterly to regret.*

---

*A number of those involved in the July 1944 plot to assassinate Hitler came from *Junker* families.

Even in Königsberg the lure of Nazism proved irresistible. Here, apathy was the main culprit; while the city's intelligentsia and middle class were alarmed by Hitler's violent and populist rhetoric, they convinced themselves it was better to do nothing, lest the communists take over instead. In this, my great-grandparents Albert and Frieda were no different. They were fair-minded, enlightened people, who privately voiced their concerns about Hitler's beliefs and methods. Judging by their friendship circle and by my grandmother's recollections, neither could be described as anti-Semitic. Frieda was a strong Christian who, when a young Inge repeated the anti-Semitic slurs of her classmates, told her daughter that all were equal under God. She would tell her granddaughters about her Jewish friends from Königsberg who had managed to escape. Recounting those stories years later, when I had started my search for answers, both my mother and her sister told me they never dared ask about those who didn't.

But while they did not vote for the Nazi Party, neither did they actively protest against it. Political protest was not a feature of either Albert or Frieda's world view. Albert's business was flourishing, their life was comfortable and secure, so they chose the easier path, dismissing Hitler as a short-term hiccup that would eventually recede. Had they known how quickly the Nazis would cement their grip on power, they might, in those early days when the penalties for speaking out did not yet involve imprisonment or death, have taken more of a stand. But hindsight is a luxury, so I cannot know for sure.

With the apathy of moderates allowing it to rise unchecked, Nazism flourished. Koch's instinct had been right. In 1928, there were only eighty Nazi Party members in Königsberg and 249 in the whole of East Prussia. By March 1933, in the elections that brought Hitler his sweeping victory, the Nazi Party won 56.5 per cent of the East Prussian vote, 12.6 per cent above the national average and the highest in the whole of Germany. It was no coincidence that the three regions where the Nazis had won the highest share all bordered Poland.

This was not the Königsberg of which my grandmother spoke in the first years that followed my discovery of the little black album. Memory is deceptive when it comes to recalling the events and places of our childhood; it tells us a story of our past, idealised and distorted by the passage of time. Loss is the most powerful of these emotional lenses, endowing the places we can never return to with a magic that magnifies the good and softens the ugly.

In the conversations we shared over the six years that followed, during family holidays in France, it was a near-perfect world that my grandmother described as we sat together on the terrace. Perhaps I would have challenged her more had we seen each other more often, but our time together was always short, and I feared that questioning her too closely would interrupt the flow of her reminiscences and break the intimacy we had so recently started to share. I did not want this newly expansive woman, lost in her memories, to revert to the reserved, closed-off person she had been. So I let her lull me into a world seemingly untainted by Europe's darkest hour. I listened to her speak of the old places, about the habits and rhythms of her life as a child. The smallest thing would prompt her to start talking: a reference to her middle name, which she had always hated; a question about the street the Wiegandts lived in; the sight of a cup that looked like one her parents had once owned. Afraid to break the spell, all I did for a time was to listen.

ALBERT BY THE RIVER PREGEL.

She spoke of a land of kindness and plenty, security and laughter. She told me the story of the monkey Albert had bought for Frieda as a pet, who had grown so jealous of Inge that he had to be given away to a friend. She described the city squares that were filled with baskets of flowers in summer, and the skating parties held on the frozen River Pregel as soon as the ice was thick enough in winter. Her stories had an almost fairy-tale quality, free of any shades of grey. They were glimpses into a life of privilege and affection in a country she loved. And I did indeed find much light-heartedness in the old pictures of that small black album, in the walking party by the dunes, in the laughing faces that sat at the Wiegandts' dining-room table. My mother had often spoken of Frieda as a woman who radiated goodness, and her memories of

Albert were of a kind and affectionate man. I read these qualities in the faces I now looked at, Albert's stout and comfortable, kind-eyed Frieda with a motherly smile on her lips. But every time I looked through the album, I also saw the stare of the cousin in his Luftwaffe uniform. It was a reminder of what these stories obscured: that the Königsberg my grandmother recounted had also been, for a large part of her childhood, a place of violence and fear.

For Königsberg's Jews, life would never be the same after the Nazis came to power in 1933, when, according to a June census, 3,170 Jews still lived in the city. Koch, who was named East Prussia's *Oberpräsident* soon after the Nazis' electoral victory, soon set about putting his mark on the region, with almost immediate effect. He combined being one of the few openly practising Christians in his party with becoming one of Hitler's cruellest administrators; though he'd been happy to put anti-Jewish rhetoric aside for immediate political gain, he was a virulent anti-Semite. Once he had power, he turned his attention to the persecution of East Prussia's Jews, starting with Königsberg's sizeable Jewish population. For them, life changed fast. Anti-Jewish propaganda soon dominated newsreels, film previews in the cinema and radio announcements. Before long, anti-Semitism was codified into the laws that governed everyday life in the Reich. It started in 1933, with the burning of books by Jewish or anti-Nazi authors. By 1935, the Nuremberg Laws stripped Germans who met the Nazi criteria of 'Jewishness' – three or more Jewish grandparents – of the right to vote and forbade mixed marriages; those with fewer Jewish forebears were defined as *Mischlings*, and the law was also expanded to include those of Romani descent and black citizens. By 1936, Jews were banned from parks, swimming pools and restaurants, and two years later from theatres, concert halls and exhibitions. Many Jewish students were removed from school and universities before being formally banned from mainstream 'German' schools in 1938. By the time war was declared in 1939, more than 250 edicts against Jews had been enacted.

No one describes this abrupt change more eloquently than Michael Wieck, in his memoir of life as a Jew in East Prussia.[2] In 1935, Wieck still attended a mainstream German school. By the end of that year, his systematic exclusion from school events had led most of his classmates to adopt, unthinkingly at first, the anti-Jewish jibes and jokes they heard every day on the radio; it wasn't long before they believed even the most perverted Nazi racial slurs. This legalised persecution sowed the seeds of a hatred that reached its peak on the night of 9 November 1938, when Inge was fourteen years old. Nazi paramilitaries and civilians destroyed and looted Jewish businesses and homes, demolished schools and hospitals, and beat up and murdered those they found there, while police looked on. The shards of broken glass that littered the streets of German towns and cities the next day led to its name, Kristallnacht.

Both Königsberg's old and new synagogues were destroyed during that night. The events, which sent shockwaves round the world, prompted many of the city's Jews to emigrate before it was too late. By 1939, the city's Jewish population had shrunk by more than 60 per cent. Those who stayed were forcibly ejected from their homes and sent to camps. In June 1942, 465 people were transported to the Maly Trostenets extermination camp outside Minsk. The few who remained were sent to the Theresienstadt Ghetto and to Auschwitz in the months that followed. It was the end of a community whose roots in Königsberg had gone back to the sixteenth century.

These were the cold, hard facts that prevented me from taking the pleasure I otherwise might have had in my grandmother's recollections of her vanished childhood. How could the Wiegandts, whom I believed to be kindly, enlightened and just, have silently stood by? When had the criminal, inhuman face of Nazism become impossible to ignore? By the time of her confirmation at the age of fourteen, my grandmother was on the cusp of womanhood, surely old enough to see the ugliness that lurked beneath the perfect life she described. Was it fear, or just apathy? There were no immediate, and no easy, answers. I did not know what Albert and Frieda made of the increased penalties for speaking out, the compulsory attendance required of their daughter at Nazi-sponsored youth events, the destruction of Jewish businesses or the brutality that became part of the fabric of everyday life.

Only some small anecdotes, that Frieda passed down to my mother, hinted at how the Wiegandts adapted to their increasingly polarised world. Albert forbade Inge to repeat the propaganda she was taught at school or in the youth groups she was forced by law to attend. Before the outbreak of war made him crave information, he would switch off the radio at the first sign of an official party broadcast. Some stories I found less easy to hear, such as that of the house Albert had bought from a Jewish neighbour who managed to emigrate in the early 1930s. The man had sought a private sale before the property was seized and Albert jumped at the chance; I can only hope he paid him a fair price, but I will never know. I was also struck by the stories that Frieda, a kind woman who led her life according to the Christian principles she held dear, chose to repeat to my mother. The memories she clung to in the years after the war were of those small acts of resistance, such as the pastor's prayers, or Max's refusal to *Sieg Heil*, rare flashes of humanity in a Germany that had lost all claim to it.

Even I, two generations later, was no stranger to the complex relationship Germans have with their past. Growing up in France, I had felt that shame every time a teacher taught my class about the

Nazis. I felt that Germans in the war divided into either the good, who resisted, or the bad, the perpetrators. I'd never thought of the people whose disagreement was quiet or unspoken, those who, for want of heroism or even simple courage, chose to look the other way, to act as the need to survive dictated. And for all the pleasure I took in our conversations, I felt that my grandmother was holding something back; she never spoke of the war years. Did she fear that recalling a time in which darkness could not be absent would break the enchantment she had woven around the memories of her childhood years? Or were there unpalatable truths that she did not want to reveal? I did not know then that it was not just the war, but a part of herself, one that defined and shaped her, that she persisted in concealing. I may never have discovered it, if it hadn't been for a blow that shook the even tenor of her life, six years after I'd called her from Kaliningrad.

Chapter Three

A FUNERAL

It was a death that caused the first crack to appear in my grandmother's carefully curated life. Or more specifically, a funeral, that of her husband of almost sixty years.

Vati was my grandmother's crutch, her mainstay; since he was the younger of the two, we had always assumed he would outlive her. When he passed away suddenly, at the age of eighty-two, we feared grief would overcome her.

In July of 2012, my mother, my brother, my aunt and I met in Kiel a few days before the ceremony, to help my grandmother with the arrangements that were needed in the aftermath of Vati's death. Horst Irmen, or Vati, as we all called him, was born and lived all his life on Germany's northern shore, his weathered face a testimony of hours spent walking along its windy beaches. He had made a simple request in his will: an atheist all of his adult life, he'd never liked the idea of a coffin and wanted his ashes scattered over the deep.

We hired a small, wooden boat to take us from Strande, a seaside village on the Jutland Peninsula, on a sunny Tuesday morning in July. We headed for a small patch of water about a kilometre off the coast, the spot where, according to German bureaucracy, Vati's urn could be deposited into the water legally. There were only twelve of us on board, our immediate family, Vati's closest cousins, and a couple of old friends; the drawback of old age is that you outlive the people you have known the longest.

Below deck, a feast of shrimp, smoked eel, rye bread and slices of raw onion with bowls of sour cream had been laid out, next to the framed photograph of Vati that usually stood on my grandparents' bookshelf. Schnapps and beer flowed freely; it was a typical northern German wake. My grandmother was very quiet, staying below, hiding behind dark glasses, wrapped, despite the warm July weather, in a leopard print coat of fake fur that dwarfed her bird-like frame. She had shrunk into herself and spoke very little, gazing into the distance, oblivious to the photograph of Vati beside her. I put an arm around her shoulders; she felt so small it was as if I encircled her completely, but she barely reacted to my touch. We'd all had the same thought since Vati's death: how could she, so dependent on her husband, possibly manage on her own?

The ship stopped by a single red buoy that marked this maritime graveyard, the shoreline and its houses just discernible in the distance. I helped my grandmother up the stairs and we all gathered by the boat's edge to watch the urn being dropped into the sea. A gaudy pattern of seashells gave it an absurdly Mediterranean air, a final jest from a man whose entire life was spent by the icy currents of the Baltic. It floated for a brief moment, an unlikely patch of ochre in the blue, before it sank. The sun was getting stronger but my grandmother, now quietly weeping, remained wrapped in her winter coat. Vati's younger cousin, Christian, cleared his throat. He'd prepared a few words and spoke about their shared holidays, Vati's happiness with Inge, his joy at the birth of his two daughters. Much affectionate laughter followed an anecdote of a fishing trip they had taken together one summer.

My brother caught my eye and we shared a moment of complicit unease. Christian's speech was a sincere eulogy to a well-loved man, from someone who had known my grandmother and Vati extremely well for many years. But for all this intimacy, neither this man, nor most of the people around him, knew that Vati was not my mother's biological father, or that she was born long before Vati and my grandmother met, though he had loved her as if she were his own. I glanced at my mother to show her my silent support; she was standing just too far away for me to take her hand. She smiled at me, the same sad smile she had worn since we set off. I looked over at my grandmother who stood, her face inscrutable and sphinx-like, swathed in her folds of fake leopard skin as if she hadn't heard the words at all.

The days that followed passed in a whirl. My brother and I, after that shared glance, did not mention the speech at all. We were busy helping my grandmother tidy their flat and making arrangements for her to have help around her home, as she was getting frail and would not be able to live on her own without it. But there was little to do in Kiel, and I walked for hours, thinking over the speech. I thought of the stories my grandmother had told me in the six years since I had phoned her from Kaliningrad, the childhood she had lovingly described. There was a gap in the narrative, a story that was as yet untold. There were the years of her first love, of becoming a woman, of war. The years with that man, my grandfather, whom she had presumably loved before Vati, and about whom I knew so little. I knew from my mother that he and Inge had met in Berlin, where she had briefly attended college during the war, and that, though he had survived the war, they had not reunited.

But I, one generation down, with my new-found knowledge of my grandmother's youth, did not want the story to end there. I had learnt to know Inge, the child, through our conversations about Königsberg. Now I wanted to know Inge, the woman. I wanted to hear about her love story, to hear of how my grandparents first met, what had passed between them, and why they parted. I wanted to know why my grandmother never spoke of him. What had happened in those intervening years, between the childhood idyll she had described, and her life in Kiel?

My grandmother and I didn't spend much time alone in the days after Vati's death. The bustle of family, each solicitous in their different ways, and the tiredness that the shock brought on, shortened our conversations. It was only when I went to bid her goodbye on my last day, kissing her cheek, that she pressed an object into my hand. It was solid, and loosely wrapped in crumpled silk paper.

'I want you to have this,' she said.

Before I could thank her, she turned and started to walk back to her bedroom.

It was a bracelet of gold plate, about two centimetres wide, the solid kind that clicks shut, beautiful in its simplicity. As I closed my fingers around it, I noticed the mechanism was broken and the clasp locked. Try as I might, I could not prise it open.

We had anticipated that Vati's death would leave my grandmother bereft, but her resilience astonished us all. Within days, she adapted her routine to his absence, resuming her life and her outings seemingly unperturbed. It was not that she didn't mourn him; her anguish at his death had been sincere. It was rather that once the ceremony was over she decided to consign him to the past, and did so almost ruthlessly. She spoke of Vati very little, though he had been her constant companion, and within a month she expressed her intention, aged eighty-eight, to find another man. She even attended a *Kaffee und Kuchen* afternoon at the crematorium that had handled his body, telling us it was as good a way as any to make new friends. Her toughness impressed me but it hurt her daughters.

They saw a callous practicality in her fortitude, a betrayal of the man who had loved her so much and for so long.

But every mind will buckle if put under too much strain. Psychologists have a prosaic metaphor for this: repressing trauma, they say, is like stuffing a duvet into a cupboard and shutting the door. The door will only hold for so long, until the smallest bit of extra pressure forces it to burst open and everything comes spilling out. In my grandmother's case, her mind rebelled about two weeks after the funeral in the form of waking dreams.

We had all gone back home for a few days, leaving my grandmother under the eye of a watchful housekeeper and neighbour, when my mother received a phone call at 7 a.m. saying she had disappeared. The visits from the dead had begun.

They came to her when she slept, when she woke, when she made the coffee, when she put on her coat, their voices clear, as though they had never been gone. Her father was the first, that morning, suggesting they go out for breakfast; they used to like their outings so much. She wore a new dress and carefully put on lipstick before calling a taxi, asking the driver if he knew somewhere nice. The young man at the hotel was very kind, showing her to her table, though it was early still, not yet 7 a.m. She ate well for the first time in days: cold ham, smoked fish and a boiled egg. The waiter came back several times and stayed by her table to chat. He was Kosovan, he told her, and had been in Germany for five years.

'My father suggested we have breakfast at a nice hotel which my mother would like.'

The young man smiled.

'I know they're dead,' she said.

'People can be dead,' the young man said, 'and feel like they're with us still.'

By the time she returned home her daughters had had such a fright that they took turns to come to Kiel after that, to keep a close eye on her. She told them that she was not mad, she did not mistake the dead for the living, but she knew the taut threads that bound her mind to the life she had meticulously built had snapped. The doctor told her that she was dehydrated and gave her sleeping pills. But the people had kept coming.

Her mother was next, sitting on the end of her bed, her hands clasped on her lap, looking at her with large, kind eyes that promised to ease her troubles. Soon, Albert and Frieda were joined by others. Some names I recognised, such as Gisela, my mother's aunt, the sister of her mysterious real father; she had died in the late 1960s. Others, I did not know: Lotte, Mütterchen and, a name which my grandmother only spoke in a whisper, 'Buschi'.

She knew it was just a matter of time before she saw his face, and when it came, it made her heart skip a beat. There he was, with the smile that she had worshipped, one corner of his mouth turned up more than the other, shy at first and then facetious. His voice was still that of a boy, though she knew he had died an old man. He was humming that song he liked, the one they had secretly danced to in the upstairs corridor, the sound from the gramophone coming through the open door of his bedroom. *Doo wah, doo wah, doo wah, doo wah / Doo wah, doo wah, doo wah, doo wah.*

Only when my mother turned round to ask her to repeat what she'd just said, did my grandmother realise she had been humming it too.

Chapter Four

'BEI MIR BIST DU SCHÖN'

A month after Vati's death, at our family home in south-west France, my grandmother sat alone in the shadows of the shuttered dining room, eyes closed, clicking the fingers of her right hand, her left tapping the table, marking time. The music drifted in from the terrace and travelled through the long, low-ceilinged room to reach her, its chords muted and the swinging beat softened by distance, but she recognised the tune. They were delicate hands, the skin stretched, diaphanous over stiffened joints, a fine web of blue veins marring its whiteness. Her nails, painted bright red, flashed as her fingers snapped and drummed on the dark oak table, thudding on cracks filled and smoothed by years of polish. Old age largely confined her to stillness, but as she sat at the end of the table, her cup of tea grown cold, she danced again in her mind, lost to the music.

It was a late August afternoon, in those dead hours when the heat, thick in the air, precludes activity. I had come here for our annual family gathering and was lounging on the terrace in an old cane chair, listening to Ella Fitzgerald, enjoying the heavy stillness and the warmth of the terracotta stones beneath my bare feet. Everyone had disappeared indoors and the noisy house was suddenly quiet.

My grandmother's stay this year had been unusually long, as we had not wanted her to remain alone at home. The wanderings of her mind, which had so concerned us in the weeks following her husband's death, had stopped. She was almost back to her usual self, her small yet persistent demands still capable of driving my usually calm mother close to the brink of nervous collapse. But she sought out my company more often now, every conversation opening another window into her past. The stories she told were still of East Prussia, but the Inge of her recollections was slowly getting older. I tried, on my part, to find out more, from my mother, my aunt and other family members. I gleaned bits here and there – of college years in Berlin, of a friendship with my grandfather's sister, which had led to their first meeting – but their knowledge was piecemeal at best; only my grandmother's telling could bring these fragments together.

I hadn't noticed her at first, a solitary figure seated indoors at the far end of the table. The soft tones of 'If Dreams Come True' shifted to swing, the beat surging from the small speaker as it started playing *Bei Mir Bist du Schön*, a popular dance-band hit of the 1930s and 40s. I rose to join her, worried she might be feeling isolated, but the expression on her face gave me pause.

My mother had told me that my grandmother had loved to dance and had attended forbidden parties in wartime Berlin where musicians were trained to switch from swing to a government-approved foxtrot at the first sign of the authorities. The story had the unreality of a time long past and the glamour of fiction, its image of a free-spirited girl at odds with the unadventurous and critical elderly woman I knew. I remembered that story as I watched her now, oblivious to the world around her, entranced by a music that was bringing glimpses of that girl back to life. When the last note of the song had finished, I went to sit beside her.

'*Magst du die Musik?*' I said. Do you like this music?

'*Ich kenne dieses Lied,*' she answered, opening her eyes again. 'I know it well. She was singing it, the day I arrived in Berlin.'

*

The summer Inge turned fifteen began much as usual with the Wie-gandts' annual holiday on the coast. Their plans never varied much: in June, Frieda and Inge started their preparations for Rauschen, where they spent most of the summer. Albert joined them mainly at weekends, though he always took two weeks off in August. It was 1939 and they had been there two weeks already, staying in their usual boarding house, a white stone villa from which a narrow sandy lane snaked down among the pines and straight to the sea. Inge could see the Baltic from her bedroom window and would fall asleep listening to the crashing of the waves on the shore. In the morning, they would sit down for breakfast with the lady who rented them their rooms, a pleasant, buxom woman in late middle age who always called her 'Ingechen' – 'little Inge' – with that very East Prus-sian habit of adding the suffix 'chen' to everything you held dear. In previous years Inge had counted down the days to their holiday in Rauschen, but that summer she had grown blind to its beauty.

Rauschen was a windswept resort by the Baltic with pine forests and sixty-metre-high dunes separating the town centre from the sea. Its beach stretched for miles into an endless expanse framed only by the water and the sky, its sand so fine a gust of wind would fill the air with it. It was one of the smaller of East Prussia's coastal resorts, attracting visitors from all over Germany in its earlier days. Only a short train journey from Königsberg, it served as a summer base from which Albert could return to town as often as his busi-ness required, allowing his family to spend the whole of the summer holidays together. But Inge, on the cusp of her fifteenth birthday, dreamt of excitement and company. The wildness of the dunes and the quaintness of the town were lost on a teenager who wished only for dancing and boys.

She did not notice the lines deepening in Albert's face or the tension that was growing more frequent in the adult conversations around her. There was much talk of the threat of another war; it was written on every furrow of her father's brow, and in her mother's attempt to change the subject every time the issue came up. But all she could think of was how bored she was, a boredom so intense it ached.

Albert could not help but see his daughter's listlessness. He'd noticed her long silences and often asked her why she looked so sad. She told him, somewhat snappily, that she hated holidays and that no one understood her, to which he only smiled. The summer had started badly when Christa, the friend of all her past holidays, wrote to her in June to say that her parents had decided to spend the summer in Cranz, a more fashionable resort thirty kilometres farther east, instead of taking their usual rooms near the Wiegandts in Rauschen. Christa's parents were regulars from west Germany who had come to the East Prussian coastline every year of their childhoods and had continued to do so with their own families, in spite of the travel complications wrought by the Danzig Corridor. A redhead with a taste for mischief, Christa first met Inge as a toddler playing among Rauschen's dunes and the girls had been firm friends ever since; Inge couldn't remember a summer without her.

Frieda's suggestion that she invite Christa to come to Rauschen for her birthday helped lessen her disappointment. Inge's summer took an even better turn when Christa wrote to suggest Inge return with her to Cranz for the rest of the holidays. Frieda and Albert, seeing the change the letter made in their daughter, accepted at once.

Now Inge sat on the station platform, impatiently awaiting Christa's arrival, her suitcase for Cranz already packed, save for the dress she had set aside for her birthday dinner the next day. It was not the siren's outfit she had so coveted a few weeks before for her confirmation, but a fashionable blue silk, which Frieda had reluctantly agreed to buy her. She had allowed Inge to meet Christa alone; the villa was only a fifteen-minute walk from the station. The platform was quiet apart from a group of young men in soldiers' uniforms, who were standing together talking. Inge sat on a bench pretending not to notice them; she knew they were looking at her. As she smoothed away a stray curl, she thought of that line in Christa's letter: 'You are rotting away in Rauschen! You'll see how much fun we'll have here in Cranz.' Christa understood exactly how she felt.

She jumped up as the train pulled in. One of the boy soldiers turned towards her and said something, but the whistle of the engine drowned out his voice. She saw her friend almost at once and ran to embrace her. Her arm linked to Christa's, Inge glanced over at the boy and smiled, before walking away towards the villa.

Two days later, she was in Cranz. The girls set off the day after Inge's birthday, and the journey there had been filled with anticipation. The pastel houses, the centre's cobbled streets and the shops and cafes in this more fashionable resort were all she had imagined. Christa's older brother came to meet them at the station and took them straight to a cafe terrace to eat strawberry and vanilla ice cream. They watched the holidaymakers and the groups of young men who loitered on the promenade, trying to catch Inge and Christa's eye. The seafront here was less steep and free of trees, leading straight into the town, so the promenade was a constant bustle of activity. Almost as soon as Inge took the first bite of her ice cream, a band struck up a tune.

Inge and Christa spent their mornings at the beach, took boat trips along the coast and spent their afternoons at the cafes by the seafront. Those late afternoons were the highlight of their day; Christa's brother, Franz, acted as chaperone, so that the girls enjoyed almost total freedom. They laughed and flirted with Franz's friends or the boys in cafes who came up to their group and asked the girls to dance.

The dancing was Inge's favourite part; it was the summer she discovered live music. She danced between the cafe tables, on the terraces, along the promenade, oblivious to the gaze of the older folk who watched her. The music was swing, an American variant of jazz that had taken Germany by storm in the last few years. Though the bands were the second-rate kind that played holiday resorts and often mangled the tunes, their beat and energy were a musical epiphany for Inge. It spoke to every frustration of her fifteen-year-old self, and dance was their release. She had the summer of her life and its recollection, when she described it to me seventy years later, still made her laugh with joy.

Those weeks in Cranz would mark the end of Inge's carefree childhood, for when she returned that September, two things happened that would change the course of her life. The first was her decision, having had her first taste of freedom, to leave Königsberg as soon as she could. The second was beyond her control.

On the first day of September, Inge stayed home from school, after complaining to Frieda of a sore throat the night before. She looked at the clock on her bedside table: it said 9.45 a.m. She'd slept late, and felt better for it; she decided to get up and go to the kitchen to make herself a cup of coffee. She put on her dressing gown and her slippers. Her mother was in the kitchen; to her surprise, her father, who ought to have been at work, was sitting by the radio.

'How are you feeling, *Liebchen*?'

Her father glanced at her and smiled. She noticed the circles under his eyes; he'd been up late the night before, listening to reports of something happening in Poland.

'The Reichstag has been called in extraordinary session; the Führer is about to speak,' he told her.

Inge shrugged and turned to find the coffee pot was almost full, the coffee was freshly made and still hot. The speech her parents had been waiting for began shortly after 10 a.m. The shouts and cheers that resonated through the airwaves and filled the kitchen announced that Hitler had arrived. She listened to the start, something about Danzig, as she poured herself a cup of coffee and added two teaspoons of sugar. She decided to take it back to bed. As she walked out into the corridor that led to her bedroom, she heard something about Polish soldiers firing that made her father gasp, and stopped, halfway to her bedroom, to listen. Someone had turned the sound up so loud she could hear everything. German forces, Hitler said, had come under attack from Polish soldiers.*

'Since 5.45 a.m. we have been returning fire. And, from now on, bombs will be met with bombs.'

The shouting and cheering coming from the radio almost drowned out the rest of Hitler's speech. She walked back to the kitchen where the door stood open and saw her parents holding each other tight. They had not heard her come back. Shutting the kitchen door quietly behind her, she turned and went back to bed.

The days that followed meant little to Inge, though she felt a kind of excitement in the air. To her parents, the declaration of war was a catastrophe, though one many had foreseen. Hitler had pursued an aggressive foreign policy since 1936, when he re-militarised the Rhineland, Germany's border region with France. It was a direct breach of the Locarno Pact – an extension of the agreement at

---

* This report of Polish aggression was a lie. On the evening of 31 August, a group of SS men disguised themselves as Polish insurgents and seized the German radio station at Gleiwitz, one of a number of incidents giving the appearance of Polish aggression against Germany to provide Hitler with a pretext for the war.

Versailles – and hugely popular with voters as a show of German resurgence. The annexation of Austria, and then the Sudetenland, part of Czechoslovakia, had followed two years later, and still European powers had sought to avoid war. The invasion of Poland made the conflict, which the Wiegandts had hoped could yet be avoided, inevitable. Frieda was fifty-three and Albert fifty-nine; the memory of the previous conflict was fresh. They had survived the wreckage of their generation, and now it was their daughter's turn to witness the destruction of the next.

However, although Albert and Frieda were surely not alone in greeting news of the conflict with consternation, in those first few months of the war, life went on as normal for most East Prussians. Daily adjustments were minimal at first. A rationing of sorts had been in place from late August, as war looked increasingly inevitable. For the young, free of their parents' scars, war even held a certain glamour. Hitler had brought back conscription in 1935, but many students were, in those early days, able to postpone their service, delaying the grim reality to come. For Inge, war brought little change, save the sight of young men in uniform.

That September, Christa, who was a year older than Inge, was sent to finishing school in Ilsenburg, a small town near their home in Harz, Saxony. Christa wrote often, suggesting that Inge join her the following year when she would finally be allowed to leave school. Cranz had given Inge a taste for change, and she was determined to seize this chance. She knew her parents were unlikely to object, though Ilsenburg was almost 1,200 kilometres away. She had travelled to Harz the previous autumn to stay with Christa's family and the three-week visit had been a great success. Albert and Frieda trusted Christa's parents.

The Wiegandts knew they had to make a decision about Inge's future. They were ambitious for their daughter and wanted her to complete her education as far as she was able. She was still very young, and though she was intelligent she lacked the patience or application to excel academically. Albert correctly diagnosed Inge's lack of interest in her studies as the product of boredom, and thought a change would do her good. With war underway, it would have been natural for Albert and Frieda to refuse to send Inge away. But Albert remembered how he had longed for a different life as a young man, and knew his daughter needed a little excitement; this was as safe an option as any.

The Ilsenburg finishing school was typical of its time. It was no trailblazer, no hotbed of radical ideas. It offered little by way of academic study; young girls from good families were taught cooking, *Schliff* – the German word for etiquette – and dancing, with perhaps a little French. Albert was old-fashioned, he liked women to be feminine and often told Inge he couldn't bear girls who didn't know how to cook. He told her she could try the finishing school for a year, and then decide if she wanted to pursue her studies further.

But the war Inge had so far managed to ignore put paid to her plans. The woman running Christa's course wrote to Inge to say that she was sorry, but the limitations of rationing were forcing them to close. If Inge could wait until the war was over, the school would be happy to take her then. To a fifteen-year-old impatient to grow up, she may as well have told her to wait a hundred years.

But no wartime privations could stop Inge's determination to get out of Königsberg. With Christa's finishing school no longer an option, she turned to her mother's friends for help and they proved effective allies. They were on the whole younger and more modern than her parents, and believed that a change from the provincial horizons of Königsberg would be the very thing Inge needed. It wasn't long before one of them asked her if she had heard of the Lette Haus, a college for the higher education of women in Berlin. Her niece had studied interior design there, she said, and it was known as the best place in Germany for young women to study. She gave Inge the address and the girl sent off a letter of enquiry almost at once.

The Lette Haus was founded in the nineteenth century by Wilhelm Lette, a lawyer and social reformer, and was much more than an ordinary finishing school. It strove to provide young women with a solid education and professional training, a flavour of feminism counterbalanced by courses that provided the skills that were considered essential to become a good housewife in Nazi Germany. Needlework and cookery aside, its focus was on the arts, and its design, fashion and photography schools were well respected. Inge was full of enthusiasm for the idea, but Albert met her suggestion with a flat refusal.

It was not the dangers of war that worried Albert. Germany was militarily strong; newsreels broadcasted images of an army that conquered all before it, and belief in the Luftwaffe, then Europe's largest air force, was absolute. Most Germans believed the capital invulnerable to foreign attacks. Unlike London, where evacuations started as early as 1939, there was no move, in the early years of the war, for women and children to leave the big cities in Germany. For those Germans like the Wiegandts who weren't singled out for persecution, their country felt safe enough. Though the war had started at East Prussia's borders, as it progressed the fighting was in the west and seemed remote enough, at least to Königsberg's civilians. Hitler's invasion of Poland had removed the buffer zone between East Prussia and the rest of Germany, uniting the country once more. While Germany was at war with the West, on its eastern border there was, for now, no threat of war. To the surprise of Western governments who had hoped to secure the Soviet Union as a military ally against Hitler, Germany and the USSR signed a ten-year non-aggression agreement, the Molotov–Ribbentrop Pact, in August 1939. Its premise was simple: in return for the agreement, Hitler promised Josef Stalin part of eastern Poland, 10 per cent of Finland, as well as Lithuania, Estonia and Latvia. Britain and France's offer to the USSR had simply not been as advantageous.[1]

But Berlin presented other dangers to a father of a pretty and flirtatious girl. In the 1920s the city had acquired a reputation for glamour, decadence and promiscuity. Nazism had done much to dampen this, but Berlin's reputation remained broadly unchanged. Inge mapped out her campaign to win Albert over carefully. The new term started in September and it was already April; she was determined not to miss a moment of it. She spoke of the Lette Haus's famous cookery school and the refinements she would learn. Because Nazi law required young unmarried women to be 'usefully' occupied, she asked Frieda's professor uncle to help find her a work placement with a colleague in Berlin. She showed Albert the professor's letter, which was full of praise for their decision to send her to the Lette Haus. 'A Lette Mädchen!' he had written, referring to the nickname given to those girls fortunate enough to secure a place at the exclusive Berlin college. 'That is no small thing.' Unbeknownst to Albert, she had already sent a letter applying for their September course. Their reply said that Inge could have the last remaining place, but they would need the completed forms within a week.

Albert was no match for the combined pressure from his daughter and his wife's friends. He capitulated within a week and as soon as he had signed the form Inge took it to the post office. She trusted no one to send it but herself.

*

Inge and her mother arrived in Berlin at the beginning of September 1940, to settle her in to her new life as a Lette Mädchen. Preparations had not gone entirely smoothly and Inge had spent her last few weeks at home living in constant fear that her father would change his mind. Finding accommodation had been the greatest sticking point. Her late registration meant the Lette Haus's residential dorm was already full; a pastor's daughter, also from East Prussia, had taken the last remaining bed. Inge would have to find lodgings independently of the college, an idea which Albert at first rejected outright. He had noticed the amount of effort and expenditure that had gone into his daughter's new wardrobe, which seemed to have been purchased with dancing and socialising in mind, rather than work and study. The idea of Inge living outside the college, and the freedom this would give her, made him nervous. Berlin was a big place, and she could easily fall in with the wrong set. Inge pleaded with him, insisting she would be far too scared to go out on her own. Fortunately, the Lette Haus's director came up with a solution, suggesting Inge should lodge at a boarding house a short walk from the college. It was run by an acquaintance of his, he said, and in the past he had recommended it to some of their most respectable students. The widow who owned it kept a close eye on her charges. Albert allowed himself to be placated and, to Inge's relief, he permitted her to leave Königsberg.

Frieda and Inge arrived at the boarding house, a large and pleasant villa set back some distance from the road, on a sunny Sunday morning. The weather was warm and the French windows to the sitting room were wide open, framed by a yellow climbing rose still in bloom. As Inge and Frieda walked through the garden and up to the front door, they saw a girl at the piano, playing and singing a contemporary song. The music carried out into the garden, its catchy tune prompting Inge to clap her hands with delight.

'Do you know the song, *Liebchen*?' Frieda asked.

Did she know it! She and Christa had danced to it all summer long in Cranz. The song, '*Bei Mir Bist du Schön*', had been one of the biggest swing hits of the late 1930s. Frieda asked Inge, somewhat cautiously, as the owner of the boarding house appeared on the threshold, if she thought the owner was Jewish.

The song may not have been known to Frieda but, musical as she was, she'd recognised the genre and, most importantly, the lyrics: the girl was singing them in their original Yiddish. Swing music had long been singled out by the Nazi authorities, who saw it as *Entartete Musik*, modern music which, along with modern painting, they considered harmful and decadent, part of what they labelled 'degenerate art'. The overwhelmingly popular song in question particularly attracted their ire. It had been written for Broadway by the Jewish American composers, Jacob Jacobs and Sholom Secunda, for the Yiddish language comedy *I Would if I Could*. Joseph Goebbels, Germany's minister for propaganda, had singled out the song, banning it two months before Kristallnacht as 'non-Aryan', along with the works of the Jewish composer Irving Berlin. He followed this up by creating, in spring 1939, an index of 'undesirable and harmful music'.

From 1933, the Nazis had tried to ban jazz and particularly its newest form, swing, which they saw as the embodiment of American decadence and its African American and Jewish influences. Hitler hated it and radio stations were told not to broadcast its tunes, with some, like Berliner Funkstunde, banning them from its airwaves the moment he got into power. This did nothing to dim swing's popularity, however, with Germans instead tuning in to foreign stations such as Radio Luxemburg or the French Poste Parisien, which continued to play the latest American dance tunes. Despite the Nazis' efforts, jazz and swing continued to be hugely popular, and nothing illustrates the Third Reich's failure to crush it more than the popularity of the song Inge and her mother heard as they arrived at the boarding house that day. The song Inge had recognised was one made popular in Germany by Swedish singer and actress Zarah Leander, but sung in the original Yiddish of the Broadway show.[2]

The red-haired Leander was a star in late 1930s and 40s Germany, a fame she gained partly due to her more glamorous compatriot Greta Garbo's decision to reject Hitler and emigrate to the US. Staying in Germany was a decision that would kill Leander's post-war career but which, in 1938, allowed her to be popular enough to take a risk and record '*Bei Mir Bist du Schön*', though the song's Jewish origins were by then well publicised.*

It was a choice of song that also said much about the boarding house Inge was about to lodge in. It was a liberal environment, a far cry from the buttoned-up society Inge was used to in Königsberg, bringing to her life a flavour of political controversy that thrilled her. The woman who ran it was not, as Frieda suspected, Jewish; however, she had close friends who were and helped them as best she could. The run-up to the war had not brought about the immediate violence many German Jews had feared; some still felt that their connections could save them and took the risk of remaining in Germany during those last few months of peace, but for most people leaving was quite simply too expensive, or meant abandoning loved ones. In the early days of the regime, their hounding was carried out by means of bureaucracy, with daily life made more difficult to bear with every new decree. Once war broke out, food rations for Jews were cut, their movement curtailed and

---

* Leander's general willingness to turn a blind eye to Nazi persecution makes it unlikely that this was an act of political defiance. Leander's most famous surviving recording of the song is in Swedish, though she was also said to have performed it in Yiddish. Yiddish recordings were first mistaken for German dialect, before being banned, though they continued to circulate on the black market.

every aspect of daily life made increasingly impossible, a situation that could only be tempered by the kindness of friends. By 1939, evictions had started and a curfew was imposed on Jewish residents. By 1940, Jews were no longer allowed telephones or ration cards for clothes.

The girls who lodged at the boarding house lived three to a room. An only child who had never had to share anything, Inge was appalled at first by the arrangement, but was soon won over by the camaraderie and companionship she found in her room-mates. The singer at the piano who had so enchanted her on the day of her arrival had turned out to be one of them, a pretty girl who moved with quiet grace, with nut-brown hair and a heart-shaped face. Inge learnt that she was a student at the nearby Medau school of music and dance. The girl's beauty and sophistication fascinated Inge and made her feel clumsy and provincial. She longed to have her as an intimate friend and took every opportunity to be in her company. But the lasting friendship she craved never had a chance – three weeks after Inge's arrival, she found her room-mate in their bedroom, sobbing as she packed her belongings. The Medau school had told her that her three-year course of study had come to an end, even though the academic year still had nine months to run. She was one of their best students, but staying there was no longer an option.

'She said to me, "What do you think they'll do to us next?"' my grandmother told me as we sat together at the living-room table. 'I was so stupid, so ignorant. I asked her what she meant. I said it was so unfair that it couldn't be right. I told her that if she wrote to the director to tell him, they'd realise it was all a mistake. I thought that would comfort her. Comfort her! I remember her staring at me. "Don't you know?" she said. "Don't you realise that I'm Jewish?"'

My grandmother and I sat in silence as the final Ella Fitzgerald song came to an end and the heat of the day slowly crept through the open door. I had so many questions that I did not trust myself to ask. Could anyone in Germany in 1940 really have been so unaware of what was happening around her? How much of it had been ignorance and how much wilful blindness? The Holocaust was not a subject I had ever discussed with my grandmother, though my mother had spoken of it freely. She was of a generation brought up in the aftermath of the war, defined by the guilt of its parents, and had been a student in Paris in the 1960s, a time of reckoning for young Germans. My mother had found a redemption of sorts for her Germanness in how she raised her family. Her closest friend, with whose children my brother and I grew up, was Jewish and we participated in as many of their family's religious festivals as we could. It became such a part of our lives that, aged ten and nominally a Catholic, I felt more comfortable explaining the significance of Passover than that of Good Friday.

I had always reasoned that my mother was just a small child when the horrors of Hitler's regime were laid bare for all the world to see. She could bear no responsibility for them and that had been a comforting thought. When it came to my grandmother, those reflections sat less easily. It was the unspoken shame of any German family and it had hung between us when she accompanied my mother and me to a friend's wedding in a west London synagogue a few months earlier. She had been full of enthusiasm for the ceremony and its rituals, but I had still shirked from asking the questions that lingered in my mind.

What had been the fate of the girl at the boarding house, that friend of my grandmother's who had wept so bitterly? I tried to entertain the fantasy that she could have been one of the very few to have stayed in the country that late into the war and still have made it out. But what we know of the restrictions of the time make this highly unlikely; once war had been declared, the borders had been closed. Escape from Germany for Jews after 1939 was almost impossible.

I still wasn't sure exactly what I feared finding out when I asked my grandmother about her youth, but now it was too late to stop. Every time we talked of the past, another question came up. I wanted to know more about those years in Berlin during which she'd left childhood behind. My mother had told me it was where her parents had first met. How did my grandfather, whom I had never known, come to meet a sixteen-year-old girl living at a ladies' boarding house? Why had he disappeared from her life so completely? As I looked at my grandmother, trying to recall her lost friend, I came to realise that I had no idea who this woman, whom I had known my entire life, really was.

'I was so stupid,' my grandmother said. 'They were terrible times, such terrible times. No one should ever live through them again. But I was sixteen, so irresponsible. And so very stupid.'

She fell silent again for a while, and I saw the red-nailed fingers tremble as she wiped away a tear. When she spoke again, it was almost in a whisper: 'I can't even remember her name.'

PART II

Chapter Five

VOGELSANG

A shift had taken place in my grandmother's stories as she spoke of those years in Berlin. The naive child from provincial Königsberg was gone. In her stead was a girl, almost grown up, yearning for life and excitement, ready to seize whatever opportunity came her way. One memory stood out for her, more vivid than the rest. That of a white villa at Vogelsang, a place of laughter and grand parties, where she came to live soon after starting at the Lette Haus. She spoke its name – the German word for birdsong – as if it were music.

My grandmother spent two of the happiest years of her life here. It was where she first built a future away from her parents, where she met the family that would so closely shape her life, where she fell in love, where she first experienced heartbreak.

Years later, as I sought to learn the details of her story, I went to see the house she had described so fondly. I wanted to see it for myself, to stand where she once stood. Walking through the prosperous neighbourhood of Dahlem, I soon found Vogelsang, one of its smartest streets, an avenue of cobbled stone divided by a garden of slender silver birches. It certainly retained the glamour my grandmother saw in it seventy years before.

The house where she once lived was large, three storeys high, with a pillared portico setting off a balcony covered in pink roses and a red tiled roof with gabled attic windows.

I rang the doorbell, but no one answered, so I sat on a bench among the birches. Two lovers had carved their initials on the tree trunk. I wondered if my grandmother had once done the same.

For all its beauty, Dahlem is a neighbourhood with a tainted past. It was home to many senior Nazis, most of whom lived in villas seized from their Jewish owners. Something about the villa in Vogelsang had been troubling me ever since I arrived in Berlin. A search in the Bundesbank's archive revealed it to be part of a block built in the 1920s for the use of the senior directors of the Reichsbank, the name of the German central bank before the war.

During the war, it was the residence of the Reichsbank's vice president, Kurt Lange. My grandmother had mentioned his name, but little else about him. An ambitious bureaucrat, he joined the Nazi Party in 1930, rising to the rank of minister of the economy when Hitler came to power, before his appointment to the central bank. A photograph in Berlin's Bundesarchiv shows a bald, square-jawed man who would once have been handsome before middle age brought a certain heaviness to his face. It accompanies a profile of Lange, part of a brochure about the Reichsbank in wartime; the brochure includes snapshots of the central bank's officials, Lange in the background, engaging in target practice in an underground shooting range. A few pages earlier, a full page is devoted to a slogan: '*Kämpfen-Arbeiten-Opfern*' – 'Fight, Work, Sacrifice'.

It moved me to be standing in the place she came of age, but the emotion was tainted by new doubts, brought by the knowledge that she, whom I'd always been told had no Nazi associations, spent what she described as her happiest years in the house of a man who was part of Hitler's government machine.

Inge spent her first weeks in Berlin in what she described as a state of constant bewilderment. No other city in Germany could have offered a greater contrast to the provincial and conservative familiarity of Königsberg. Throughout the 1920s, Berlin had been

KURT LANGE.

the centre of Europe's avant-garde, a cultural, religious, sexual and political melting pot known as the 'reddest city after Moscow'.* It carved out an identity by rejecting the traditional Germany to which authoritarians and nationalists aspired, contrasting with more conservative cities such as Munich, where far-right groups had been allowed to flourish. Only 1.6 per cent of Berliners voted for the Nazi Party in 1928. Over the next five years, by targeting the city's large number of unemployed, the Nazis managed to bring that vote share up, but the 31.3 per cent of votes they won in March 1933 was still one of the lowest in the whole of Germany.

By the time Inge arrived at the Lette Haus, the city's radicalism and independence had been cowed. But some independence of

* This phrase was coined by Goebbels, or the Nazis generally.

thought remained, even in the safe confines of the Lette Haus, which pushed its students to become something more than the child-bearing *Hausfrauen* on which Hitler modelled his ideal of German womanhood. Its alumni had included some of the most daring figures in art and fashion circles in the 1920s. The story of one Lette Haus student stands out, illustrating just how starkly Nazism changed Berlin's fabric and society. Else Neuländer-Simon, a photographer who went by the name of Yva, opened her own studio in 1925, a few years after her graduation. Her work was often commercial and focused on fashion and stars of theatre and film. What made it groundbreaking was its decadence. She portrayed her subjects as 'New Women', strong, independent, sensual, part of a push for female emancipation that caused much debate in Weimar Germany, and in the rest of Europe. She was hugely successful, and regularly featured in the illustrated magazines that Inge was so fond of reading. Yva managed to keep her studio going throughout the first years of Hitler's administration, but her pseudonym could not disguise her Jewishness for long. By the late 1930s, the stars who had courted her deserted her completely. Little is known of her war years, but at some point in 1944 she perished in a concentration camp – the exact date and place of her death are unknown. Today, her work has been all but been forgotten, though some of it lived on through that of her apprentice, Helmut Newton.

As she walked across the Viktoria-Luise-Platz with Frieda on her first morning, Inge was oblivious to the persecution that would eventually kill Yva. By the time they reached the imposing building which dominated the square, her excitement had turned to dread. Frieda, who had stayed in Berlin to settle her daughter that first week, was not allowed to come further than the reception, and for the first time in sixteen years Inge was on her own. It took all her courage to walk to the front desk, where a woman with elaborately coiffed hair took her name before directing her to a room off the main corridor. She was early; only three girls had arrived before her, sitting in a row of chairs. She took them in at a glance. Two of them were dowdy, wearing unremarkable clothes, their hands and ankles neatly folded; one had absurdly thick glasses. The third, whom Inge was told to sit next to, looked much more promising, a tall blonde girl, very chic, with her hair in the rolls Frieda would not yet allow Inge to wear, saying she was still too young. Inge's hand self-consciously went up to her unruly dark curls. Her eyes met the blonde girl's, and they smiled at each other.

The course director, a tall, forbidding-looking woman in a long black dress, asked the girls their names. When the blonde girl's turn came, she mumbled, 'Schimmelmann.'

The director's eyebrows shot up.

'Come, Gisela, that's not your whole name.'

'Gisela von Schimmelmann,' the girl replied, looking straight back at her.

'But that's not everything, is it?'

'That's the only bit that matters.'

Inge did not know what this exchange was about, but she caught the girl's eye in a silent show of support. She knew they would be friends.

Gisela – or Gigi, as she soon asked Inge to call her – was the youngest child and only daughter of Carl-Otto, Graf Schimmelmann and his first wife, Dorothea, née von Wedel. Her family was aristocratic, wealthy and, by the time she met Inge, tainted by scandal. Her mother, Dorothea, had shocked fashionable society by falling in love a few years earlier with the family lawyer, Kurt Lange, a rising figure in Nazi bureaucratic circles. She had divorced Gisela's father, a handsome but dissipated man who had already gambled away much of his fortune and amassed large debts. The scandal of the divorce had been fuelled further by his decision to marry a young English woman in London, whom he then brought back to Germany. Society gossip dined out on the tribulations of the von Schimmelmann family for years; it explained Gisela's reticence to make a parade of her name.

GISELA AS A GIRL.

Gigi was a shy girl with a rebellious streak, who immediately took to Inge. A year older, from far out east, Inge had heard none of the gossip about Gigi's family. Both girls were little inclined to follow rules and they soon became inseparable. They sat beside each other in class, gained a large circle of acquaintances and were among the most popular girls at the Lette Haus, but their friendship admitted no other intimates. From Gisela, Inge learnt to be more poised and sophisticated in her manners and dress, while Gigi adopted some of Inge's vivacity. Inge's letters home were full of Gigi and of the places they had been together, with a line added here and there to say that she was studying hard, which was a lie.

Gisela lived with her mother and stepfather in Dahlem. One morning, a few weeks after they had first met, she asked Inge to come home for dinner with her family. Dahlem was a few stops away on the U-Bahn, a novelty for Inge, who'd only ever taken Königsberg's trams. She was nervous of the family at first. The house was grander than any she had seen before, a large villa set back in a beautiful garden, with a butler, a cook, a gardener, a chauffeur and maids; the largest staff Inge had been used to consisted of a cook and a housemaid. It was a comfortable modern house, with none of the constraints of old family places. By 1940, Kurt Lange was the joint director of the Reichsbank and the house had come with his new position. He greeted Inge politely, but it was Gisela's mother, Dorothea, whom Inge was immediately drawn to.

Dorothea was tall, slim and blonde-haired, with a warm and sensitive heart. In her youth she had been famous for her beauty as well as her fearlessness on horseback, and she possessed an impetuousness that made her prone to making impulsive decisions. Her family were *Junkers* whose loyalty was to the military, their horses and their country. She married her first husband, Carl-Otto, at the age of nineteen. He was then a 26-year-old handsome army major and heir to one of Germany's richest and most prestigious families. After their first child was born, he took Dorothea to the family seat at Ahrensburg, near Hamburg, a massive, stately edifice by the side of a lake. By the age of twenty-seven, she already had three children, of which Gisela was the youngest.

Carl-Otto's gambling habit and large and expensive estate had by then cost him much of his fortune. Multiple mortgages on the land gave his lawyer, a young and ambitious Kurt Lange, cause to come often to the family's home at Ahrensburg to advise him on

DOROTHEA WITH CARL, WOLFGANG AND GISELA.

how to keep his creditors at bay. Lange first caught sight of Dorothea riding into the courtyard there, her hair loose on her shoulders, her colour high from the outdoors. He had been captivated by her beauty. Carl-Otto's frequent absences and the loneliness of her life in the country had damaged Dorothea's marriage. Lange's air of authority, his purposeful manner and his energy soon seduced her. She was a woman who loved wholeheartedly and without caution; before long, she had agreed to run away with him.

By the time of Inge's first meeting with her, Dorothea's relationship with Lange was showing some cracks. Lange's ruthless ambition allowed very little to stand in his way and he spent less and less time with his wife as he rose through the Reichsbank. His absences triggered what her family described as a tendency to melancholy, or in today's terms, a predisposition for depression. These had been aggravated by personal tragedy. Three years earlier, her eldest son Carl had died of meningitis at the age of seventeen, while staying on his uncle's estate in Denmark. He had been sent there with a view to becoming his uncle's heir and had died before his mother could reach him to say goodbye. Maybe it was those past hardships that led Dorothea to look so kindly upon Inge, alone in Berlin, with her parents so far away. She warmed to the girl at once; her own family had roots in East Prussia and she knew Königsberg and the coast well. Inge, hearing her talk the first time they met, of her home city, of childhood holidays by the sea, of the forests that turned into dunes, felt almost as though she were back at home.

Dorothea knew the last few years had been hard for her children. The scandal of her second marriage and the gossip that ensued had been bad enough, but the death of their older brother had been the hardest blow. She tried to make up for these difficult

DOROTHEA AS A YOUNG MOTHER WITH CARL.

years by being as liberal and loving towards them as she could. In Inge, she saw a spontaneity her own daughter lacked, and she hoped this friendship would be the tonic her family needed. She soon grew to love the girl whose petite stature and naivety made her seem younger that Gigi, even though she was one year her senior. There was always laughter in the house when Inge came to see them, first one evening a week and then every weekend. Soon Mütterchen, as they all called Dorothea, asked Inge if she would come and live with them. The nickname – little mother – was a very East Prussian one and says much about their closeness; Inge would call her that all her life. Albert and Frieda heard a great deal about Dorothea's kindness to their daughter in Inge's letters home. After a few weeks, Dorothea had written them a friendly note to ask if Inge could come and live in Dahlem, and the idea delighted them. It quietened all Albert's fears about life in a boarding house. Once she lived with a family, he thought, she would not be left quite so much to her own devices.

Inge adapted quickly to life with the von Schimmelmanns, fitting into the family as if she'd always been a part of it. The politics of the household were interesting. Emboldened by her wealth and her position, Dorothea was free in her criticism of the regime, and the openness of their talk shocked Inge at first. Frieda and Albert would have agreed with much of what Dorothea said, but would never have dared to admit it outside their closest circle. By 1940, it had become the default for most Germans to outwardly voice approval of the regime, though for many this was little more than lip service.

How the Nazis managed to maintain their grip over the German population is something that continues to divide historians to this day. One cannot explain away the hold of Nazism over an entire people by saying they were simply terrorised into it; but terror, and its threat, was nevertheless one of the key elements of the regime's control. The Nazi Party was, at least in the early years of its rise to power, a hugely popular one. Its most successful propaganda in the pre-war years relied on playing on established beliefs and preju- dices – fear of communism, recovering national pride, community, cultural anti-Semitism (then prevalent across Europe), as well as on touting achievements that were grounded in reality: reduced unemployment, order on the street, a revival of Germany's inter- national standing. But at the heart of the regime lay a system of violence and intimidation. From the earliest days of the Nazi regime, Hitler focused on suppressing dissent among those sec- tions of the population who weren't true believers. The result, as historian Richard Evans describes, was a regime that aggressively targeted certain groups, and dominated the rest of the German population through a system of coercive control.[1]

The measures they used for this coercion were wide-ranging. Numerous laws were put in place, setting out a plethora of offences from telling jokes about Hitler to listening to foreign radio stations, to refusing to enrol your child in the Hitler Youth, to name but a few. The means of their implementation were equally broad and relied on many agencies. They relied, in part, on official agents such as the secret police, known as the Gestapo, the criminal police and the SS – the Nazi Party's paramilitary arm. But the largest part of this was achieved through vast num- bers of lower-level Nazi officials such as the block wardens who reported on entire buildings, the members of various Nazi organ- isations, and vocal party members who could, through a simple report of careless speech, cause an arrest, a deportation, or even an execution. Although the zealous believers represented a minority in a population of 80 million, they still numbered enough to achieve total control. Retribution, even for party members, was swift, and brutal violence became normalised.

Civil liberties were entirely destroyed. Censorship was total, eventually covering all newspapers, music, literature, radio and film. Police were allowed to open letters and tap phones. It was illegal to spread rumours about the government, or to discuss any alternatives to the regime. It was illegal to belong to any political grouping apart from the Nazi Party, or to any non-Nazi organisations apart from the army, churches and their lay groups. German citizens could be detained indefinitely, without trial, in protective custody or concentration camps. Children who didn't attend Hitler Youth meetings faced leaving school without being awarded a diploma, and civil servants who didn't join the party were threatened with losing their jobs. Millions of youths were indoctrinated from a young age into a belief system in which violence was the norm. There was no obvious route for dissent that would not result in severe punishment, or even the endangering of one's life and the lives of one's loved ones. As a result, many Germans who did not share Nazism's ideology chose the indifference of silence.[2]

Dorothea despised the Nazi party's populism, its violence, its control over every aspect of life; she frequently made jokes about Hitler. Though he served in Hitler's government, Kurt tolerated and occasionally even took part in such conversations. He was a man who believed in little apart from himself; he had joined the party purely because he saw in it the chance to rise.

Before long, the family had nicknamed Inge '*Pünktchen*', or little dot, as they were all very tall, and she barely five foot three. Her letters home in her first few weeks at the house in Dahlem were full of Gisela, Dorothea and her life in Berlin. But there was another member of the family whom she was growing close to, whom her letters home did not mention at all: Gisela's older brother, Wolfgang, whom his family called 'Buschi'.

The first time Inge saw him was across the dinner table, the second time Gigi invited her to the house, just a few weeks before asking her to move in. The soup had already been served when he came in, mumbling apologies for his lateness. He was very tall and wore a long jacket in the English style. His blonde hair was much longer than that of most boys of his age, and flopped across his forehead. He barely spoke during the meal; she noticed he hardly touched the food on his plate, veal escalopes in green sauce. Every time he caught Inge glancing at him she quickly looked the other way. He had a serious face, she thought, and nice blue eyes.

The talk at dinner was of a reception they would give the following week. 'It will be a big party,' Gigi had told Inge earlier that day. 'It's for my stepfather's work.' Dorothea had ordered a new dress for Gigi, and asked Inge if she would come too.

Kurt smiled at Inge kindly, before he turned to Wolfgang. 'If you won't cut your hair, at least you could make sure you attend next week,' he told Wolfgang, only half in jest.

'I do not kiss the gloved hands of the rich,' Wolfgang retorted quietly, in a tone that just managed to escape insolence.

Dorothea gently put her hand on her husband's arm, and Inge stifled a laugh. After dessert was served, Wolfgang excused himself and got up from the table. As he turned to leave the room, he caught Inge's eye, and winked. She felt her cheeks burn.

Wolfgang was a young man of nineteen, a highly intelligent boy whose shyness hid a sensitive character. He had been very close to his older brother Carl, only three years his senior, and had been devastated by his death. Carl had been an extrovert and his father's favourite. With his penchant for sports and danger, he had been the opposite of his quieter, studious younger brother, who preferred books and inventions to physical activity. Wolfgang's natural dislike of pomposity and his diffidence made him, in many ways, ill-suited to his sudden position as his father's heir. He was an idealist with a natural sense of fairness, which often brought him into conflict with his stepfather. He frequently expressed his dislike of Nazism and its creed. While Lange was a Nazi by opportunity rather than conviction, he and Wolfgang often clashed. His relationship with his father was also complex; though Carl-Otto tried to do the right thing for his children, his authoritarian bent made him badly equipped to understand his intellectual son. Wolfgang was exceptionally close to his mother, sharing with her a sensitivity that meant they both felt emotions and disappointments deeply.

Wolfgang had so far escaped serving as a soldier. Born in 1921, he should have been among those called up in March 1941, but had managed to defer his call-up through family connections and by invoking his need to finish his studies. He dreaded the prospect of military life; the qualities that so endeared him to his family made him poorly suited to life as a soldier. While studying engineering, he had found a job in a factory, and enjoyed the work. Gigi hinted darkly to Inge that he had even dabbled in student socialism. She told Inge that he tried to hide his wealth; he never wore a coat to work because his clothing, he said, would show at once where he came from. The subterfuge backfired one day when his colleagues, taking him for a poor student unable to afford winter clothing, clubbed together to buy him one, delivering it to his home, much to his embarrassment.

Gigi did not take her brother very seriously and told these stories with a touch of mockery. But impressionable as Inge was, they sparked in her something of hero worship, which Wolfgang could not help but notice. She would lurk in the corridor outside his room while he listened to music, jazz and swing records he'd bought on a trip to England, where he'd spent a few months at school, and then in Denmark. One day, she plucked up the courage to talk to him about his music, and from then on they became inseparable. The tall student and the pretty brunette girl from Königsberg had discovered that they shared a passion for jazz. In another era, it might have been a teenage romance that lasted only the course of a summer, but in a world that would soon be dominated by war, the darkness of the times and their shared love of forbidden music quickly turned their mutual attraction into a love affair that defined the rest of their lives.

Chapter Six

SWING TIME

There's something else that makes this tune complete ...
It don't mean a thing if it ain't got that swing
– 'It Don't Mean a Thing (If It Ain't Got That Swing)', Duke Ellington

If war, bringing with it the shadow of death, would become the driver of Inge and Wolfgang's romance, swing was its soundtrack. In the spring of 1941, almost two years into the war, life in Berlin, on the surface, continued relatively undisturbed. The German Army seemed unstoppable. By early April of that year, Hitler's forces had invaded and occupied Poland, Denmark, Norway, the Netherlands, Belgium, Luxembourg, France, Yugoslavia and Greece, and were a year into a sustained bombing campaign of Britain. In North Africa, Field Marshal Rommel's Afrika Korps was sent in to back up Mussolini's troops, to drive back the British and control the region. Royal Air Force raids on Germany had been largely unsuccessful so far, because Berlin, more than 900 kilometres from British shores, was at the far reach of the British bombers' range. As a result, the city's infrastructure was unscathed, food supplies had not yet dwindled and civilian morale was high.

After eight years under Nazi control, Berlin had lost the cultural edge and decadence that had made it famous across the world a decade earlier, but to sixteen-year-old Inge, brought up in a sheltered family in the backwater of Königsberg, its nightlife was a revelation. Through Wolfgang, she now discovered a real music scene and the nightlife of a capital city. Gisela always joined them on their outings, allowing the three of them to go out unchaperoned and leaving them to enjoy Berlin's wealth of tea dances, bars and nightclubs with a degree of freedom Inge had never experienced before. While Berlin's jazz scene could not compare with that of London or New York, it still provided music of a quality Inge had never heard before. Until the early 1930s, and during the brief reprieve offered by the 1936 Berlin Olympics, when the Nazi regime, mindful of its international image, temporarily toned down the worst of its anti-Semitic propaganda, Berlin hosted some of the world's top performers. Their influence continued to feed the musicians who had stayed and who tried to offer the latest American jazz and swing hits to eager audiences of mostly teenage fans. For teenagers like Inge and Gisela, swing provided an escape, a means of asserting individuality that was almost irresistible in an era in which the lives of 'Aryan' teenagers were closely monitored.

National Socialism believed it could forge the tastes and morals of a new generation of Germans through total control of their minds and activities. From 1936, all 'Aryan' children over the age of six had to join a Nazi youth movement – all other organised youth leagues had been disbanded three years before. Anyone with Jewish ancestry was banned from organised activities. This was reinforced by the introduction in March 1939 of *Jugenddienstpflicht* – youth service duty – which made such membership mandatory even if parents objected.

Boys were expected to join the *Hitlerjugend* – the Hitler Youth – where they were taught to fire rifles and march in formation, while girls attended the *Bund Deutscher Mädel*, which trained them to be wives and mothers, with some physical education thrown in. Young men and boys were expected to keep their hair short and dress in conservative and almost military fashion; young women were to style their hair in traditional German braids and to leave their faces free of make-up.

Everything about Wolfgang stuck out from his more conservative peers. He owned a collection of swing records you could only buy on the black market. Like other swing enthusiasts, he loved all things American and British; he got on well with his father's second wife, and his year at school in Britain had instilled a love of the English language. Inge's devotion to the genre was perhaps less sincere, as it was initially motivated by a desire to impress him. She started to dress like the girls she saw when they went out dancing, dropping the more conservative hair rolls she'd so admired on Gigi just a few months earlier, letting her curly hair fall loosely to her shoulders, shortening her skirts and buying herself bright scarlet lipstick that scandalised her mother when she wore it during the Easter holidays in Königsberg. She learnt to revere Benny Goodman and Louis Armstrong, dismissing her former idol Zarah Leander as 'Nazi approved'.

Her worship of Wolfgang had inevitable consequences. By the spring of 1941, the two were deeply in love. Gisela became the couple's confidante and partner in crime. The trio were typical *Swingjugend*, swing youths, as they called themselves, young, well-off and from backgrounds whose liberal bent gave them the confidence to rebel against Nazi rules. Though it fell far short of active resistance, it was a spiritual rebellion against a regime that sought to dictate everything from the way youths dressed, to their hobbies and thoughts. It flourished in bigger cities such as Hamburg, Berlin and Frankfurt, especially among upper- and middle-class youths, who had the money and leisure to go to parties and purchase banned records.

Swing's increasing popularity became a thorn in the side of the Nazi regime, which was bent on shaping young people in its image. But the government never fully succeeded in its attempts to ban it, and Nazism's relationship with jazz and swing remained a complicated one, at least for the first half of the war. Joseph Goebbels, the Minister of Propaganda, feared too strict a crackdown on dance venues in wartime would dampen German morale. His attempts to introduce Germany's own brand of 'new dance music' were a failure and crackdowns on orchestras found to be using English jargon or playing 'Jewish' tunes simply led to new ensembles appearing elsewhere. The censors, more often than not, were forced to turn a blind eye.

Goebbels had also been warned that young Germans, eager for dance hits, would turn to foreign sources for their music if thwarted at home, something which indeed many of them did. The BBC cleverly sandwiched its news broadcasts with the latest hits to maximise its appeal to German audiences, and by 1943 it had attracted as many as 3 million clandestine German listeners, including many young soldiers. This became so widespread that Goebbels was forced to make musical performances for the Wehrmacht, the German Army, exempt from the restrictions imposed on civilian venues.

So great was swing's appeal that Nazi propaganda tried for a while to use it to further its own ends. In 1940, Goebbels decided to create his very own swing band, Charlie and his Orchestra, which would prove to be one of the regime's most ridiculous efforts.[1] The band recorded covers of famous American hits, sung in heavily German-accented English and with specially adapted

Nazi lyrics. These were aired every Wednesday and Saturday at about 9 p.m. for the benefit of British audiences. The results were clumsy at best. Bing Crosby's wildly popular 'Makin' Whoopee', reworked by Charlie and his Orchestra, replaced the light-hearted 'Another bride, another June / Another sunny honeymoon' with the more sinister 'Another war, another profit, / Another Jewish business trick'.

Charlie and His Orchestra's musical gems, perhaps unsurprisingly, left the British public cold. But they did acquire one loyal listener, who found their songs immensely entertaining – it was said that Winston Churchill never missed a broadcast.

For young people like Inge and Wolfgang, being a dedicated swing fan was not without peril. The streets around Berlin's nightclubs frequently sported signs stating that swing dancing was *verboten*.[2] Before long, Inge was following Wolfgang to clandestine parties, semi-private gatherings in dance halls and apartments.

With Wolfgang to look out for them, the girls painted their nails red and went out late to nightclubs or to dances in old town halls and basements. It was only at night, when dancing, that they really felt free from the stifling edicts of the Nazi regime. To Inge, those were months of discovery, as she realised how small her world in Königsberg had been. Men started to notice her too, and she soon discovered her power over them; she was not averse to making Wolfgang a little jealous occasionally, but she was always faithful to him. One evening, a Norwegian she was dancing with tried to insist on taking her home with him; only her pleading ensured the evening did not end in blows.

Unwanted sexual advances were not the only danger. Revellers were always at risk from raids by the Gestapo. Organisers would deploy a couple of watchmen just outside the venue to watch out for late-night patrols; if any were spotted, a signal was given and the music would switch to the safer Nazi-tolerated foxtrot. For all the danger it involved, the time Inge and Wolfgang spent at dances, away from prying eyes at home, allowed their relationship to blossom. The threat gave a sense of romance to everything they did; Inge would remember those years as wonderful and terrible in equal measure.

In time, it was a romance which Wolfgang's mother Dorothea could no longer ignore. She loved Inge like another daughter and saw the pleasure Wolfgang and Gigi took in her company. The house, which had been so quiet since her eldest son Carl died, was suddenly filled with laughter. Shy Gisela was full of enthusiasm and vitality, while Wolfgang, who had been rather withdrawn and solitary, was turning into a happy and confident young man; but it was impossible not to see that Wolfgang had fallen in love with Inge. The situation left Dorothea deeply conflicted. She didn't want to hinder her son's happiness, but she had also promised Inge's parents that she would look after her as if she were her own daughter and Inge was still so young.

Her own marriage was under pressure. Word of her outspoken views about the government had reached the ears of some of Kurt's colleagues and he had warned her to keep quiet, though she knew that privately he agreed with much of what she said. She was starting to loathe the ambition she had found so attractive in him, seeing his rebukes as the betrayal of a man who had once admired her for her independence of thought. The feelings of melancholy that had intensified since her eldest son Carl's death started to plague her incessantly. She knew she was allowing her children too much freedom; even Kurt warned her that she was taking a risk in allowing Inge and Wolfgang to go about so often together, with only Gigi for company.

Dorothea knew that the war might take her only surviving son from her, and that she was powerless to prevent it. His year's deferment was almost up and the military was becoming more intransigent as the need for soldiers increased, with Hitler gearing up to expand his empire farther east. For Wolfgang, military life beckoned. Dorothea felt that the only thing she could give him now was his freedom and this made her reluctant to hinder his happiness, comforting herself with the thought that his feelings for Inge might only be a harmless crush. She noticed the covert glances he cast at Inge over the dinner table, his reluctance to look anyone in the eye whenever she was mentioned. Early one morning, unable to sleep, she watched from her bedroom window as the two sneaked back into the house at dawn, holding hands. By the autumn of 1941, Wolfgang's infatuation with Inge was an open secret, yet still Dorothea could not bring herself to put a stop to it.

Wolfgang found concealment increasingly difficult. Once, when Dorothea told him they would find a way to keep him from being forced to be a soldier, he exclaimed, 'If you want to hide me, it won't work. I'm so in love with Pünktchen, it would be very hard for me to stay away.'

He'd spoken the words in a light-hearted tone, but Inge's blushing face led Dorothea to take the girl aside.

'Buschi says he loves you. How do you feel about him?'

'It's all a silly joke,' Inge said, trying to laugh it off.

Inge, who usually confided everything to Dorothea, was wary of telling her how she really felt. She feared that Dorothea would feel duty-bound to tell her parents, who would come and take her away. In secret, she and Wolfgang were mapping out their future life together. They planned to marry as soon as he returned from the war, something which remained a somewhat abstract concept, at least to Inge. After his studies, he would find work as an engineer and they would live together in Berlin or perhaps even travel the world. Wolfgang told her that when the time came, he would write to her parents to formally request her hand. He warned her that his father might make difficulties and Inge knew, though Wolfgang wouldn't say it, that this was because the circles her family moved in were not as smart; Carl-Otto hoped that his son would make an advantageous marriage. Regardless of these obstacles, he promised her the world and she, with all the conviction of first love, thought nothing could stand in their way.

Chapter Seven

THE BETRAYAL

I would have liked to hear my grandmother recount their love story without knowing how it ended. To imagine it as a love forged in wartime that had endured the test of conflict and time, a tale a happy couple might tell their grandchildren after many years together. But I already knew that this was not to be. I knew that he had survived the war, that they had stayed apart. The story of their romance had long been mired in silence; what I wanted to know, was why.

I might never have found out that it had been love, and not war, that caused the first great pain in Inge's life, had I not experienced heartbreak myself. I was in the thick of that pain, hard and sharp, which hits you like a punch to the stomach – the one that comes with betrayal. In December 2012, the end of an affair had brought me to France earlier than I had planned, well before the start of my family's Christmas celebrations. My grandmother's recognition of my pain pierced her reserve, reviving memories of her first heartbreak seventy years before.

My grandmother was already a week into her month-long visit. Only my mother and aunt were there, my brother and his family were not due to arrive until the following week. She was visibly frailer, which made the journeys from her home in Germany more arduous, but she still doggedly undertook them twice a year. Winter frosts give the south-west of France a delicate prettiness, its outlines sharper, its colours less vivid than those of summer. But consumed by heartbreak, I could not see its beauty that year. Instead I stayed indoors and often joined my grandmother in the darkened sitting room where she spent most of her days.

My family, whose love is of the prying kind, had left me well alone for once. I needed refuge in silence and found it, unexpectedly, in her quiet companionship. There was understanding in her silences, in her lack of questioning, that led me to talk. Almost before I even knew I'd begun, I'd told her everything, the instant mutual attraction, the charge in every touch and word. How he'd told me he was already separated from his long-term partner, a half-truth told in the intensity of that first meeting. His frantic and insistent courtship, and the year in the shadows that followed, waiting for him to change his life so I could be a part of it. The excitement of secrecy, the emptiness of bank holiday weekends, and dinner parties attended alone. That first time I'd walked away, when he'd begged me to come back, before finally asking me to risk it all. The promises, the elation, and then, perhaps predictably, his last-minute change of heart. How, after the tickets were booked, he had sat in that cafe unable to meet my eye, and how I knew, without him even having to say it, that he had gone back to her.

She listened quietly without interrupting, her eyes intent and fixed on my face. She took in every detail, her gaze never wavering. When I finally stopped speaking, she said nothing for so long I wondered if I had been mistaken. Perhaps she had not been listening at all, until she gently took my hand.

'*Ach Süße*. I know, it happened to me too.'

And then she too, started to talk, continuing the story of her and Wolfgang's doomed romance.

*

The blow fell in late spring 1942, on an unusually warm May morning, when Inge had been living at the house in Dahlem for more than a year. The letter was brought in on a tray while the family were at breakfast in the garden room and Wolfgang was just minutes away from leaving for work. It was addressed to him, on official paper.

Inge watched him open it in silence, and saw Dorothea staring fixedly ahead, her face frozen. Gisela, who had been buttering her toast, paused with her knife in mid-air. Wolfgang's skin was ashen. They all knew what it must contain.

He read the telegram out loud, in a voice that shook slightly. The message was short and to the point: it summoned him to report to barracks in three weeks. Inge didn't even have time to hear Dorothea's gasp or see her take her son into her arms. Unable to hide her feelings any longer, she burst into tears, and ran out of the room. Wolfgang left for work and Dorothea went to bed, her face turned to the wall. Only Gisela came to hold her as they both wept at the news that marked the end of Wolfgang's youth.

There was a party in a private dance hall in central Berlin that night, organised by a student friend of Wolfgang's. It was an event of the kind that had flourished since under twenty-ones had been banned from attending nightclubs the year before. The United States' entry into the war in December 1941 had led to a renewed crackdown by the authorities on followers of American culture, driving the *Swingjugend* further underground. The party was invitation only, held in strictest secrecy, the consequences of being arrested having become more severe. In August 1941, more than 300 teenage swing fans had been arrested in Hamburg and a number sent to concentration camps, an ordeal that some of them did not survive. The following January, just a few months before Wolfgang's summons arrived, the *Swingjugend* had drawn the attention of two of the Holocaust's most senior architects and enforcers. Heinrich Himmler, head of both the SS and the German police, wrote to Reinhart Heydrich, chief of the Reich's Main Security Office, calling for the 'evil' of swing to be 'radically exterminated' and its organisers 're-educated' by a few years of hard labour and beatings.

But the weight of Wolfgang's summons to war gave him and Inge a new sense of recklessness. The party was in the basement of an office building in East Berlin, the concrete rooms made welcoming by red velvet sofas and cushions on the floor. The light was dim and a large stage dominated the main room, which was filled with people. Once they arrived, Gisela discreetly went to join other friends, leaving Inge and her brother alone. That night the band played Duke Ellington's 'It Don't Mean a Thing' twice, and Inge and Wolfgang did not leave each other's side, holding each other close; Inge would remember that song for the rest of her life. They did not return to the house on Vogelsang until late into the night. With just three hours left before the rising sun would wake the household, Inge, for the first time, allowed Wolfgang into her room.

After Wolfgang's departure in early June, the household did its best to return to normal. He had not been sent straight to the front but to a training facility some hundred kilometres away, where he would spend the next few weeks waiting to be told where his regiment would be deployed, something he would find out with only a few days' warning. While Wolfgang was learning the rudiments of life as a soldier, Dorothea pulled every string she could think of, pleading with every acquaintance to help ensure her son would be sent to the Western Front. No one in the household had dared suggest the possibility Wolfgang might be sent out east, where his own father was serving as an officer.

The war was preparing to enter its bloodiest chapters. Germany's fragile truce with the Soviet Union had ended the previous June when Hitler, emboldened by the army's successes in Western Europe and North Africa, set his sights on conquering the Soviet Union and invaded its territory. That winter, tales of atrocities committed against Jews and the local population of Eastern Europe started to filter back to civilians back home. The first winter offensive had taken its toll on a Wehrmacht ill-equipped for the harshness of the Russian climate, and while the Germans had yet to suffer defeat on the ground on a significant scale, morale had been dented. Hitler, who took pride in his own hardiness, had refused to heed meteorological forecasts warning of the early and intense winter that hit Russia in 1941, with disastrous consequences. The army's failure to supply its troops with proper winter clothing left thousands of soldiers maimed by frostbite. Soldiers were so ill-equipped that in December Goebbels broadcast an appeal for warm clothing to be sent to the troops. These stories were impossible to suppress; they were told in army messes, and filtered home in coded letters that soldiers wrote to their loved ones. A college friend of Inge's said her brother had told her that his regiment had crossed paths with troops on their way home from the Eastern Front. Something unusual struck him in the returning soldiers' wide-eyed stares; he was told later that their eyelids had frozen off.

In this climate, the best Wolfgang could hope for during his few weeks' training was that he would be sent to the Western Front, where the fighting was less fierce, the weather less brutal and food was in better supply. After Wolfgang's departure for training, the way Inge saw the world changed. In the past, she had cared little for people's accounts of the front but she now became hungry for the smallest detail, never missing an official broadcast and keeping an ear out for any uncensored news that filtered out. For the first time she noticed the absence of men on the tram she took to her classes, in the street, in the shops. Rationing was getting stricter, with goods harder to come by, and the war was slowly reaching the everyday lives of those Berliners who until then had been able to ignore it.

The girls had transferred to new courses at college, Inge to study interior design, and Gisela fashion. Inge was glad to leave behind the hours she'd been taught to stitch, darn and cook, and threw herself into her studies. She regularly received letters from her parents, who wrote with news of friends, of day-to-day life in Königsberg, where it seemed little had changed. But Wolfgang's absence hung heavy about the house, in his empty place at the table, in the quiet of the upstairs rooms, where the gramophone in his room no longer played his favourite records. Gone, too, was the nightlife they had so enjoyed; Inge spent most evenings at home, as Wolfgang had been the instigator of their outings. The one tea dance to which Dorothea took her and Gisela to cheer them up ended with Inge bursting into tears. She no longer had the strength to hide her feelings.

Dorothea, who now knew the depth of Inge's attachment to her son, pitied her. Wolfgang had departed in early June, and would not be granted leave until just before his deployment. It was now mid-July. She pretended not to see the letters that arrived, addressed to Inge in her son's hand, several times a week. They were the only times the girl, who looked pale and had lost much of her vivacity, came alive again. He wrote of future plans, describing their life together after the war. He spoke little of his day-to-day life as a soldier, save for details of army meals or to describe others in his regiment. Though only twenty-two, he was older than most of the recruits, some of whom were as young as seventeen, as the German Army now allowed men to enlist two years ahead of their compulsory draft. Those young boys showed a zeal and enthusiasm for war that Wolfgang simply could not understand. He hated the brutality of life in the army, and the war that he did not believe in fighting.

Dorothea, who had allowed her children to voice their criticism freely in the house, now wished that she had taught them to stay quiet instead; these were dangerous times to speak one's mind. It was bad enough as a civilian; Germany's entire legal system was designed to shut down dissent. As the war raged on, the intelligence agency, known as the SD, was ever keen to pick up on any signs of public anxiety and the Gestapo was swift to crack down on any 'defeatist' talk. But as a soldier, Wolfang would no longer enjoy the safety of closed doors behind which he could vent his anger.

The Wiegandts had not seen their daughter since Christmas, as Inge had cancelled a planned visit in May, saying she was too busy with her new course, but really in order to spend the last few days with Wolfgang before his enlistment. She was due to return to Königsberg for the summer holidays in July, and from there to travel to Rauschen, where her parents had reserved their usual rooms at the boarding house. Frieda had written to ask whether she wanted Gisela to come and join them there for a few weeks and who Inge wanted to invite for her eighteenth birthday celebrations.

Inge's letters home had lost much of their zest and excitement and even talk of a birthday party failed to spark her interest. She wrote only of her studies. Albert welcomed her new seriousness as a mark of his daughter growing up, but Inge's tone worried Frieda, who read it as a sign of unhappiness, though she didn't suspect its cause. Dorothea was concerned about Inge too, noticing how little she ate at breakfast and how withdrawn she had become. She thought Inge's long silences and her growing habit of skipping meals were down to her missing Wolfgang. She no longer worried about the relationship between the two young people, believing that war and separation would bring it to a natural end, or at least force them both to wait until they were a little older.

One morning, Inge did not come down at all and Dorothea, full of concern, went up to her room. There was no answer to her knock, so she called out and tried the handle, only to find the door locked. After a few moments she heard the key turn and the door slowly opened. Inge was sitting on the edge of her bed. She had not changed out of her nightdress or brushed her hair. As Dorothea looked at the girl's face, it was not her unkempt appearance that betrayed her, but the fear in her eyes. She understood almost at once, taking Inge's face in her hands, asking if she was ill, but she knew the answer before Inge shook her head.

When Dorothea asked Inge whether she'd been sick, the girl could not bring herself to look her in the eye. She asked if she had missed her period, and Inge nodded slowly, before bursting into tears in the older woman's arms.

'That too, in these terrible times,' Dorothea said as she hugged Inge close.

'What am I going to do?' Inge said, looking up at her, her face still wet.

'You must marry, and soon. It's the right thing to do.'

Dorothea knew the phone call would devastate Inge's parents. She thought of Frieda's visit a few months before, remembered how she had thanked Dorothea for looking after her daughter. After trying to console Inge, she had, with the guilt of that meeting in mind, spoken to her in a more severe tone than she had ever used before. Her conscience told her that this was her fault for failing to separate the lovers, but it was too late now.

Inge listened behind the door as the phone call took place.

'I'm sorry,' she heard Dorothea say. 'I was unable to prevent it. But I love your daughter and I want her to marry my son. We'll make it come right.'

Wolfgang was due back for a short leave the following week, ahead of his deployment. Although Dorothea had been counting the days until she could see her son, she now dreaded his return. They must marry, she thought, even though they were both so young. She wondered how her former husband, full of pride in his only remaining son, would take the news and knew there would be trouble ahead. Carl-Otto still supported his children financially and much would depend on what he had to say.

Inge had written to Wolfgang telling him of her pregnancy before Dorothea discovered it. He responded to her letter at once, promising to look after her and to put things right. He would find the right moment to talk to his father; the plans they had made for a life after the war would just have to be brought forward. Despite these reassurances, he was terrified of telling Carl-Otto, who he knew would not approve. He did not know that the news had already reached the rest of the household. When he received his mother's letter, he knew the meeting could no longer be delayed. He and Gisela were due to meet his father on his next leave, as they did every quarter, in the same restaurant in Berlin as always. He wrote to his father saying he needed to speak to him after lunch.

In Berlin, Inge helped Gisela prepare for lunch with her father. They were to meet at the restaurant at 12.30 p.m. At 11 a.m., Gisela suddenly remembered that her nails were still painted red.

'The old man will go crazy!' she said to Inge. 'He's so strict, I know what he'll say.'

Inge ran at once to the chemist for a bottle of nail varnish remover.

As she cleaned off the last smear of red with a piece of cotton wool, Gisela said gently, 'You know, Inge, the old man doesn't like trouble. He's already had quite a bit, since marrying the English-woman, now that he's a German officer. He won't want any more.'

'What do you mean?' Inge asked

'About you,' she said. 'He won't want any trouble about you.'

Carl-Otto von Schimmelmann was a proud man, who held high hopes for his surviving son and heir. Although he had lost much of the family fortune, his children were still financially reliant on him. Kurt Lange, while enjoying a lavish lifestyle through his work, had few means beyond his salary, and was in no position to support his stepchildren as they neared adulthood. Carl-Otto had read the letter Dorothea had sent him with consternation. If Wolf-gang had hoped to find him a sympathetic listener, he was deeply mistaken. Carl-Otto flatly forbade the marriage.

While he told his son he was too young to marry, as Wolfgang had feared, his reasons lay mainly in the fact that he did not think the match prestigious enough. Inge was from a respectable, com-fortable background, but she did not meet the social ambitions he had entertained for his son. Carl-Otto was by then heavily in debt; even the sale of the family estate had not ended his financial troubles, and he hoped his son's marriage might restore the status and wealth his family had once enjoyed. He told Wolfgang that he must finish his military service and his studies before he could think of marrying at all. After the war, perhaps they would reconsider, but if he married now, he would be cut off without a penny.

Inge waited for Wolfgang's return that day, sitting by the window. Her parents were on their way from Königsberg. She hoped that everything would be settled by the time they arrived. Gisela's words troubled her, but she tried to put them out of her mind.

She jumped as she heard the car pull into the driveway. Only Gisela stepped out. It was another hour before Wolfgang returned. She ran up to him as he walked up the driveway; one look at his face was enough.

Gentle, shy Wolfgang, who had only ever sought rebellion in music, was not strong enough to stand up to his father. Faced with the full weight of Carl-Otto's disapproval, he had given in. Perhaps he'd told himself that he would work things out with Inge eventually, that this was only a delay. He told her he was sorry, that he would explain – but she would not listen. His weakness at the moment she had needed him most betrayed every pledge and declaration that he had ever made her. She did not want to hear his protestations. She ran from him, leaving him standing in the hall. That was to be their parting: that evening, a taxi came to take him to his father's hotel.

Dorothea tried to intervene. She was devastated by the outcome of Wolfgang's conversation with his father. Inge was their daughter's best friend and, while the match would not be a grand one, it was hardly disastrous. The girl was living in their house as a family friend, and Dorothea felt that they had deeply failed both Inge and her parents in their duty of care. Kurt agreed with her, but his position as the man who had enticed Dorothea to leave Carl-Otto made it impossible for him to intercede.

As for Wolfgang, while she deplored his lack of courage, she could also sympathise with it. She knew the power Carl-Otto exercised over his children; she herself had experienced his influence during their marriage. She felt helpless. That night, she held Inge in her arms, and sobbed.

While Inge had been living in Berlin, Frieda and Albert's life in Königsberg had continued to run along well-ordered lines. Their lives and social circles followed the strict morality of a provincial town and were rarely touched by scandal. Like many others, Albert's business had suffered from the wartime economy, especially during those later years. Grain shortages had increased the cost of making schnapps, and rationing curbed demand for imported wines. But he had laid aside enough money in the years before the war broke out to secure not only his and Frieda's future, but also that of his daughter. He still owned the house he had bought from his Jewish neighbour a few years before, which he rented out until the time would come, he hoped, for Inge to live there with her own family.

Though Russia, which shared a border with East Prussia, had again been declared an enemy, the Wiegandts' life in Königsberg reflected little of this new menace. East Prussia's geographic isolation shielded its German population from the most obvious signs of war. Its rich agriculture offset the worst of rationing's restrictions, at least in the countryside. Beyond periodic troop movements through the region and the absence of fathers, brothers and sons, there was little to be felt of war at all. From the quiet and safety of Königsberg, Albert worried about his daughter. Concern about air raids, infrequent though they still were, and about the war, which he had started to think the Allies would probably win, had replaced the fears that had occupied his mind when Inge had first asked to move to Berlin, fears more typical of the father of a teenage daughter. But in a future that war had made uncertain, Inge's prospects shone bright. He was proud of her achievements in Berlin, her enthusiasm for her studies and her connection with the von Schimmelmann family. He loved the new sophistication that set her apart from her peers on her visits home. Inge's move to the house in Dahlem had brought the Wiegandts great comfort. They had met Dorothea and her husband, and seen how the family had taken to their daughter.

Dorothea's phone call was the blow that ended all these hopes.

Frieda answered the phone, her hands still full of the linen she'd been mending. Albert was standing beside her. He saw his wife's face suddenly freeze, and the dishcloths she'd been carefully hemming fall to the floor.

His first thought was that Inge had been injured in an air raid. The truth, when he learnt it, brought a mixed relief. To Albert and Frieda, seventeen-year-old Inge was still a child. But though they were in many ways typical of their generation, their reaction to Inge's news set them apart. Their first instinct on hearing of her pregnancy was to protect their daughter, rather than to condemn her. Within an hour of Dorothea's call, Albert had written to Wolfgang's father to request a meeting. The next morning, they were on their way to Berlin.

Frieda collected Inge as soon as they arrived and took her to a hotel. There was no sternness in that first reunion; Inge flung herself into her mother's arms. She was a little shy of her father at first, fearing his reproaches. Instead, he wept as he held her, his tears hurting Inge more than any disapproval could.

Frieda's meeting with Dorothea was a quieter affair. The women talked for a long time, Frieda discovering in Wolfgang's mother an ally who was prepared to fight Inge's corner. Frieda's kindness moved Dorothea, who felt her helplessness acutely; it made Wolfgang's father's behaviour even harder to bear.

The next morning, a letter from Carl-Otto arrived at Albert's hotel. In it, he restated his opposition to a marriage between Inge and his son; it was the beginning of a furious row. The two men met in a Berlin restaurant. Carl-Otto refused to budge, and Albert stormed out. An angry exchange of notes followed. Finally, Albert requested a meeting with Wolfgang, hoping to appeal to the boy's sense of responsibility. But there, Carl-Otto played his trump card. He told Albert that his son had just received his call-up, and would be leaving for the Eastern Front that very day. The timing might have been a mere coincidence, but Wolfgang believed for the rest of his life that his father had orchestrated it.

After the terrible failure of the Battle of Moscow the winter before, the Eastern Front was the destination every German soldier feared. The Battle of Stalingrad began at the end of August and would, over the coming months, prove one of the bloodiest of an already brutal conflict. Forced to fight in a war he did not believe in, the summons had come as a death sentence for Wolfgang.

'My Buschi, he let me down,' my grandmother said. She was still holding my hand and I felt her grip tighten. Her feelings were still raw seven decades later. 'I still don't understand it, after everything he said.'

Her nails were digging into my skin, but I did not withdraw my hand.

'After everything we both felt. All the promises he made. He had told me, again and again, that it would be all right. I will never understand.'

Later, I thought of the selfishness I'd always seen as self-indulgence, which I now realised might have been her protection. I remembered the stories my mother had told me, incomplete and sketchy, of a wartime marriage later dissolved. She had told me that the ceremony had taken place in Königsberg without the groom's presence; a hat had been placed on a chair in his stead. Was this story true, or had it been invented to preserve my mother from the strong stain of illegitimacy? I imagined Inge as a lone bride in this ridiculous scene, just eighteen and heavily pregnant. Who had put the ring on her finger? Whose hat had they used?

It was a story from a time when respectability mattered, though the war had eroded social norms to an extent. Conflict forced even unimaginative people into unconventional choices; it made a habit of deception and led the prudent to become reckless. Something about the strangeness of the ceremony's detail made me think the story could have been true. But whatever legality had been given to her circumstances, it did not lessen the strength of the betrayal in my grandmother's recollection. She remembered only that Wolfgang had buckled under his father's pressure and broken the promise he had made as he held her close during that last dance in Berlin. She remembered that she had been forced to realise that a love she had thought stronger than war itself had been fragile, in the end. Seventy years later, the bitterness of that hurt still stung her.

And yet, much as she had revealed, there was still so much more to this story that I wanted to know. My grandmother still spoke of Wolfgang as the love of her life. I knew they had met again after the war had ended, after my mother had been born, and I wondered why nothing had come of that reunion. My mother, who must have asked herself that question throughout her childhood, had come up with her own explanation, which had become the prevailing family narrative: that the Wolfgang who met Inge after the war was a soldier who had spent three years in Russian captivity and had returned a broken man, drained of all emotion. His teenage sweetheart was by then a woman, a mother and a refugee, who had seen death and deprivation first-hand. They'd met again as adults, shaped by hardships. Survival had taken up all their emotional resources, extinguishing that earlier teenage love.

While this had the ring of truth, something still didn't add up. Life in a Soviet camp would not have led him to forget a sweetheart whose memory might have been one of the few things keeping him alive. My grandmother, who felt so strongly about him decades later, must surely have still loved him when he first returned. Surely, she would have wanted her daughter to have a father in her life.

The pain of betrayal felt by my grandmother and the memories of my own hurt still fresh in my mind, I wondered, for a moment, whether Wolfgang's story was a lie – if perhaps he hadn't really loved her as she'd loved him; if my great-grandfather's disapproval of the match had been little more than an excuse; even, for a while, if he had been a prisoner at all. It was the moment I stopped just being a listener, and decided to seek out the truth.

Chapter Eight

AN UNCERTAIN FUTURE

Sifting through the past can be a slow and painstaking process. But sometimes the clues you look for come unbidden, and when you least expect them. A few months after I began searching for further details of my grandmother's past, my mother gave me a book of Friedrich Hölderlin's poems. She'd found it at the back of a cupboard in one of her unsuccessful attempts to sort through her papers. She didn't remember how she had come by this gently worn, slim paperback volume, which had my grandmother's name inscribed on the flyleaf. As I opened it, a photograph fell from where it had been tucked between the pages of a poem called 'The Oak Trees'. It was black and white and a little faded, showing a group of holidaymakers on a beach. The figures were standing by a wooden jetty on a sunny summer's day, somewhere in East Prussia.

At the front, to the right, was an older woman – Frieda perhaps, though I couldn't be certain – wearing what would today be called a jumpsuit in a bold floral pattern, and a string of pearls. She was laughing as she held a ring in her left hand and a ball in her right, her arm raised mid-swing as though she were about to throw it. Second from the left was my grandmother, standing next to a muscular young blond man, who was almost a paragon of healthy German manhood. She was wearing a dark short-sleeved jacket over a bathing suit in a pale Liberty print, its bottom half gathered in puffs, and smiled as the wind blew her hair away from her face.

INGE AND FRIENDS BY THE SEA.

I didn't know the young man's name, but the fact he's there at all dated the photograph to no later than 1941, Inge's first summer back from Berlin. After that he, like all young men of his age group, would have been called up to the front.

It was a moment of light-hearted joy frozen in time, a holiday snap like many others, taken in Cranz, perhaps, or Rauschen; there was nothing written on the back to identify its location. I was not sure why it moved me so. The knowledge, perhaps, as I held it in my hand seven decades later, of what was yet to come for that carefree little group. It showed a final fleeting summer of youth and innocence, a world about to shatter, not just for Inge by Wolfgang's betrayal, but for a whole generation, who would soon be swept up by a tide of brutality in which they would all but disappear.

I thought about that last time Inge came home on holiday, the summer the photograph might have been taken. She was then a

Lette Mädchen, the darling of her mother's friends, the envy of her peers, full of tales of her studies and life in a grand house in Berlin. A year later, she faced a different return, back to a provincial town and its conservative bourgeois circles, whose codes she had failed and from which she had fallen. She was no longer a young woman with a future, but one disgraced, bearing a child without the clear promise of a marriage. It must have been hard for Albert and Frieda too, part of a generation whose lives were bound by convention and to whom change did not come easily. Did Inge think of this on the train ride back east and wonder if life could ever be as it once was in that snapshot, surrounded by friends in a moment of carefree fun?

For Inge at least, the East Prussia she returned to in the late summer of 1942 had changed very little. The fear of air raids that had started to prey on civilians' minds after the bombings of Lübeck and Cologne that spring had not yet reached the region. Königsberg and its streets had been shielded by its remoteness. But though the city had been spared for now, its younger generation had not. August 1942 was a turning point for Germany in the war, and Hitler's determination to break Russia had set the country on a course from which it would not recover, sealing the fate of East Prussia, the homeland the Wiegandts held so dear. The young man who stands beside Inge in the photograph would probably have been a soldier, sent like most East Prussian recruits to the Eastern Front. If he had not been killed by 1942 his chances of survival would have grown slimmer by the day. In the summer of 1944, the German Army would lose a million men, dead, wounded or missing, in the space of just 150 days. As for the women in the picture, they would almost certainly have already lost friends, husbands, sweethearts, or brothers. In early 1945, the lucky ones among them would face flight and displacement; those less fortunate, who stayed behind, are likely to have endured the unspeakable horror of gang rape by the Red Army.

Inge could not have known all this as she looked out of the window at the beauty of the landscape, made richer by the hints of early autumn colour, as the train took her eastwards to her home. But though she was then just eighteen, the last few weeks had divested her of her naivety. She was returning a different woman, with new-found cynicism, and eyes that noticed things she would previously not have seen.

'My stomach was getting rounder,' she told me. 'I wanted to scream, to ask why he had let me down, but his father wouldn't allow me to see him. All those who wanted to help me, Mütterchen, my mother, my father, were powerless. There was nothing to do but to go home.'

If I were to pinpoint the moment I felt my grandmother dropped the last of her guard towards me, I would date it to our moment of shared hurt at a man's betrayal. The thoughts she shared with me from that time were no longer those of a naive girl. They were self-critical, raw, angry and sad: those of one woman opening her feelings to another.

They marked Inge's last night in Berlin with a quiet dinner in the hotel. She and Frieda set off early the next morning on the long train journey home, while Albert stayed behind to do battle with Wolfgang's father. Inge hadn't seen Wolfgang since the day he had told her his father had forbidden their marriage. She thought of him constantly, with both pain and worry, wondering where the war would take him, still holding on to the hope that everything might eventually still come right. In the meantime, there was nothing for her to do but wait quietly, resignedly, all her gaiety gone. She dreaded the questions she would face back home, the shame, the disappointment of the friends who had argued so strongly in favour of her going away.

As she got off the train, she was immediately struck by how few signs of conflict the streets of Königsberg bore. Though Berlin's infrastructure still worked, war was visible on every corner, and in the back gardens where more and more private shelters were being built. The increasing frequency of RAF raids had prompted the German government to step up civilian defences in the northern part of the country. A couple of successful incursions on Berlin had caused relatively minor damage – it was only after the United States, with their longer-range aircraft, joined the war that the air raids on Berlin became more severe – but had significantly dented morale, hitting the city many Germans had believed beyond the Allies' reach. Three concrete towers, with walls four metres thick, were built in the capital's parks, complete with radar equipment and anti-aircraft guns. Though there were only enough public bunkers in Berlin to accommodate 10 per cent of its inhabitants, the towers were visible signs that the city was readying itself for attack.[1]

War fatigue had set in. Berlin was a city where cynicism towards politicians was second nature, and Inge had grown used to talk of possible defeat, to jokes and comments critical of the regime. Since Wolfgang's departure for the army, she had been more alert to these changes in morale or mood, hoping that the end of the war would bring Wolfgang back to her. In Königsberg, by contrast, one could be forgiven for thinking the war had never happened. People went about their daily business and enjoyed *Kaffe und Kuchen* at the city's cafes. The region itself was still undamaged, and only the military hospitals and training camps set up across the province served as reminders that Germany had been in a state of war for over three years.

It was a pace of life in which Inge, as she awaited the birth of her child, found a degree of comfort. It felt as if time had stood still, giving an illusion of peace that made what came after the end of their life in Königsberg, when the tables finally turned, even more shocking in its brutality.

To the extent that war made itself felt for people like the Wiegandts, it was in the privations of daily life. East Prussia's urban areas had been hit by an acute shortage of food and coal. That spring, food rations were cut across Germany, reducing the allowance of meat and fat by a quarter, and there was a dire shortage of fresh vegetables, as much of the agricultural produce was reserved for army use. While those in the countryside found ways to supplement rations, in Königsberg itself people had little option but to turn to the black market, which flourished.

With most German men between the ages of eighteen and forty-five at the front, Polish and French prisoners of war and workers from occupied territories farther east had been forcibly brought in as manual and agricultural labourers. By mid-1942, though Germany had not implemented the mass evacuations that the British had put in place at the start of the conflict, many schoolchildren and mothers with infants from big urban areas such as Hamburg or Berlin had been relocated to East Prussia, at the time still considered one of the safest regions in the Reich.*

There were also other, daily reminders of Nazi brutality, for those who chose to see them. The persecution of East Prussia's

---

* The bulk of evacuees arrived in 1943 after more severe air raids started.

Jews had now been going on for a decade, increasing in intensity every year. Even before Königsberg's Jewish population had been all but eradicated in 1942, in 1940, 1,558 mentally and physically disabled inmates disappeared from East Prussian institutions and were transported to the Soldau camp in Poland, where they were later killed with a mobile gas van.[2] Their families' enquiries were met with a bureaucratic silence as Erich Koch, who had been running East Prussia as though it were his personal fiefdom since 1928, ensured their tragic fate was never publicly disclosed. By then, the Nazis had also started to crack down on what they saw as evidence of moral decay in women whose menfolk had gone off to fight, focusing particularly on reports of romantic liaisons with POWs. By contrast with the inhumane treatment meted out to many prisoners of war, whether civilians or captured soldiers, evidence suggests that in East Prussia, POWs and civilian workers, mainly from France and Poland, were often relatively well treated by the farming families whose land they had been sent to work on, and with whom they lived in close proximity. Sexual relations with prisoners of war resulted in public humiliation for these women and death by hanging for the men involved. In the first half of June 1942 alone, Königsberg's state court passed fifty-six such death sentences.[3]

Both Inge and my mother told me that Frieda used to end her prayers with the words: 'God help us and those less fortunate to live through these terrible times.' Frieda, Inge said, tried, in her small way, to counter the normalised world of violence with small acts of charity. These were far from heroic, but in the early days of the regime, both she and her husband, through Albert's contacts from the wine trade, helped find sponsors abroad for those Jewish friends who emigrated in time. As the persecution grew harsher, she brought those who remained presents of money or food while she still could. She included the widow of Albert's friend Max, whose arrest and probable death in custody had made her a social outcast, in every family gathering. No one ever knew for certain how Max had met his end, and his wife's mind had grown unbalanced.

These were tiny, almost insignificant gestures, but they were enough, at the very least, to expose Frieda to disapproving talk, in a world where to be noticed held dangers. I used to think that, living in those times, I would never have been able to keep myself from speaking out. Now, as I learnt to know the Wiegandts and their lives, I was no longer so sure. No one can take their capacity for heroism for granted.

But the war had yet to meaningfully change the Wiegandts' lives. A couple of days after their return, Frieda took Inge straight to Rauschen on the coast to give her time to rest and adjust. She thought the fresh air and happy memories of childhood summers might help reconcile her daughter to the changes she would be forced to make to her life and would postpone the inevitable awkward and painful questions from well-meaning friends and neighbours. In Rauschen, the impact of war was more visible. Her regular group of friends wasn't there that year and the beaches were quiet. Those hotels not given over to housing evacuees from the big cities in the west were boarded up, and only a handful of cafes remained open to holidaymakers. Christa, her companion of past summers, had stayed home to help her mother, who was struggling to cope with the loss of Christa's older brother Franz. He had died while serving as a soldier in Ukraine, and her father was away with his regiment somewhere in the Caucasus.

In Rauschen, Inge walked for hours along the familiar beaches. As her pregnancy started to show, Albert and Frieda explained to friends that Inge's fiancé was at the front fighting the Red Army. Her pregnancy drew its share of condemnation in Königsberg. She had heard the whispers from some of the women who knew the Wiegandts as she queued for rations, seen the look the neighbour's wife gave her every time she passed her on the stairs. Only the proprietor of the Cafe Berlin, who had known her since she was a little girl, acknowledged her pregnancy with nothing but warmth, insisting she sit at the best table with such kindness it almost hurt. But as the weeks went by, and reports from the Eastern Front grew graver, the glances of those who had judged her at first gradually softened.

For a regime rigid in its adherence to traditions and conservative in its views of women, condemning female emancipation as a feature of communism, Nazism's attitude to unmarried 'Aryan' mothers was curiously liberal. The motive behind this was predictably sinister; alarmed by the declining birth rate, the regime was fanatically pursuing any policy that would increase reproduction among 'racially pure' Germans. Women were celebrated solely for their capacity to bear children. The growing losses at the front had raised the prospect of a future in which women would significantly outnumber men, prompting talk in Nazi circles of actively promoting single motherhood and encouraging German soldiers returning from war to father children outside their own marriages. In a plan Hitler outlined in 1944, he envisaged a 'post-war polygamous utopia' where single German women would be used to increase the 'Aryan' population.

Until such plans could be developed, the state provided assistance to single mothers in the form of fresh linen and other household goods, as well as medical care. During the war, to make the birth of those children considered to be racially worthy both legally and socially acceptable, measures such as 'war marriage' and 'long distance marriage' were implemented and made policy priorities.

*

As autumn and then winter came and the US air force intensified its aerial attacks on Germany, Albert and Frieda drew comfort from the fact that their daughter was safer in Königsberg than she would have been in Berlin. Both Dorothea, who remained in Berlin, and Gisela, who moved in with her father's family near Munich, away from the danger of bombings, wrote to Inge regularly. Dorothea, blaming herself for failing to prevent the pregnancy, had been a little more reserved than usual towards Inge in the immediate aftermath of its discovery, but Inge's return to her parents' home soon removed this sense of awkwardness, allowing both women to resume their intimacy. They wrote to each other every week. News of Wolfgang was sporadic at best and Inge knew only the little Dorothea was able to tell her: that he was somewhere on the Eastern Front. Inge did not know exactly where he was, though she had heard that the offensive to capture Stalingrad, which had begun in August, led by the 6th Army, a field unit of the Wehrmacht, was taking up much of the military's resources.

Inge listened for every news bulletin of the battle, but the accounts on Germany's Rundfunk radio and the newspapers – carefully controlled by Goebbels – only ever consisted of praise, lauding the 6th Army's endurance, and continuing to speak in upbeat terms of Germany's imminent victory. In early November, Hitler declared that only a few pockets of Stalingrad were yet to be conquered. It was only through Frieda's uncle, who listened to the BBC in secret, that they learnt the truth – that the Wehrmacht had been cut off following the Red Army's successful attack. None of the official broadcasts carried this news, but it soon became apparent that the Wiegandts were not alone in having found alternative sources of information. A friend of Frieda's, whose son was also at the Eastern Front, came round the next day to give them the news and seek comfort for her worries, which she dared not reveal in public. From December 1942 on, the official broadcasts that carried the news sanctioned by the regime became thinner in content and more infrequent.

In mid-December, Inge finally received a letter from Wolfgang, dated a few weeks earlier, the envelope tattered, the military stamp revealing little of his location. She did not know whether he had hesitated before sending it, or if it had simply been slow in getting to her, for military mail was often subject to lengthy delays. In it, he asked for her forgiveness and spoke of the months they had known together in the words of someone who would never again live to repeat them. It held nothing of the tone of the optimistic and impulsive boy she still loved in spite of everything; it was a letter from a man resigning himself to likely death. That Christmas, Frieda included Wolfgang in the family's prayers.

Now, even in the relative quiet of East Prussia, fear started to set in. The changes were few at first; people ceased trusting the authorities, treating any broadcast or official speech with scepticism, and a new self-awareness started to emerge. As the bombs started targeting other German cities, people talked of them as the world's revenge for the atrocities their country had committed. Now that Germany's defeat was becoming more and more likely, ordinary Germans found it harder to ignore the evidence some had previously turned a blind eye to. Reports of atrocities committed against Jews and Soviet civilians out east, and the existence of camps where mass murder was being committed, had started to filter through.

It's hard to establish how much people knew, and when they knew, about the death camps. Knowledge and popular opinion are hard to measure in a totalitarian regime, and the silence of shame that followed in the post-war years compounded this. The phrase 'we knew nothing about it' comes up regularly in Germans' accounts of life under Nazism, when asked when and how they found out about the death camps, the existence of which were never made public by the Nazi regime. In his study of what Germans knew about mass murders, *'Davon Haben Wir Nichts Gewusst!'*,* the scholar of Nazi Germany, Peter Longerich, concludes that by the last eighteen months of the war, the 'final solution' was an open secret. Historian Nicholas Stargardt also found references, in letters home from soldiers in the early stages of the war, to mass executions and extreme violence, a few expressed with moral outrage, others in a matter-of-fact tone. Some soldiers writing home from Poland and Ukraine, for example, chillingly sent rolls of film home to be developed that included executions of civilians and the rounding up of Jews.[†]

My grandmother found it hard to talk about these atrocities. 'Did people know?' I once asked her. I did not need to specify exactly what my question referred to for her to understand.

'They knew. But they did not want to see.'

I have spent a long time trying to understand what she meant. In those last two years of the war, she was a young mother, barely out of her teens, in love and alone. Anticipating the Soviet invasion everyone knew was coming, Albert and Frieda were struggling to come to terms with the idea that the life they had built, the only one they had known, would probably soon be lost. I imagine that, given all this, to dwell on the horrors which were being whispered, and in which the entire nation was silently complicit, was simply too much to process. My mother told me that in her adolescence, the euphemism of 'those horrors' was used by her mother and stepfather, but details were never specifically discussed. Even at school,

---

* *We Didn't Know Anything About It!*
† German forces treated Soviet civilians and captured Soviet soldiers with particular brutality.

in the immediate aftermath of war, where she was taught by teach-ers who would have been in their twenties during the conflict, and some of whom had served as soldiers, it was not touched upon. For that generation, shame was expressed through silence. My moth-er's first exposure to the full horror of the Holocaust came when she watched documentary footage of the liberation of Dachau. 'I remember watching, the knot in my stomach, the shame, the tears. I can still feel them today,' she said. It would only be in the late 1950s and the early 60s that Germany would truly start a collective process of coming to terms with its national shame.

For many Germans who lived under Nazism, fear must also have played a part. Longerich observes that most Germans reacted to the growing persecution of Jews with neither active resistance, nor active participation. He suggests that most disapproved of the violence against Jews and other minorities, but what appears as indifference could also be seen as a feeling of powerlessness, brought on by fear of arrest and other reprisals.[4] In the last eight-een months of the war, public talk of the final solution was shut down, with the Nazi regime ruthlessly punishing 'rumour-mongering' about the extermination of Jews.[5] The historian Richard Evans concluded that as defeat loomed, those Germans who knew the details of the death camps started repressing this knowledge, in fear of the retribution they knew would eventually come.

At the start of 1943, Germany no longer looked victorious. In spite of the regime's best efforts to control public opinion and crack down on what it saw as defeatism, voices critical of the war were starting to make themselves heard. They belonged to anxious fam-ilies, and to those soldiers who had set out to fight to prevent their own sons from facing another conflict, or to restore Germany's standing in the world; in the brutality and grimness of life on the Eastern Front, they saw nothing worth upholding, and presaged only defeat. However hard the Nazi regime tried to control the message, the truth of Hitler's disastrous winter campaign against Russia was starting to reach civilians. While soldiers were forbidden to talk of their experiences on the front, parents and wives learnt to read between the lines and the increasing death toll was becoming harder to hide.

On 30 January 1943, shortly before 11 a.m., Albert, Frieda and Inge sat at the kitchen table and tuned in to the Rundfunk, which was broadcasting a speech by Reichsmarschall Hermann Goering, marking the tenth anniversary of the day Hitler had been named Chancellor. To their surprise, instead of the much-trailed broadcast, they heard a performance of Bruckner's 7th Symphony; a neatly timed RAF raid on the Rundfunk's Berlin headquarters on Masurenallee, the first committed in daylight on the capital, had forced the speech to be postponed by an hour. Preparing for bad news, Frieda made coffee, using the last of the carefully hoarded beans her uncle had given them for Christmas, seeking a semblance of normality in this familiar ritual.

When the speech finally began, they listened in silence to Goering's words, his strident tones betraying the fury the forced delay had provoked. His voice rose to a shout as he mentioned Stalingrad, causing Frieda and Inge to start in dread. He did not speak of defeat, instead lauding the battle as an example of epic heroism, likening the 6th Army to the warriors in the Battle of the Nibelung, the Nordic epic immortalised by Richard Wagner in his opera. It would, he assured listeners, in coming years be seen as a cornerstone of Germany's *Endsieg* – the final victory.

I imagine the three of them sitting there, waiting for a hint of truth amid the propaganda. Goering's speech took place five days after Germany's forces in the Caucasus had started their retreat and a day before General Field Marshal Paulus, the 6th Army's commander, formally surrendered.

'Wanderer, when you arrive at Sparta,' said Goering, 'report that you have seen us lying here, as the law commanded ... Should you come to Germany, then report that you have seen us fighting in Stalingrad as the law, the law of national safety, commanded.'

Goering's words, most shrill when lauding a battle he already knew was lost, crafted what was to become the Stalingrad myth. When Goering likened what was left of the 6th Army to the 300 Spartans who had held out at the Battle of Thermopylae, he raised his voice as if to give credence to what would become one of the regime's most ill-judged lies. The 6th Army had effectively been abandoned by the Reich. Those soldiers who listened to the broadcast on radios from the ruins of Stalingrad, starving, covered in lice and surrounded by the frozen corpses of their comrades, likened the experience to that of listening to the eulogy at their own funerals. Speaking later that evening at a rally at Berlin's Sports Palace, Goebbels mentioned Stalingrad only in passing as the 'heroic battle of our soldiers on the Volga'. What Goering and Goebbels were doing was paving the way for a deception of monumental proportions, which asserted that every soldier as well as the generals who led them had died in the fighting. In reality, more than 91,000 men, their leader Paulus included, were preparing to give themselves up to Soviet captivity.

As the speech ended, the Wiegandts stared at the silver pot on the table between them in which the coffee had grown cold. Inge and her mother remained seated, lost in thought, while Albert stood up to switch off the radio without comment, and walked out of the room.

Three weeks later, Goebbels declared Germany was in a state of 'total war' that would require the efforts of every man, woman and child, but by then trust in the regime had been severely damaged. It was at that time, my grandmother told me, that she had understood that Germany's defeat was no longer a question of 'if', but of 'when'.

When the 6th Army's defeat at Stalingrad was finally announced on 3 February 1943, clear guidelines were issued to the press in the regime's daily media directive:

The heroic battle for Stalingrad has ended. In several days of mourning the German people will honour the brave sons, men who did their duty to the last breath and to the last bullet, and as a result have broken the backs of the Bolshevik assault on our Eastern Front. The heroic battle for Stalingrad will become the greatest of all the heroic epics in German history. The German press has one of its greatest tasks before it. In the spirit of the special OKW communiqué to be issued later today the press must report the stirring event which outshines every feat of heroism known to history, in such a manner that the sublime example of heroism, this ultimate, self-sacrificing dedication to Germany's final victory, will blaze forth like a secret flame. The German nation, inspired by the deathless heroism of the men of Stalingrad, will draw even more powerfully than before on the spiritual and material forces which assure the nation of the victory it is now more fanatically than ever resolved to win.

German radio rose to the occasion as instructed, by declaring that the battle for Stalingrad was over, and that the nation's soldiers 'had died so that Germany could live'. The broadcast concluded with a muffled drum roll and lines from the song *Ich hatt' einen Kameraden*, before three days of national mourning were declared.

The implication that all, to a man, had heroically perished was one of the most misguided falsehoods in a campaign that would turn out to be both a military and a PR disaster for the Nazi regime. In the whole of Germany, and particularly in East Prussia, the shock of the defeat confirmed a growing belief on the home front that the war had turned against them. The Wehrmacht Information Office was worried that word of the near starvation and disease-ridden conditions endured by German soldiers at Stalingrad would reach civilian ears. So desperate were they to conceal the truth that, under Goebbels' orders, they intercepted the last few bags of letters written by the 6th Army's soldiers to their loved ones. Those letters were never delivered but, despite officials' best efforts, the truth still leaked out.

Keen to reach a German audience of families increasingly frantically seeking news of their sons, husbands and brothers, both the BBC and Radio Moscow read out the names of German prisoners daily. For anxious relatives, illegal foreign broadcasts were often the only hope of gaining any news of the 91,000 captive soldiers. For Allied forces, this new audience provided the ideal opportunity to seek to undermine support for Hitler on the home front. Inge, too, listened for news of Wolfgang, whom she thought might have been among them, and to learn the fate of those childhood friends who would never again share her summers. It was no coincidence that by 1943, 3 million Germans were clandestinely listening to the BBC, though to be caught doing so would land you in prison. That February, anticipating the advance of the Red Army, Albert started to think that, perhaps, he should make plans to move the Wiegandts' most valuable possessions to west Germany.

Two weeks later, Inge, whose child was almost due, received a letter from Dorothea. She hoped, as she opened it, that it might contain news of Wolfgang. But Dorothea wrote only of her worry; she had been without news of her son for weeks. She'd had a dream, she wrote, that he had called for her. It had woken her from her sleep. The Eastern Front seemed to have swallowed him up; a well-meaning friend, whose own son had been reported missing, had told her to prepare for the worst.

I don't know whether Inge still hoped then that Wolfgang might yet return to her alive. She faced the likely prospect of having to raise a child alone, without a father in its life, during a war that seemed without end. Childbirth itself, which Frieda spoke of only as a pain that brought much joy, a description Inge found unhelpful at best, held as much uncertainty for her as fear. Deprived of life as a married woman, too young to have friends who were also expecting children, she had no one to turn to save her parents. I imagine not knowing whether Wolfgang was alive or dead made her loneliness even more acute.

It was in this time of sadness and uncertainty that she gave birth to a little girl, on 6 March 1943, in the same bedroom she had slept in as a child. The pains started in the middle of the night. Focusing on every step, she made her way to her parents' bedroom and knocked on their door. They called the midwife at once, who arrived an hour later. Frieda held her hand and stayed by her side, wiping her forehead and trying to ease her pain. The midwife, a lanky, grey-haired woman, did not mention the father's absence. She had probably seen enough individual tragedies so far in this war to know never to ask. Instead, she smiled broadly as she placed the healthy baby girl in Inge's tired arms.

During the past weeks in Rauschen, and in those moments when she had faced the stares of other women as she walked Königsberg's familiar streets, Inge had wondered how she would take to the child whose conception had caused her life to change so dramatically, and whose father had let her down. Would she love the baby, as Frieda assured her she would? Or would there always be something of bitterness there, a living reminder of the life that might have been? But all doubts and regrets were forgotten the first time she set eyes on her daughter. Inge saw in her face, in her fine blonde hair, her nose and her blue eyes that opened as if to look straight into hers, the image of Wolfgang. But all the love she'd felt for him was nothing next to what she felt at the sight of her baby. In that moment, the wounded girl was gone; she had become a mother.

Albert, for whom Inge's pregnancy had brought much disappointment and anguish, became a slave to the little girl the moment

INGE AND BEATRICE.

Frieda placed her in his arms. The baby was a smiling, happy child, who offered the promise of another future, after the war was over; a new reason to live in their increasingly uncertain world. For Dorothea, writing to Inge of her joy at the baby's arrival, it fed the hope she held in her heart that her son was still alive. Along with her letter of congratulation, she sent Inge an embroidered lace blanket and a plain, heavy, gold-plate bracelet, a small trinket, she wrote, that could withstand the grasp of a baby pulling at her mother's hand. She suggested Inge call the baby Irina Antoinette, family names from the von Schimmelmann side. Inge, who had been reading Dante, chose instead to call her Beatrice. She wrote to Dorothea that she had also given her the middle name Solveig, meaning 'she who walks with the sun', because her daughter had arrived on the eve of spring, bringing optimism despite the fact that the future was growing darker by the day.

Part III

Chapter Nine

TRAPPED

'Adolf,' she said, her voice low and disdainful. I looked up with a start. Christmas had come and gone and it was spring again, the first week of May. We were sitting in the garden, although it was still a little cold. I watched her draw her shawl closer around her. She had returned to France earlier than usual that year, as my cousin was getting married a week later.

My grandmother spoke to me more freely now, though she always waited till we were alone. She had been telling me about my mother as a baby, how she had become her entire world. How her father, who had found it hard to accept his daughter's pregnancy, smiled the moment his granddaughter was put in his arms. How he sat beside her cot, reading a book when she slept, and whispered to her when she cried. How that first Christmas Frieda made her a dress of white wool, edged in lace she had cut away from the collar of her best dress. It was a quiet, contented picture of family life, which that name suddenly shattered. I had never heard her speak it before.

'That day in July ... We heard about it on the radio. Everyone around us pretending to be outraged that someone had tried to kill Hitler. And all we could think, my mother and father and I, was "if only".'

More than a year had passed since Inge had given birth. She had come to motherhood full of fear of what people would say, of how she would cope, a single mother with a child. But it had been a time of wonder.

The baby, a pretty blonde and blue-eyed child with a round face and dimpled cheeks, had breathed new life into the Wiegandts' household. In the first months of Inge's return to Königsberg, the atmosphere had been one of tension and worry. The worry was still there, but Albert's expression was softened by the smiles he gave his granddaughter, and in place of the newspaper he always used to carry there was now, more often than not, a doll or a children's book. Frieda was always sewing, cutting up her old dresses to make clothes for her granddaughter with a zeal that made Inge laugh: 'Mutti, at this rate she'll have enough clothes to last her till she starts school!'

Albert and Frieda doted on their granddaughter. She had quickly become the centre of their existence. The months flew by, marked by milestones that at times allowed them to put the war to the backs of their minds: the sound she had made, which Frieda insisted was the word 'ma'; the first, faltering steps she took before falling into her grandfather's outstretched arms. Albert had lost his heart to her completely. She played with him for hours, sitting on his lap as he read her stories. They had games of their own, such as when she would take all the keys out of the cabinet, and he would, laughing, show her how to put them back. As Albert watched her he frequently remarked, as if speaking to himself, that she was, after all, a particularly sweet child.

Though by July 1944 the authorities were discouraging all but essential travel,* and further cuts in food rationing and an influx of refugees from the west had forced even more of the boarding houses to shut down, Albert had insisted they go to Rauschen in

---

* A stricter prohibition of travel was put in place for civilians on 17 July 1944, by which time the Wiegandts would already have been in Rauschen.

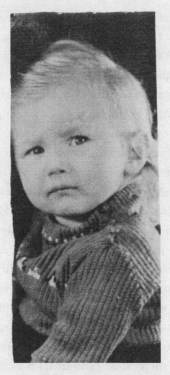

BEATRICE, AGED ONE.

July as was their tradition. He said that two weeks of sea air, away from the heat of Königsberg, would be good for Beatrice, who had turned one a few months before. Through this enforced repetition of their childhood summers, Inge knew her father was putting off the thought that their imagined future, and the life of comfort he had built over so many years of hard work, might be about to end.

The Wiegandts' last summer holiday in Rauschen at once held the familiarity of old times and the ominous stillness of an era drawing to a close. The landscape's windswept beauty was unchanged and the sea unusually still; on the promenade along the seafront, sheltered from the gusts that buffeted the beach, people still took their daily walks, while children armed with buckets and spades built castles in the sand below. The changes that Inge noticed lay not so much in the absence of the band that had played on the hotel terrace every summer afternoon, or in the want of ices served with whipped cream, nor could it simply be explained by the lack of the young men who used to linger by the beach, hoping to flirt with the groups of girls who walked laughingly past. It was something in the atmosphere itself, in the stooped shoulders of the old men who sat playing chess in groups, and in the thin and drawn faces of the women who watched their children with a new intensity as they played, the sense of a people waiting for the reckoning to come.

They shared their boarding house – the one they had always stayed in – with a mother and two boys who had been evacuated from Hamburg. The landlady complained to Inge that they stole some of her rations. By 1944, East Prussia was teeming with evacuees, mostly women and children, sometimes entire school classrooms with their teachers, who had been sent to the safety of this quiet, agricultural land. More than three quarters of a million people had come there fleeing the air raids that started targeting Germany's major cities in late 1942, intensifying the following year, around the time of Beatrice's birth. While East Prussia was still being spared the intensity of the bombings, suffering only a few incursions from Soviet fighter planes earlier in the conflict, it now faced a different menace. Germany's repeated defeats on the Eastern Front had raised the threat of invasion by the Red Army, and many evacuees were now trying to make their way back home to the west. Through the summer and autumn of 1944, the Eastern Front drew nearer as Germany started to lose its hold on the occupied Baltic territories, and the first waves of refugees had arrived from the town of Memel, making their way west across the border with herds of cattle and horse-drawn carts, harbingers of the exodus to come.[1] Once the Baltic territories were secured, the invasion of East Prussia lay next in Stalin's sights.

MAP OF THE RED ARMY ADVANCE, 1945.[2]

As the news grew worse for Germany, Inge argued with her parents again and again, insisting they leave for the west. Although the D-Day landings in June spelt the end of Germany's dominance of the Western Front, shortly afterwards Dorothea wrote to Inge urging them to leave East Prussia, for the talk in Berlin was that the

Eastern Front was all but lost too. Faced with a choice between British or American forces, and the Red Army, it was safer to go west.

Albert said he would think about it, but he would not be rushed. Inge reluctantly agreed to his request for this final holiday, hoping that the compromise, which would allow him to see the dunes he loved one last time, would help her convince him. But once there, as she sat by him on the sand one afternoon, and watched him smile as he encouraged her daughter to walk towards him, picking her up every time she fell on the soft sand, she decided that she would speak no further of flight while they were here.

In the late afternoon of 20 July 1944, the four of them sat down at a cafe, tired and happy, the glow of the sea air still on their skin, Beatrice drowsy from play. The sun was warm and the cafe terrace busy with its clientele of elderly men and women, and mothers with their children, sitting gossiping and drinking ersatz coffee. The Wiegandts were laughing at Beatrice's attempt to beat the table with her spoon when suddenly a hush fell and the waltz that had been playing on the radio stopped. A crackling voice said an emergency announcement would be made shortly, and the proprietress rushed to turn the volume up as people strained to hear. There had been an attempt on the Führer's life, the voice said. He had escaped unharmed.

Inge heard a woman gasp. Another crackle, before the voice resumed.

'The attempt which has failed must be a warning to every German to redouble their war effort.'

The shocked silence was followed by an outcry so loud it drowned out the rest of the broadcast, as if the cafe's guests were competing as to who could be the loudest to voice their condemnation. Raised voices berated whoever was responsible, condemned the treason, called for the harshest of punishments and thanked

God for the Führer's survival. Only the Wiegandts sat quietly at their table in stunned silence, not daring to speak or even to look each other in the eye, lest they betray what others, surely, must also be feeling. Inge listened to the scolding that came from all around them. A phrase ran through her head, a phrase she knew her parents were thinking too, but didn't dare to speak aloud: *If only*.

The assassination attempt had taken place at 12.42 p.m. at Hitler's military headquarters in the east, known as the Wolf's Lair, in the Masurian woods just 115 kilometres south of Königsberg. Colonel Claus Schenk von Stauffenberg, a senior officer in the Wehrmacht, had planted a bomb in his briefcase, during a meeting with Hitler and his general staff. While the bomb went off, Hitler escaped with only a burst eardrum and blast injuries.

The Wiegandts left the cafe shortly after. Dinner that evening was quieter than usual. It was perhaps telling that even in the privacy of their own home, none of them dared dwell on the hope, quickly snuffed out, that the announcement had stirred up. They didn't stay up to listen to Hitler's speech at 1 a.m. that night.

Reprisals against the plotters were swift. Von Stauffenberg was arrested and shot the same night. Eight of his co-conspirators were hanged with piano wire from meat hooks, and their executions filmed and broadcast to senior Nazi officials and the armed forces.

In the months and years to come, remembering the home she had lost forever, Inge would frequently think back to that golden afternoon, which had driven out all thoughts of the war for a few precious hours, and the moment in the cafe that had both raised and dashed the promise of peace. She thought of the relief she had heard people express at Hitler's survival at the cafe that day. She could never decide what it was that had driven it – fear, years of brainwashing, or simply an instinct for survival.

By summer 1944, many Germans had lost confidence in their country's ability to win the war. The most brainwashed still believed in the existence of the *Wunderwaffe*, or miracle weapon, which government propaganda promised would lead Germany to victory. It is a term still used by Germans today, to describe a universal solution to every problem, with heavy irony. Most knew the war was as good as lost, even if they dared not say it. The possibility of a Russian invasion was on everyone's mind, colouring every decision, every judgement; Inge was astonished to hear one of her mother's friends, who had become an outspoken critic of the regime after her husband's arrest for listening to illegal broadcasts, describing Hitler as Germany's only hope.

The German people's continuing loyalty to the Führer, or rather their lack of mutiny in those later stages of the conflict, is difficult to understand. The historian Richard Evans writes that as defeat loomed, those Germans who knew the details of the death camps started repressing this knowledge, in fear of the retribution they knew would eventually come.[3] This fear drove some Germans to develop a warped sense of loyalty in the last few months of the war. In her autobiography of life as an Englishwoman in Nazi Germany, *The Past is Myself*, Christabel Bielenberg recalls an innkeeper from the Black Forest, on leave from the Eastern Front, telling her: 'If we are paid back one quarter of what we are doing in Russia and Poland, Frau Doktor, we will suffer, and we will deserve to suffer.' With the knowledge that Germany was teetering on the brink of the abyss, many civilians, even those who previously did not support the Nazis, considered Hitler's survival to be Germany's last chance.[4]

The July 1944 plot to assassinate Hitler not only failed to overthrow his government, it led to a sharp radicalisation of the regime, and a renewal of popular support for his leadership among the many who feared Hitler's death would plunge the country into chaos.[5] Almost overnight, the government sharpened its efforts to repress dissent: thousands were arrested on suspicion of involvement, or simply for anti-Nazi activities. The regime had long been willing to take whatever measures were necessary to keep the population under control, but after the July plot even a careless remark expressing scepticism at the outcome of the war could result in arrest. During the course of the war, some 20,000 German soldiers were executed by the authorities, 500 times more than had been put to death in the First World War, compared with forty in the British Army, or 103 in the French. It took very little, in the German Army, for a soldier to be seen as undermining the war effort. As the Eastern Front collapsed in the final months of the war and soldiers separated from their regiment, or feigning detachment, sought to make their way back west, reprisals became even harsher. One commander, Colonel-General Ferdinand Schörner, ordered 'stragglers' to be hanged from trees with a sign stating 'I refused to protect German women and children' suspended round their necks.[6]

Though exact numbers for civilians who suffered a similar fate are hard to come by, the toll is known to have been even worse. By the end of the war, the mere telling of a joke at the Nazis' expense, already an offence under the law, could result in being killed.[7]

In East Prussia especially, with an increasingly fragile Eastern Front in such close proximity, civilians looked to the future with a sense of foreboding. Its population had been conditioned by years of Nazi propaganda against the 'Bolshevik menace', and people lived in dread of the Red Army's advance. For those like Albert and Frieda, who had lived through the First World War, memories of the invasion of East Prussia by the Imperial Russian Army were still fresh. The Russians had then come as near as forty kilometres from Königsberg; villages had been burned, hundreds of civilians killed, thousands had been deported to remote areas of the Russian empire, a third of whom did not survive. It was a different Russian army threatening them now, one whose reported brutality far exceeded that of the Tsarist forces, driven by revenge for the 27 million Soviet soldiers and civilians killed in this war.

Despite this growing realisation that the end was near, East Prussians went about their lives with a strange sense of apathy, not entirely wanting to believe that all was lost until they absolutely had to.

The zeal with which the authorities implemented the state of 'total war', first called for by Goebbels after Stalingrad, took a particularly extreme turn in East Prussia following the failed July plot, with devastating consequences for the civilian population. Erich Koch had been appointed Reich Defence Commissar, a role that gave him extensive powers over the organisation of civil defence. As early as July, Koch took measures to make East Prussia a symbol of Germany's last stand, conscripting women and any men who'd been spared from the fighting by virtue of extreme youth or age to help dig trenches, fortifications, bunkers, tank traps and roadblocks. Even Albert was summoned to bolster Königsberg's defences, despite being lame from his old leg injury, only to be sent home by the overseer, who was exasperated at his slowness. The defences on East Prussia's border, vastly neglected until now, became a matter of national priority. Koch convinced Hitler to build an *Ostwall*, a wall across the eastern perimeter to guard against Soviet incursions. As defensive measures went, it would prove as effective as a house of straw.

Koch's edicts also ended the Wiegandts' hopes of an early escape, through his successful move to quash any talk of early evacuation of the region, which he viewed as defeatist. The efforts to prevent departures started that summer, from about mid-July.

Goebbels, who as well as being propaganda minister, was, as *Gauleiter* of Berlin, responsible for the capital's civilians, negotiated the evacuation of 170,000 Berliners who had taken refuge in East Prussia. With Hitler's support, Koch restricted the number to 55,000, and from this point on trains leaving East Prussia were carefully controlled; the crackdown on civilians suspected of trying to leave became ever more draconian.[8] By the time the Wiegandts returned from their holiday, it was impossible to do so. Albert's desire for a last holiday at his beloved East Prussian coast would have consequences for which he would blame himself for the rest of his life.

By autumn, the Wehrmacht had advised that civilians close to the eastern border should be moved. Once again, Koch intervened, warning that an evacuation might lead to a stampede of people from the region. By early 1945, power had disproportionally drained to regional party chieftains such as Koch, with the result that the Wehrmacht's recommendations were widely ignored – a fact said to have reduced some commanders in the regions to fits of uncontrolled, if futile, anger.[9] What had started as a move to control departures from East Prussia now, with Hitler's backing, became an outright ban. The punishment for anyone who was so much as suspected of making preparations to leave was summary execution on the grounds of *Wehrkraftzersetzung*, the undermining of military morale. This included the civilians living nearest to the front, who instead of being allowed to heed the advice given to them by the army, were instead given spades and ordered to dig defensive trenches. Soldiers fared little better; the fighting had turned into all-out slaughter, with 5,000 German soldiers dying every day.[10] Over the space of 150 days, more than a million men were recorded dead, missing or wounded, a disaster that made even the Battle of Verdun, the bloodiest of the First

World War, and the disastrous defeat at Stalingrad pale in comparison. Of Wolfgang, there was no further news, and Inge had given him up for lost.

The Wiegandts returned from Rauschen on Saturday 26 August and went to bed early; Beatrice had been fractious on the train journey back. The evenings were getting shorter, with a chill in the air announcing that summer was drawing to a close. Inge was woken in the early hours by the sound of her daughter's crying. As she picked her daughter up, she heard another noise, the roar of an engine, distant at first, but getting louder. She opened the window to find that it was not yet dawn. The roar turned to a whine. Holding Beatrice in her arms, she ran to her parents' bedroom, shouting at them to get up, and the four of them ran down to the cellar.

The Wiegandts crouched in terror with their neighbours in the bowels of the building. In the darkness of the cellar, they could only speculate on what was happening outside, listening for every sound, alert to every smell, wondering whether this was the end that they had known must eventually come. They came up a few hours later to see smoke in the distance. The Lancaster bombers had missed their target and Königsberg's centre had escaped unscathed; the smoke in the distance showed the bombs had only hit the east of the city. Later that morning, Inge helped her mother move an old mattress and some blankets to the cellar, in case they were forced to wait out further attacks. They devised a makeshift table from a case of Albert's vintage port.

Just three nights later, a siren roused them shortly after midnight and the family again made their way to the cellar. Frieda carried her granddaughter, who was sleepily mumbling something.

'What is it, *Liebchen*?' Frieda whispered.

Beatrice mumbled the word again. Inge realised she was trying to say the word 'ball'.

Although it was a cloudy night, that time the Lancasters did not miss. Four firebombs were dropped on four separate targets, setting most of the city centre alight. Though the distance lay at the limit of the Lancasters' range, meaning the RAF's n5 Group only succeeded in dropping 480 tons of explosives, fewer bombs were needed as Königsberg's narrow cobbled streets and tall buildings made it particularly vulnerable to incendiary devices. The intense din of the anti-aircraft guns firing at the Lancasters soon told Königsberg's inhabitants that this raid would be far more severe than the last. From the darkness of the cellar, the sound of the bombs falling was a deafening roar, the stillness that followed giving way to a crackling and splintering that the Wiegandts soon realised were flames consuming nearby roofs and beams.

At dawn, they emerged to find much of the Paradeplatz gone and the streets behind it still ablaze. The heat and smoke were still intense. Fire spread quickly in the city's old medieval structures. In some streets the heat from the cobbles was so intense it melted the shoes of those who ran across them and burned the soles of their feet. The Wiegandts' building had escaped the bombs and blaze, but three streets down, others had not been so lucky; the residents of an entire block of flats had perished in the cellar, burned to death. Flames even lapped the Pregel River, as the bombs that destroyed the city's bridges ignited the timber pilings along its banks. In the days that followed, Inge heard accounts of entire families perishing in the inferno.[11]

The bombing had lasted only an hour, but the flames burned on: 41 per cent of the city's housing and 20 per cent of its industry were destroyed in that second raid.[12] Inge went back to the flat to collect a few things; it was, she thought as she watched the embers glow from her bedroom window, what hell must look like.

The Cafe Berlin had escaped unscathed for the moment. Walking past its window, Albert saw that the proprietor had stubbornly set out the tables and chairs. He stopped to sit at one of them and, head in his hands, wept for the city he had lost.

The Wiegandts slept in the cellar for the next three nights, partly out of fear, and partly to avoid the burning ash the wind carried across the streets, from parts of the city that were still in flames. As those who survived the bombing of Königsberg tried to pick up what remained of their lives in the weeks that followed, they forgot, for a while, that an even greater threat still lay on the province's eastern borders, where the Wehrmacht's defences were fast being eroded.

But on 20 October 1944, East Prussians got the first glimpse of the horrors to come, when the Red Army first breached the *Ostwall*. For years, Nazi propaganda had fuelled civilian fears of the Soviet soldier; but when the day came, official plans to evacuate failed completely.

The small village of Nemmersdorf lay in the path of the Soviet Army as it pushed westwards. Like most of the region, it had not been evacuated. Koch had refused to countenance the move despite the Wehrmacht's numerous requests. There was heavy mist on 20 October 1944, and as the trucks planned to evacuate civilians failed to turn up, people fled in panic, some in horse-drawn carts that queued to cross the only bridge over the Angerapp River, some by foot across the fields and forests, as news came that 'Bolshevik' soldiers were just a couple of hours' march away. By the early hours of 21 October, it was already too late to escape.

It's hard to know definitively what happened at Nemmersdorf, as the events that took place there were seized upon and distorted by Nazi propagandists keen to exploit the tragedy to shore up hatred of the enemy, and are still the subject of controversy.[13] That atrocities were indeed committed seems hard to dispute, as part of the problem in determining with certainty what happened is that hardly any of the civilians caught up in the assault, including women and children, and French and Belgian POWs, survived to bear witness. It was the first German village that lay in the Red Army's path, the first chance of revenge for the brutality the German Army had inflicted on all those they'd encountered. The massacre at Nemmersdorf was no different to many conducted by the German Army in Soviet territory.[14] For the Nazi regime, the grim fate of the villagers who were left behind became a propaganda gift, with the party's mouthpiece, the *Völkischer Beobachter*, reporting on the 'fury of the Soviet Beasts' who had mutilated children, raped and murdered women, and nailed corpses to barn doors. The Nazi propaganda image of the 'Bolshevik' that would come to pillage and rape was now a reality.

The tragedy at Nemmersdorf stoked the fear that had, over the summer, crept into East Prussians' minds. And these were anxious times for the Wiegandts, who were trapped in the place that had for so long been their refuge and their home. The week after Nemmersdorf, they waited, listening to the radio most of the day, awaiting an order to evacuate that did not come. Instead, in a surprise counter-attack, the Wehrmacht pushed the Red Army forces back over the line. The move gave East Prussia a short period of grace. This time could have been used to evacuate its civilians to safety but, though the army knew that it could not hold out much longer, Koch refused to evacuate anyone except for those civilians who lived within thirty kilometres of the front. The end, Inge felt, was drawing near, but still all she could do was wait.

A strange quiet descended on Königsberg in the run-up to that Christmas; it was a time Inge would remember standing out for being strangely ordinary. Neighbours came round with greetings and small gifts, and on Christmas Eve Frieda's uncle joined them, bearing a quarter-pound of sugar, a packet of real coffee and a rag doll for Beatrice. No one talked of the wounded soldiers who kept arriving in Königsberg hospital, their injuries testimony to the situation that was fast deteriorating just a few hours' march away. In his diary of life during the Russian invasion and occupation of East Prussia, the doctor Hans von Lehndorff, in his hospital ninety kilometres east of Königsberg, wrote:

Christmas, for those who could still stay in their own homes, could be celebrated almost as if in peacetime. Even hunting was reinstated, and people met, to see through the end of a year once more in the old fashion. Fourteen days later, it was all over.[15]

But the quiet of that Christmas was a prelude to the storm of revenge and suffering to come.

It was a New Year's Eve tradition among East Prussian families to heat the room as much as you could, to keep the dead you wished to remember warm. The Wiegandts had never followed the custom that keenly and coal shortages in the war had led to it being dropped from many homes altogether. But this year was different, and they followed all the old rituals as if to imprint them forever in their minds. On 31 December, Inge sat by the fire and watched as her father broke up an old chair, throwing it into the hearth with abandon. He followed it with handfuls of their carefully hoarded coal. Frieda watched him with sad eyes. It was as if, Inge thought, they knew they would be honouring the old traditions for the last time. Watching her father stoke the fire with quiet intensity, Inge knew that in his heart he was already saying goodbye to the city he held so dear.

The change, when it came, did so with the suddenness of a nightmare.

In the third week of January, the Eastern Front crumbled. On 20 January 1945, Koch finally agreed to allow civilians to evacuate, but panic had already spread, and the words 'the Russians are coming' were on everyone's lips. The neighbour's wife told Inge that special invitations were no longer needed to take a train west. Albert immediately hurried to the station to try and secure tickets, but it was so packed with people he couldn't even make it through the main doors. He tried again the next morning, but by the time he arrived the trains packed with civilians trying to flee were being sent back; as it swept towards Berlin, the Red Army had taken the Danzig Corridor, and East Prussia was now surrounded. The only remaining way out was by sea.

As the Red Army drew ever nearer, thousands of refugees made their way to Pillau, the nearest Baltic port to Königsberg, or to Gotenhafen to the west. Many did so on foot, across the frozen lagoon and along the Frische Nehrung, a narrow spit of coastland seventy kilometres long and two kilometres wide, which was still, for now, under German control. Like the Wiegandts, many stayed in Königsberg, awaiting a clear evacuation plan which, though it had been drawn up in the second half of 1944, never came. Without a central office, gathering points or an organisational body to direct and guide the 2.5 million people who were desperate for a way out, chaos descended. Most relied on word of mouth. The first ship designated to take refugees from Pillau did not arrive at the harbour until two weeks after the Soviet offensive was launched, by which time hundreds of thousands of people already lined the shores.[16] From 21 January, the German Navy, or Kriegsmarine, headed by Admiral Dönitz, set out to rescue those it could. Even then, East Prussia's civilians were not considered a priority. Though the war was all but lost, ships had to keep space for military equipment, coal and soldiers, restricting the number of civilians who could be taken aboard.[17]

On top of the failure of the authorities came the added burden of a particularly bitter winter. Thousands of refugees froze to death on the trek to the shore, or as they waited for the ships to carry them to safety; children and the elderly were particularly at risk. There was little shelter along the way, and both the ships and the convoys which crossed the frozen lagoon frequently came under attack from the Russians. The lagoon, though it was covered by a thick layer of ice, became a watery grave for many, engulfing part of the convoys when a bomb fractured the surface, or when it simply buckled under the weight of the wagons crossing it. None of these hardships befell *Gauleiter* Koch, who, having been so loud in denouncing those who tried to take flight, was among the first to leave the province. He commandeered two steamers for his personal use, taking not a single refugee aboard with him.

Left to fend for themselves, encircled by a Red Army that was drawing the noose tighter around them, civilians became increasingly desperate. For Albert and Frieda, those last days of January were a time of bewilderment; they did not know what to do. As 150,000 refugees from all over East Prussia descended on the region's capital in the hope that the old fortifications might yet protect them, having failed to secure an escape by train, Inge knew her parents were close to despair. Aged just twenty, with a small child, surrounded by chaos and panic, any hope of her family's survival would be down to her.

'My parents were overwhelmed, they were almost ready to give up,' my grandmother said. She shivered slightly, though we had moved from the garden into the kitchen; May was too cool a month for her to sit outdoors in the early evening. She was still talking; at least an hour had passed since she had started her story. I looked up at her face, to see her eyes staring into the distance. 'But I was not ready to give up.'

Chapter Ten

THE FLIGHT

There were people everywhere, in doorways, in cafes, bedding down in stairways, in the ruins of buildings, desperate people come to seek shelter within the city's walls, hoping to be saved. Everyone here knew the battle was lost, yet the SS were still on patrol, snatching boys who looked close to sixteen from their families, boys who had arrived in Königsberg seeking protection from the Red Army, only to be hurriedly enlisted and sent to be slaughtered at the front. A woman shouted that the Russians had broken into Pomerania, that the western border had fallen. A man started running, though there was nowhere to go.

Inge knew time was running out, but didn't know who to call or where to go, so she returned home. As she walked through the door, she saw her neighbour on the stairs. They'd sheltered through the bombings together, shared their food on Christmas Eve. He held a suitcase in his hand. He told her he was going to his daughter's house in the suburb of Amalienau and from there to Pillau, a port forty kilometres away. There were ships there, he said, taking people to safety in the west. She clutched his arm as he tried to walk past her.

'Help me,' she said. 'I don't know what to do.'

Inge almost ran up the stairs to her parents' apartment, through the front hall and into her father's study, where they kept the telephone. She picked up the receiver, letting her breath out at the sound of the ringtone; incredibly, despite the chaos, the lines were still working. She dialled the number she'd been given and counted the rings. One, two, three … At the fourth, a man answered. He was calm, almost detached, as he listened to her frantic enquiries. He asked for her name when she told him how she had got his number. His tone became more friendly; he told her that he knew her father, and that he'd often bought wine from him. There was an operation underway, with the help of the Kriegsmarine, he said, getting people away by sea. The man told her that she had to get to Pillau, from where a passenger ferry, the *Göttingen*, would leave the next day. He could secure them tickets, but they'd have to get there by dawn to be on board in time.

She looked at her watch. The time was 5 p.m. It was the end of January and outside the window the sky was dark. She knew they wouldn't be able to go by car, as all the petrol left in the city had been requisitioned for the use of the army. A horse and cart could perhaps get them there in time, though the roads were frozen and the snow deep, but it would take too long to find one as demand was so high. The man had told her that a *prahm* – a transport ship for soldiers – was due to leave Königsberg at 9 p.m., taking people up the Pregel River and through the Vistula Lagoon to Pillau. He didn't know how many they'd allow on board, but she reasoned it was their only option.

Inge found her parents in the sitting room, her daughter asleep in Frieda's arms. She told them they must go now, at once. She braced herself for a fight, as they'd been reluctant, until now, to admit that life as they had known it was over. But to her surprise, they nodded. She never knew what it was that finally shook them out of their torpor, but it was as if that night was their own moment of reckoning. Perhaps they too had spoken to the neighbour, or maybe it was the thought of Beatrice, quietly sleeping, that finally caused them to act. They had an hour, at most two, to pack up their life. The *prahm* they needed to get to was in a harbour an hour's journey away and sure to be crowded.

Without saying a word, Frieda put her granddaughter down and walked into her bedroom, returning a moment later carrying her jewellery box. Calmly and deliberately, she went in and out again, bringing two evening turbans and, on a third trip, her sewing box. When Frieda sat down and handed her daughter a needle, Inge understood that her mother had really taken her words to heart. Picking up one of the turbans, she started to sew the jewellery into its heavy silk folds.

As the women sewed, Albert placed all his important papers in a leather pouch: the deeds to the apartment and to the house he'd bought for his retirement, his company's share certificates, his licence to trade and make liquor. A lifetime of hard work and success reduced to a few bits of paper, which Inge knew, but did not say, were probably already worthless.

They packed four suitcases, all they could carry. A change of clothes, the silver candlesticks Frieda had been given on her wedding day, and some food for the journey; it was remarkable how quickly they filled up. They decided to keep their clothing to a bare minimum, favouring space for valuables, but Frieda insisted that they each put on two jumpers. Inge put on the good winter coat she'd bought in her Berlin days and Frieda wore the mink Albert had given her for Christmas a few years before. All the time, a voice in Inge's head was urging her to hurry.

She started to walk towards the front door, heart pounding, her daughter now wide awake but quiet in her arms. But the sight of her parents, looking suddenly old, their faces drawn with resignation and worry, made her pause for a moment. Albert was standing in the middle of the room silently watching Frieda, who was sitting at their dining table, an album and some framed photographs before her. One by one, she carefully placed in her pocket those she had chosen to take with her. Inge would never forget that moment: her mother's figure framed and softened by the dim light of the room, sitting for a last time at the round, polished mahogany table, carefully preserving, in those few snatched moments, the story of their past.

It felt like the middle of the night by the time they set off, though it couldn't have been later than 7 p.m. They boarded a tram bound for the west of the city, but had to walk for the last thirty minutes. As they neared the quayside, almost an hour later, crowds were already starting to mass. Inge had taken the pram for that part of the journey, but now she abandoned it, as the man on the phone had told her she would not be able to take it on board. A woman appeared out of nowhere and already had her hand on its handle.

'Are you leaving this behind?' she said, ready to snatch it. Inge nodded, and watched the woman disappear into the night with her bounty.

It was a bitterly cold evening and snow began to fall. The Wiegandts moved slowly, weighed down by luggage, their arms stiff in the two jumpers Frieda had told them to wear. In ordinary times, they would have made for an odd group, in their thick boots and coats, silk turbans heavy with jewellery sitting askew on their heads. But here, among a crowd of people who, like them, had hastily gathered only what they could carry, they looked like they belonged. Inge led the way, pushing through the crowd, her daughter on one arm, a suitcase in her other hand, while Frieda and Albert followed behind her, getting jostled around, slower than her, their age suddenly a burden. Somehow, they got on the transport ship. Albert and Frieda gave up the suitcase that contained the silver; the official who took it assured them that their luggage would be sent on another ship. Inge refused to hand over her suitcase, trusting it to no one but herself.

There were at least 150 people on the deck, on a ship with a capacity of sixty. They were packed so tightly that Inge did not feel the cold. Albert sat on his suitcase beside her, his head cast down, Frieda's consoling arm around his shoulder; a long thin piece of leather lay in his lap. In the thick of the crowd, someone had cut through the strap and taken the pouch that contained all his papers.

'What does it matter,' Inge heard Frieda whisper. 'It will all go to the Russians anyway.'

The ownership of a home, of the business he'd built, his retirement plan, the sum total of a life of hard work and success, snatched away in just a few seconds.

Theirs was the last ship to make it out of the lagoon. A few hours later, the Red Army blocked the entrance to the Königsberg canal.

They arrived in Pillau late in the night, but even in the darkness Inge could make out the shape of the crowd, a dense mass of bags and people grouped together on the shore. They waited for daybreak in a hall at the harbour. Albert, Frieda and Beatrice fell asleep huddled on the floor, but Inge, too anxious to rest, studied the other travellers. They were mainly women and children and the occasional elderly man, most carrying one or two cases. She went to the window and looked outside, where empty carts stood, brought by those who'd hoped to take with them as much as they could of their lives. A white goat tethered next to one gleamed in the moonlight. A woman had just told her that some families, failing to find lodgings and desperate for a passage out, had bedded down among the dunes, though the temperatures dropped to -15°C at night.

As dawn started to break, they made their way outside. Looking over the quayside, Inge saw row after row of empty prams on the edge of the port. They had been abandoned by mothers as they made their way aboard the ships that would carry them to safety with their children in their arms; an accidental memorial to East Prussia's last generation.

The *Göttingen*, a large ship, towered over Pillau's narrow quay. She was bound for Swinemünde, a harbour on the German side of the Danzig Corridor – a journey that, under normal conditions, took only a few hours. Records compiled during the evacuation document the *Göttingen* as carrying 2,464 wounded soldiers and 1,190 refugees that day, but the real number of civilians is likely to have been closer to 5,000. The *Göttingen* was not the only ship that left Pillau that day. Also listed as having departed are the *Monte Rosa*, a transport ship for the wounded, the hospital ship *Matero*, the training vessel *Nautik* and the much larger *Groenland*, the *Irene Oldendorf* and the *Eberhart Essberger*. Some carried wounded soldiers, some exhausted troops. All of them took refugees aboard. There are no reliable figures to gauge how many people made it onto those vessels. Official numbers only registered those with tickets, but naval crews were conscious that the Red Army was drawing ever nearer, and faced with a crowd of desperate women, many of whom were carrying infants, they allowed thousands of additional passengers onboard.[1]

Amid the people fighting to get on the *Göttingen* from a narrow quay, Inge somehow found an officer who directed her to a man with a list of passengers. She anxiously watched him check it; the Wiegandts' names were on it. He handed her four tickets, though the crowd already on deck suggested they were letting on many more people than had tickets and that space would soon run out. Passengers were being lifted up in large baskets; the boat either had not put out, or did not possess, any ramps. As Inge watched people shoving and pushing their way to the front of the queue she knew they couldn't wait much longer.

'Stay here,' she told Frieda, thrusting Beatrice into her arms. 'And wait! I'll find a way. We won't stand a chance with you tagging along behind me.'

Inge made her way to where some officers stood. As she pushed her way forward through the crowd, she noticed a handsome *Oberleutnant* looking at her.

'Have you lost someone?' he asked, coming to stand beside her.

'No,' Inge smiled, in the most beguiling way she knew. 'I'm looking for accommodation.' She fought to keep the urgency out of her voice. Stay calm, she told herself, keep smiling.

The officer returned her smile. 'I can offer you my cabin.'

'Oh, how small is it?' Sound playful, said the voice in her head.

'Not so small,' he said. 'I'm supposed to share with a colleague, but I'll tell him to go somewhere else.'

He wrote the cabin's number on a piece of paper. She felt his fingers linger as he put it in her hand and told his colleague to let her go to the front of the queue.

'You'll be safe now, I'll be back before you know it.'

She watched him wink as he disappeared round the corner.

Inge whipped her head round to where her parents stood. 'Come, quickly,' she hissed, as loudly as she dared.

They were lifted up in a large basket that swung and dipped at every gust of wind. Frieda clutched Inge's hand, her face white with terror. Twice she thought the basket would tip them out into the sea below.

The cabin was a large one, and well furnished, with four berths on each side. Sighing with relief, Inge put her daughter, who was rubbing her eyes, down to sleep.

She sat with Albert and Frieda and waited. When the officer came to find her, Inge stifled a laugh at his shock.

'Sorry,' she said, smiling as she stroked her sleeping daughter's hair. '*C'est la guerre*, no?'

Inge anxiously waited with her parents and her daughter for the ship to depart. Six others had joined them in the officer's cabin. It had been several hours since they had boarded just after dawn, but the ship had not yet been cleared for departure. Every time it was about to set off there was a further delay. The open sea carried the threat of Russian submarines, watching for German vessels to torpedo, so any ships leaving had to travel in convoy. As the wait lengthened into hours, a rumour went round the anxious passengers that the Soviet air force was targeting any ships that stood in the harbour.

Despite the cold outside, heat and humidity rose quickly. Even inside the private quarters, the stench was overpowering, the air heavy with the smell of sweat and faeces. People were crammed into cabins, bedded down in the narrow corridors, huddled in groups in the ship's dining room. Due to the sheer volume of people, the ship's toilets had stopped working hours before. Many of the passengers were ill after travelling for several days in the bitter cold, without regular food or being able to wash; people were relieving themselves into buckets. Years later, Inge said the smell of a crowd, however faint, would be enough to bring it all back. When a sailor came round to serve them thinned-out pea soup, Inge realised they hadn't eaten since they'd left the night before. She watched as her daughter, a picky toddler who'd previously always refused to eat this wartime staple, finished her bowl before holding it out and asking for more.

When the *Göttingen* left the harbour, the snow was falling heavily. It was unusually cold, even for late January, with temperatures dropping to -18°C on the open sea. Meanwhile, 200 kilometres to the west, in the port of Gotenhafen, another ship waited to set out of the Bay of Danzig. The *Wilhelm Gustloff*, named after a Nazi Party leader who'd been murdered by a Jewish student in 1936, hadn't left the harbour since the war had started more than five years before. She set off at 12.30 p.m. with about 10,000 people on board, more than double her capacity. The passengers were mostly women and children, though they also included 1,500 military personnel, so the Kriegsmarine did not designate the ship as a civilian transport.*

Like the *Göttingen*, the *Gustloff* had to sail in convoy with another ship, the *Hansa*, and two torpedo boats. Her final destination was the northern German port of Kiel, 300 kilometres west of Swinemünde. To avoid Soviet mines dotted along the shallow waters, the *Gustloff*'s captain headed for the open sea, hoping the roughness of the weather would deter Soviet submarines from travelling so far out. The plan went wrong early on. The *Hansa* was forced to turn back due to engine trouble, and torpedo boat TF1 soon followed, leaving only a small ship, the *Löwe*, following behind for protection. The *Gustloff* pressed on towards the top of the Hel Peninsula. She was travelling slowly, at no more than 12 knots.

Two hours earlier, 143 nautical miles to the east, Soviet captain Alexander Marinesko set out from the Lithuanian port of Memel towards the Bay of Danzig, where he knew German ship traffic was

---

* This designation would lead to the Soviet government defending its decision to torpedo the ship, stating it had no way of knowing it carried civilians

building. He didn't see the *Göttingen*, which, luckily for the Wiegandts, set out into the open sea only after Marinesko had passed Pillau. At the top of the Hel Peninsular, he spotted the *Gustloff*. Shortly after 9 p.m., he fired the first of his four torpedoes. Each had a special message engraved along its side:

1. *for the Motherland*
2. *for Stalin*
3. *for the Soviet people*
4. *for Leningrad*

Torpedoes one and two hit the *Gustloff* in the front half. Number three did the most damage, striking it just by the engine room. Number four jammed and failed to fire.

As the ship filled with water, passengers above and below deck started to panic. It had enough lifeboats for only half the passengers, but an oversight meant they had not been swung out, and half of them had frozen fast in their pulleys. Those that made it into the water were quickly overcrowded; many overturned, pitching their passengers into the freezing sea. Women, weighed down by heavy skirts and winter coats, found it difficult to swim properly and the water was so cold that those in the sea could survive for no more than a few minutes. Thousands more remained trapped inside the *Gustloff*'s hull. Hit in the engine room, at its very centre, the vessel sank fast. In forty minutes, she was on her side. In just an hour, it was all over. The *Gustloff*'s stern rose dramatically before the entire ship disappeared under water.

Other ships nearby tried to come to the rescue, including the *Göttingen*. Inge would always remember what she saw from the window of the cabin: the sight of the wreckage as the searchlights caught it. As the *Göttingen* drew nearer, the screams of women, the sound of crying children echoing over the water. As they searched for the few lifeboats that carried survivors, dawn broke to reveal hundreds of corpses, made buoyant by their lifejackets, bobbing up and down between the waves. 'Children shouting for their mothers, mothers without their children,' my grandmother described the scene to me. 'In my sleep sometimes I can still hear the screaming. I lost my faith in God that day.'

Though it came as close to the *Gustloff* as it could, the *Göttingen* only managed to rescue twenty-eight people. Torpedo boat T36, one of the first to reach the scene, rescued 564, among them an eighteen-year-old assistant purser, Heinz Schön. Torpedo boat *Löwe* rescued 472, the minesweeper M387 saved ninety-eight people, minesweeper M375 saved forty-three people, minesweeper 341 thirty-seven, torpedo recovery boat TF19, only seven. The *Gotenland*, a freighter, rescued two. Patrol boat V1703 found, among the corpses in a half-submerged raft, a single baby boy wrapped tightly in blankets, who had somehow survived the cold. They did not know the baby's name and later christened him after the soldier who had saved him. The young assistant purser, Schön, who had so narrowly avoided drowning, devoted most of his life to trying to record the names of all the *Gustloff*'s victims. The tragedy of the sinking haunted him until his death in 2013, when a team of divers, fulfilling his last wishes, placed an urn containing his ashes on the seabed where the *Gustloff*'s wreck still lies.

Recalling our conversation a few years later, I remembered that image of mothers screaming for their children as the water engulfed them, the sound that had haunted my grandmother until the day she died. I still found it hard to picture this sinking. The seas and the route were unfamiliar, but I wanted to learn more about this tragedy, which history had almost forgotten. What were the chances of such an encounter, in the vastness of the open sea? I found out that the rescue operation had been given the code name 'Operation Hannibal'. On a map, I retraced the routes it had taken. Using my niece's marker pens, I drew a green line for the *Göttingen*, yellow for the *Gustloff*. I marked Marinesko's route in red.

On paper, it's easy to visualise how the large and cumbersome German steamers made for easy prey: routes that I had pictured as being miles apart became a criss-cross of near misses. The Hel, a long spit of land, encloses the Bay of Danzig. The shelter it provided in peacetime narrowed the ships' route onto the open sea, making them vulnerable to attack. The *Göttingen*'s final destination was Swinemünde, and the *Gustloff* was bound for Kiel. For part of their journey, both ships took a similar route. It was only when I traced their sea voyage on paper that I realised how narrow my family's escape had been.

For the Wiegandts, those last two hours of their journey, with a handful of refugees from the *Gustloff* aboard, must have seemed interminable. My mother had once told me as a child that, during the night of the flight, Frieda's hair started to turn white. Though safety was within reach, a Red Army submarine could have ended their flight within minutes in the icy waters of the Baltic Sea. Indeed, only three weeks later the *Göttingen* would meet the *Gustloff*'s fate. Naval records show that on 23 February it was hit by a Russian torpedo off the coast of Latvia and quickly sank, killing 500 people.

Putting my home-made map aside, I again took up my grandmother's little black album, with its six photos of the Wiegandts' life in Königsberg. Had Frieda chosen them, I wondered, as she sat at the dining-room table that last evening? I read the article I'd found tucked into the album's flyleaf, about the *Gustloff*'s sinking, commemorating the tragedy fifty years later, placed alongside images of the life that they had left behind. My grandmother had told me in great detail about the shouting, the smell, the fear of that terrible day, which in the space of a few hours had made her into the atheist I'd always known her to be. Perhaps she knew that the account she gave me of that night was to be her last, for she never spoke of it again.

That evening in the kitchen in France, we both stayed silent when she finished speaking. We listened to the noises of the household around us, the sounds of a meal being prepared, of onions sizzling in a pan, the clanking of cutlery being taken out of a drawer, the dog barking, the shouts calling everyone to the table to come and eat before the food turned cold. There was something comforting in their mundanity.

I wanted to know more, of course, to find out whether the trauma of this flight held the key to the aloofness I'd observed in her since I was a child. I asked her if that day, so vividly remembered, had been the most terrible of her youth and she'd answered me almost abruptly.

'No. That time came later. The worst time was in Germany, shortly after the war ended. But I can't tell you about that. Not yet.'

Chapter Eleven

A LAST SUPPER

Night was falling when the Wiegandts disembarked in Swinemünde on the bitterly cold afternoon of 31 January 1945. The
harbour straddled the islands of Usedom to the west and Wollin
to the east. Separated by the narrowest of straits, and so close to
the mainland that, viewed on a map, you could mistake them for
a peninsula, the two tiny islands were a haven for the East Prussians arriving in their thousands, though they would offer only a
temporary respite. The front was growing ever nearer and the
islands were too close to the mainland to stay long in German
hands with the Red Army advancing, but it was the longest
journey ships like the *Göttingen* would risk for fear of being
torpedoed, while on East Prussia's shores thousands kept massing, waiting for the ship to come back for them.

The descent from the ship was perilous, down a narrow ladder
onto the quay. Inge thought Frieda, who clung to the rungs as she
descended, would faint. Inge held Beatrice tight as she made her
way down, rung by rung. With the tragedy they had witnessed
hours before still fresh in their minds, the Wiegandts could think
of little but the comfort of firm ground. They'd spent the last few
hours on the open sea, dreading attacks from the air or from submarines that lurked beneath the surface. Terror and shock had
given them the ragtag appearance characteristic of those in flight,
of prematurely old faces and clothing stiff with sweat and dirt. Inge
walked alongside her parents, carrying her daughter in her arms.

Beatrice was heavy and after the fetid warmth of the cabin, the bitterly cold air was already making Inge's feet tingle. People around her were crying from both shock and relief, but she felt only numb, as if the act of survival had drained her of tears. Her daughter started to whimper and Inge suddenly remembered that they had eaten nothing since the bowl of thinned-out pea soup several hours before. A naval officer with a schoolboy's face was directing people to the station, where trains would take them over a bridge, onto the mainland, and on to the west.*

For the last few hours, Albert had barely said a word. Now he spoke, almost reluctantly, holding his wife's hand in both of his, though he was looking at Inge.

'I know a woman on this island. She'll take us in, I'm sure. The little one is exhausted. Your mother can't take much more of this. Why not stay here, for a few days at least, and rest?'

They had no one in the west, he continued, and they needed time to work out what they were going to do next. He knew the island, as he had been here several times on his annual treatments for the rheumatism in his knee. This woman, he said, was the widow of a friend he'd met there, and had a house in Misdroy, just sixteen kilometres east along the coast. Perhaps they would be able to recover the suitcases they had lost in Königsberg.

Inge hesitated as she listened to her father. Her instinct was telling her not to stop running yet, and that time was short. As for the suitcases, she knew they would never come; they had probably never left Königsberg at all. In one night, she had become the leader of her family. But just now, with the weight of her daughter in her arms, so tired she could barely stand, it was too great a

---

* Just months later, in April 1945, the Karnin lift bridge, Usedom's main rail link to the mainland, was blown up by the Wehrmacht to hinder the Red Army's advance.

burden to bear. She nodded her agreement; the tears she had been holding back finally came. They rolled silently down her cheeks as she looked at her father. For a few days at least, she would allow herself to be his child again.

They were not the only ones who had chosen to stay. Wollin teemed with families whose exhaustion and relief at being back on land had lulled them into a temporary sense of safety. They joined a group walking from the harbour to the station, just a few hundred yards away, and caught a train that would take them the few kilometres east to Misdroy. It was a small town with stone houses painted in pastel hues, an elegant pier, and long white sandy beaches. Albert pointed out the attractions as they walked, almost as though they were there for a holiday. He led them to a cobbled street, set back from the seafront by a narrow strip of garden lined with tall birch trees, and stopped at the gate of a villa. The iron handle, Inge noticed, had been wrought in the shape of a seashell.

The gate was unlocked. Slowly, they made their way through the garden to the front door. Inge was suddenly conscious of their appearance, their coats wet with snow and the smell of travel still upon them. She removed her turban, heavy with jewellery, smoothed back her hair and turned to her mother to tuck a few stray locks back into the bun at the nape of her neck. Her father, she saw, had straightened his jacket and collar. The door opened almost as soon as they rang the bell.

A woman in her late forties stood on the threshold. She had dark red hair, and she was wearing a fashionably elegant black dress. When she saw Albert she gasped, breaking into a smile of surprised joy that lit up her entire face. She was beautiful, Inge thought, watching a myriad of emotions pass across the woman's face. When she saw Frieda and Inge, the joy gave way to something like alarm, but softened again at the sight of the child in

Inge's arms. Composing herself, she ushered them into the warmth of the hall. Albert explained that they'd arrived by boat, and that there had been no time to write. Inge glanced at her mother, whose stained dress had not been changed in forty-eight hours, the fear of the previous night still on her face and her hair greying at her temples. She passed her hand gently across Frieda's forehead, as if to smooth away her wrinkles, feeling a protectiveness towards her that she could not quite explain.

The woman introduced herself as Helene. She was the widow of a well-to-do manufacturer from Stettin, a hundred kilometres farther south. The villa in Misdroy was her summer house, but fear of air raids had driven her to move there permanently two years earlier. Her welcome was warm and genuine, and she told the Wiegandts to stay for as long as they liked, insisting that the island was still safe for now. She was polite to Albert, almost formal, though once or twice Inge noticed her using the informal second person '*du*' when she spoke to him. Frieda, warm-hearted and grateful to all those who were good to those she loved, thought her charming. Inge couldn't make up her mind, but her heart warmed towards the woman when she saw the longing in Helene's eyes as she looked at Beatrice.

The house was large, warm and comfortable. Inge was given her own bedroom, with a brass feather bed and a child's cot, intricately carved and painted white. Helene said that her husband had bought it in Prague when they were first married. She was silent for a moment, then said that their baby had died. She did not say when, nor did Inge want to ask, but it explained Helene's tenderness towards her daughter. As she lay in a hot bath that evening, enjoying the warmth, she thought of Helene's loneliness.

They remained there two whole weeks, almost able to forget the war raging around them. Though thousands of refugees had arrived in Wollin, life in Misdroy was relatively tranquil. Most of the new arrivals were housed in the schoolroom and the town hall, or on camp beds in the Kurhaus, the spa resort Albert had frequented to treat his rheumatism. To her astonishment, Inge found that the shops still accepted her coupons, which she'd taken with her more out of habit than foresight. She spent all of them at once, buying a heavy navy wool coat with gold buttons for herself, of a quality she had not seen since before the war, and a warm pullover and hat for her daughter. The purchases made Albert happier than she'd seen him in months.

'You see, what a good idea it was to come here,' he said.

Inge smiled at his delight.

'Yes, father, you were right.'

The Wiegandts knew they could not stay on the island for long. The Soviet forces were getting closer. Albert had been told at the station that there were terrible food shortages in mainland Germany, and that life was a struggle if you knew no one there. The Wehrmacht's losses on the Western Front had cut off food supplies and shortages were dire. The Wiegandts had no family and almost no close acquaintances in the west. Christa and her parents had moved in with an aunt somewhere near Munich. Albert's old business contacts in Hamburg had long since been bombed out, while Berlin was out of the question, as they suspected it would not hold out much longer.

As the Wiegandts worked out their next step, Winston Churchill, Franklin D. Roosevelt and Joseph Stalin gathered at Yalta, knowing their victory in Europe was imminent. At the week-long conference between 4 and 11 February, they carved out the occupation zones that would form post-war Germany. The summit was hailed as a victory for Soviet US relations. Swiftly, steadily, the Red Army advanced westwards.

By 13 February 1945, they had taken Budapest and were massing along the River Oder, some 130 kilometres from Berlin.

Inge wrote to Dorothea again, to tell her where they were, although she suspected that Dorothea would have to flee soon too, and might never get her letter. Naive as it sounds, the Wiegandts even talked about going to England. The reality of their status as an enemy and the gravity of the crimes of their nation had not yet sunk in.

In the end, Albert suggested Denmark, where people said there was still food left. Although Inge had never been there, Denmark held a strange familiarity for her. Wolfgang had often spoken to her about childhood summers at his uncle's estate, the beauty of the land and the kindness of the people. In her letter she had asked Dorothea whether she still had friends in the country who might be able to help them. It was the faintest of ties, but it seemed to be their only option – their lives, connections and everything they could rely on had vanished in one night; there was nothing else left.

They weren't sure how they would even get there. They went back to the army base in Swinemünde where they had disembarked. They showed what was left of their papers and asked if they could go to Denmark. It was still under German occupation, and they were told it was possible. A train was leaving the next day, which would take them through northern Germany and into southern Jutland. The officer who looked at their papers told Inge that they would only be allowed one small bag per person, with a single change of clothes in it. That afternoon, Inge wrote again to Dorothea, hoping that, if she kept writing, one of her letters would eventually reach her. The note was short and hurried. As they prepared to leave, she wrote that they were all well, even the little one. She added a postscript, a final plea that Dorothea should join them in Denmark, for there were rumours in Wollin that the Red Army would soon reach the German capital.

Back at Helene's house, Inge looked with longing at her feather bed as she prepared for the journey. Helene was crying in the kitchen. She, too, was planning to leave at the end of the month, to stay with a cousin near Heidelberg. Sitting in the kitchen, Albert told a funny story about a trip he had taken to the baths, where he had first met Helene and her husband, who were also there to take the waters. Helene laughed, which made Beatrice laugh too and clap her hands with delight. Frieda had never joined Albert on his trips to the baths, and Inge, who had never asked herself the question before, now wondered why that was.

That evening, Helene said, they would prepare a feast worthy of the time before the war. There was a festive atmosphere in the villa as they worked together in the kitchen, although they knew that they would probably never meet again. Helene laid out a white tablecloth trimmed with French lace, glasses of cut crystal and her fine Dresden china; she insisted on unpacking the silver candlesticks, which had been wrapped in newspaper and stowed in her trunk, ready for her departure. All the provisions, carefully hoarded to last through the war, were taken out to be eaten: real coffee, two jars of pickled lemons, a tin of canned peaches; Frieda even made a cake with the last of the sugar Helene had saved up, adding grated dried apple slices for sweetness. Bottles of wine were brought from the cellar, dusted, and set out along the length of the sideboard. Helene insisted Albert open them all, so they could at least try to drink them before the Russians could.

Inge would remember the sight for years: the gold edging of the delicate china plates flashing whenever the candlelight caught them; Helene, in a pale grey satin dress, sitting at the head of the table, smiling through the tears that glistened on her cheeks. As her father poured the wine, Inge noticed the label: it was marked with the name 'Wiegandt'. Her glance travelled along the sideboard, bottle by bottle, each label that of her father's business. Suddenly, she understood it all: the unease, the suspicion she had not managed to shake off, Helene's tears, masked by her smile, at their imminent parting. She glanced at Frieda, who was smiling. Did she know, Inge wondered? Or did she only see the things that would not hurt her? But armed with this new knowledge, she felt her wariness lift; there was no room for anger in her heart. What did it matter now, she thought.

The next morning, they left for the train station. They carried a small bag each, with a change of underwear and a clean rag to wash with; that was all they were allowed to take. Inge had stuffed her good silk dress, which she had taken with her from Königsberg, up her sleeve. As they left, Helene thrust a small loaf of bread into her hands.

'For the little one,' she said.

They waited for twenty-four hours for the train that would take them north-west through Germany and then north on to Denmark. They had been given no food, and ate the bread sparingly. Finally, the train arrived, its windows broken, the gaps stuffed with rags. The journey was slow, frequently interrupted by stops at army checkpoints. Inge cradled Beatrice, who had begun to fall sick and had diarrhoea. It was only then that the reality of her new existence, which she had allowed herself to forget at Helene's, sunk in. They had no home now.

In September 2018, a year after my grandmother's death, I drove the six hours west from the Vistula spit along the northern Polish coast to Wolin (to use its modern Polish spelling), trying to recreate by land part of the journey my family had undertaken by sea after they left Königsberg. I wanted to see for myself the place that had been the Wiegandts' first sanctuary after they left their home. I made my way along the western edge of what had once been East Prussia's coastline, on land that was now Polish. Its history, one of contrasts, reveals itself along the road; the dark trees of Sztutowo, once named Stutthof, and the thin railway tracks are a reminder of the concentration camp once housed in this forest. From that haunting reminder of death, on to Gdansk, with its elegant eigh-teenth-century merchant houses, once destroyed by bombs, now restored to their former glory.

Over the centuries of its existence, Wolin has known Swedish, Danish, German and Soviet control.* It is a land forged by trauma. Poland, having endured terrible brutality at the hands of the Germans, found yet another kind of suffering under Communist rule. Stalin's promise at Yalta, in 1945, to allow free elections, resulted instead in a gradual hardening of Soviet control under a communist regime that failed to offer the country the full independence it craved.

The landscape changed as I drove, the fields becoming smaller, their neat hedges taming the vastness of the forests, and the hills softening the stark, vast beauty of the east. Wolin is a gateway to the west of Europe, its coastline more sheltered, the wind less relentless than on the long wild beaches of the Baltic. In the villages, new houses mix with ancient barns, unbeautified, functional and frayed with age. Świnoujście, or Swinemünde as was, where the Wiegandts first disembarked after their crossing on the *Göttingen*, has the bustle of a busy town, with its twice daily ferries to Sweden. From there, I turned

---

* Wolin was returned to Poland in 1945 at the end of the war.

back on myself and headed east on the narrow road to Misdroy, now known as Międzyzdroje.

The tiny town is quiet out of season and still retains much of its Prussian heritage. The German border is only twenty kilometres away and both German and Polish tourists alike come here in their thousands in the summer to see the cobbled streets, painted houses and ornate pleasure pier that made the resort so popular in the Wiegandts' day. The Adler-Schiffe company's scenic tours don't take much notice of modern borders, taking in both Polish and German territory from Świnoujście to Bansin in a single trip. In the main square of Międzyzdroje, the 'Berlin' donner kebab shop advertises special deals on that most German of street foods, currywurst. This duality is constantly evoked, from the small museum dedicated to Germany's V3 supergun, to the streets named after Polish independence heroes. Międzyzdroje overcame its chequered past by making its history part of the very fabric of the town. It was, after all, what I myself was trying to do: to learn the truth of my family's story, to recognise in its shifts, its hopes and its flaws, the hybridity that shaped my own identity.

In these streets, I recognised much of what my grandmother had told me – the row of houses and the border of silver birches were just as she described. I didn't know for certain which villa had once belonged to Helene; perhaps the tall cream one with the ornate windows and the lime green facings, where a sign in the window advertised rooms to let in both Polish and German.

The Baltic Sea was calm on the day of my visit. I walked to the end of what my guidebook informed me was the longest pier in Poland. There, eyes narrowed against the sun, I could just make out the next stop in the Wiegandts' journey, as a family adrift, in search of food and a future, a thin blurred line on the horizon, a time about which Inge had only spoken in a few scattered reflections. Before her death, my grandmother had shared with me the secrets she had kept, the things she had endured in these post-war years. But despite those confidences, she had left many gaps.

Starting with their time in Denmark, her recollections – or, at least, those she was willing to share with me – were sparser. I knew the Wiegandts had spent several months there, long enough for my mother to learn to speak Danish. And it was a time that, I thought, must have marked Inge. She was a young woman of twenty, with a small child and elderly parents, neither a wife nor a widow, German and yet stateless, a victim with no right to sympathy. I wanted to know how it had changed her.

To fill the gaps in Inge's recollections, I later sought out the stories of the thousands of others who, like the Wiegandts, had arrived in Denmark as East Prussian refugees. I wondered how they were received, those wives and children of the enemy, now seeking shelter on Danish shores. After undergoing terrible journeys, they had arrived between early February and 5 May, when the country was still under German occupation. Within a few weeks of their arrival, Germany's capitulation abruptly changed their status.

I found the odd article on these refugees, or the occasional reference in a book, usually within a chapter that dealt with other aspects of the war. I had heard stories of mistreatment, told by the children of others whose families had fled East Prussia. A friend, whose mother's family also came from East Prussia, told me that her aunt would never speak of her time in Denmark as a child of five. When asked, she would only cover her left hand, which had a missing finger. They were stories told in whispers, weighed down by the emotion that can never be wholly cast aside: German guilt.

My grandmother's tendency to shift from full confidence to reserve, even after our relationship changed, continued until her death. It frustrated me, but as I found out more, I started to understand it better. Inge was given no time to make her peace with the things she had lost: childhood, ambition and love. Flight denies the luxury of time and does not allow for reflection. I suppose she only had two options: to give in to emotion and give up, or to put the past behind her and move on. It was a mindset that forged her future self: her ability to survive, always moving forward and never allowing herself to look back.

Chapter Twelve

SINS OF THE FATHERS

It's strange to think of Germans as refugees, so defined are they by the weight of their nation's crimes, but it was the reality my family faced when they found themselves homeless and with no one to turn to.

They arrived in Denmark sometime in late February 1945, just a few weeks before the war ended, one family among a quarter of a million Germans from East Prussia seeking food and shelter on the country's shores. It was an influx so large that it made up 5 per cent of Denmark's total population. Eighty-five per cent of those arriving were women and children, and a third were aged under fifteen. Most of these refugees were interned in camps until they were repatriated to Germany in November 1946.

Though Inge had told me only a few stories of the Wiegandts' time in Denmark, I knew that for a while they had hoped to settle there permanently. Their experience of displacement, just as the war was ending, was a crucial part of piecing together what must have been some of the most traumatic months of my grandmother's life and, in 2018, I flew to Copenhagen to try to discover why.

On a drizzly, cold March morning, I drove south to Sønderborg from Copenhagen to take a closer look at the town my family had first arrived in. I had little to go on. A tattered cardboard document, folded in two, with the words *Hilfspass für Flüchtlinge* printed at the top – my grandmother's ration card. It was a special one for

(Ausstellende Behörde)

Hilfspass Nr. 15/45
(Ausweis für Flüchtlinge)

Familienname: _Wiegandt_

Rufname: _Ingeborg Gertrud_

Beruf: _Architekturstudierende_

Geburtsort: _Königsberg O/Pr._

Geburtstag: _24.7.1924_

Wohnort: _Königsberg O/Pr._

Gestalt: _mittel_

Gesicht: _oval_

Farbe der Augen: _blau_

Farbe des Haares: _schwarz_

Besondere Kennzeichen: _keine_

Staatsangehörigkeit: _Deutsch_

Gültig für Dänemark
~~und für die Rückkehr nach Deutschland~~

INGE'S RATION CARD.

Unterschrift des Inhabers

Der Ausweis wird ungültig am 31. Dezember 1945.

Ausgestellt { auf Grund der Kennkarte
{ nach eigenen Angaben

Es wird hiermit bescheinigt, dass der Inhaber die durch das obenstehende Lichbild dargestellte Person ist und die darunter befindliche Unterschrift eigenhändig vollzogen hat.

Apenrade, den 17. April 1945.

Deutsches Konsulat
Apenrade
Unterschrift der Behörde

Dienst-
siegel

refugees, stamped in April 1945, weeks before the war ended, by the German consulate in the small town of Aabenraa, then known by its German name Apenrade. My grandmother had once made a reference to the naval barracks where they were first taken when they arrived, a building she remembered as being so close to the shore that you could hear the sea. And there was the story of a kind school teacher's widow who had become their friend.

Sønderborg is more than three hours' drive from Copenhagen and most of the Danes I'd spoken to thought I was mad to go there in March. It was a summer place, they said, and advised me to go when the weather was nicer. But as I watched the sleet beat against the windscreen of my hire car, I thought that the Wiegandts must have arrived on a day like this, sometime in late February. Their first sight of Denmark would have been shrouded in rain and grey mist. The road there took me through an orderly agricultural land-scape dotted with small, neat towns and on to the most southerly point of Denmark's Jutland Peninsula. It has a complex history. For centuries, it was home to both ethnic Danish and German populations. First a Danish fief, it was lost to Germany in a war in 1864, before a plebiscite in 1920 led to its reunification with Denmark.* Today, those German links remain strong.

I arrived early in the afternoon to find the sleet had given way to snow and made my way to the harbour's edge, where a ship was entering the bay. Sønderburg's houses spread out along both sides of a narrow strait, with the old town on the island of Als and its newer suburbs extending on to Jutland. A twelfth-century red-brick fortress marks the harbour's entrance, a throwback to the days of frequent naval attacks. The bleak March light lent the city the drabness of a holiday resort out of season. The beach was

---

* The plebiscite was agreed at the Treaty of Versailles.

deserted, its ice-cream parlour boarded up. Even the old houses along the bay, painted in green, orange and cream, had lost their vibrance.

Past the fortress, the harbour opened up to a full view of the bay and I scanned the horizon for something that might have once been a barracks. I spotted it almost at once, an imposing red-brick building with a military air, large, bleak and square, its windows unlit. Built in German days in 1906, by the time the Wiegandts arrived, when Denmark was still under German occupation, it was being used as a training college for the German Navy. The army, faced with the need to house thousands of refugees from the eastern territories at short notice, turned every building they could spare – colleges, schools, halls and hotels – into temporary housing.*

The building showed no signs of being occupied apart from a few cars in an adjacent parking lot; its main gate was barred by a padlock and chain. Most of the windows were boarded up so I stood on a box to look over the wall, almost stepping on a dead rat in a trap. The gate led on to a square courtyard with buildings all around it. There seemed to be hundreds of rooms. I remembered my grandmother saying that they had gathered in the courtyard with many other families, waiting to be assigned a place to sleep. They had been taken to a large hall, and some had bedded down there as they waited. Young officers, most barely out of their teens, were assigned to help the families, though the numbers of women with children, sick from the perilous conditions of travel, were already overwhelming them. The boy assigned to help the Wiegandts was a doctor's son, who introduced himself as Officer De Jong. Inge could not remember his first name.

---

* Later arrivals were taken straight to Copenhagen and on to internment camps.

'He had nice brown eyes,' Inge had told me as she described her displacement. 'He wanted to take me out for dinner and to a dance. They were all being sent to the Western Front … He went too. It was just weeks before the end, but it ended for him in the same way as it did for them all. Cannon fodder.

'I still can't believe I went to that dance. I had nowhere to live, my child was sick. But you behave strangely in these circumstances.'

I remembered her words as I looked at the old building. Deserted as it was now, there was some evidence it had been lived in not so long ago. An unblocked window to a basement room revealed a kitchen and another a few bunk beds, the bedding still on. I later discovered that the barracks had been closed down in 2013 due to cuts to the defence budget. In 2014 they were used as an emergency shelter for 300 Syrians, fleeing, decades later, from another war. Their arrival caused rifts among the local population, and the 35,000 who'd applied for asylum in the region were described by some politicians as an unstoppable wave. I wondered what kind of reception the Wiegandts had received once Denmark regained independence at the end of the war, four people out of a quarter of a million arrivals foisted onto the newly freed state. But as I looked at the austere courtyard, its prison-like aspect, it seemed remarkably unwelcoming, a place of hardship rather than plenty. I put my hand on the bare brick wall, felt its coldness beneath my palm.

There's something about physically seeing places that drives home the reality of the past. As I left the army barracks, I realised I'd never really understood what being displaced meant. The sight of these stark walls somehow revealed to me what it must have been like to leave their home and all they loved behind, obliged to start anew with no clear path or direction, hated by the people they sought shelter from. These were messy and uncomfortable thoughts. My own existence had depended on that moment of flight, on that narrow escape, which I had, for years, taken for granted. That's the trouble with digging up the past, it makes you question your own present.

The boy officer who showed the Wiegandts round blushed when Frieda asked him his age. 'Seventeen last month,' he replied. He blushed again later when he asked Inge if she would come to a dance in the officer's mess that evening. Startled, she agreed without thinking, although she was stiff from a night on a thin mattress on the barracks floor, exhausted from the journey and desperately worried about her daughter, who was still unwell.

The dance was being held near the training barracks where the Wiegandts had first arrived. It had been the commander's idea, to provide, perhaps, a few hours of pleasure for the boys he knew were doomed to die and the refugees who had lost everything. It was a ragtag assembly, baby-faced soldiers and exhausted girls in worn dresses. A small orchestra of men well over sixty, too old to enlist, was playing dance tunes. Most of the girls wore winter boots, the only shoes they owned. Their frocks were mostly borrowed and badly fitting, their own finer dresses left behind long ago.

The music stopped after half an hour and someone brought out a gramophone. Inge froze as she recognised the song, one she had often danced to with Wolfgang. Her dance partner, the boy who had shown the Wiegandts to their quarters, stood expectantly beside her, but she forgot that he was there at all. One of the soldiers whooped with delight at a favourite song; he sounded, she thought, like an excited child. Look around you, she wanted to shout, look at these boys, look at the faces of us women, look at our clothes, at the soles of our shoes. What was left to fight for?

She might have said all this out loud, had her partner not asked her if she would like to dance. Here he was, a boy who should have had his whole life before him. She looked at his expectant face and didn't have the heart to refuse. Instead she forced a smile, took his outstretched hand and danced with him most of the night, laughing when he told her she was beautiful. He asked if he could write to her and she said yes, though she had no address to give him. The next evening, she let him take her out for dinner with his few remaining kroner. Afterwards, she was angry at herself for going at all, it seemed so frivolous in the circumstances. All she had wanted for those few hours had been to feel normal again.

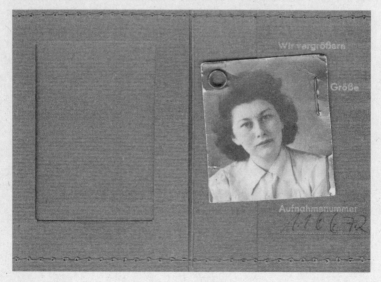

INGE'S PASSPORT PHOTO.

The next day he was sent to the front and two weeks later she was told that he was dead.

*

A few days after their arrival, the Wiegandts were moved out of the barracks to a school, where camp beds had been set up in the auditorium to accommodate the refugees. More people were arriving daily to seek shelter – sick, tired, hungry – and the auditorium was soon crowded. Some, the luckier ones, would be assigned to ethnic German families who lived in the region, but the numbers of people arriving were so large, it was becoming harder and harder to do so. To prevent chaos, the army kept a close watch on the refugees. Everyone was registered, and you could not wander far. What did it matter, if you had nowhere to go?

The Wiegandts were lucky to have been assigned a space in a corner. It gave them the illusion of a little privacy as they pushed their camp beds against the wall. No one told them how long they were to stay, or why. Until a permanent lodging was found for them, they were not allowed out. Inge watched her daughter sitting on one of the beds, staring at the room around her. She was being far too quiet for a child of her age. As the numbers of refugees grew, the food, potato soup or thinned down gruel, was getting scarcer. The overcrowding heated the room, which smelt dank from sweat. Many of the new arrivals were feverish, and as the auditorium filled up the sound of people coughing, ill from days or sometimes weeks of travel in the bitter cold, would echo through the night.

And Beatrice was getting sicker. The diarrhoea she had developed on her journey was getting worse. She had not eaten for two days, turning her head away when Inge or Frieda tried to feed her their daily soup, or the slice of bread that came with it. Inge would stay up and watch her sleep. She was losing weight fast; her skin, covered in sweat, had a yellow tinge; her eyes had lost their mischief; her blonde hair was lank and dull, and strands of it stuck to her forehead. Inge had heard a woman say, as she glanced at her trying to feed her daughter, that last week a child had died. Fear, like an icy pain piercing through her chest, crept into her heart.

Every hour, Frieda had to coax Beatrice to drink a little drop of water. Inge could barely look at her mother and father, seeing her own worry reflected in their eyes. She held her daughter's hand, the bones of her fingers lying bird-like and fragile in her palm. The German army doctor had come briefly to see her, but he had said, with a gentle shake of his head, that there was nothing he could do. He had seen it before. It was impossible to keep sanitary conditions when so many people needed shelter. Children, weakened by days of flight in the bitter cold, were always the first to get ill.

'Just give her water and keep her warm,' he said.

'This child will die if you don't do something!' Albert had shouted.

The doctor tried to calm him. It was something all children here went through, he said. Besides, there was no medicine to be had. Albert sat beside the little girl for hours, willing her to regain her strength. Twice a day he pleaded with the officer in charge of their quarters, asked for them to be moved somewhere else, asking him for medicine. The answer, though given kindly, was that nothing could be done.

Salvation came unexpectedly. A place for them came up in Apenrade, with a local resident there who had volunteered to take a family with a child. The woman taking them in had come to meet them. She was a kind-faced Danish widow in late middle age with grey hair, who introduced herself as Hanne. Her husband had been an ethnic German whose family had always lived in Denmark and she'd offered to house a family of refugees as soon as she heard of the first arrivals. Her large brown eyes showed nothing but compassion and comfort. When she saw Beatrice, lying inert in Inge's arms, she put her hand on Inge's shoulder.

'We will get her better,' she said.

Inge almost wept with relief. They set off at once; Hanne explained she lived about an hour away. Inge held her child throughout the journey.

'It will be better now,' she whispered, rocking her daughter in her arms, stroking her hair. 'Just wait.'

Apenrade was a small, quiet town. Hanne lived in the outskirts, in a pleasant neighbourhood with rows of neat wooden houses and well-tended gardens. It was a far cry from the rubble-strewn streets and destruction the Wiegandts had left behind in Königsberg. The house was painted blue with a red roof. It was a simple home, but to Inge it looked like paradise.

As soon as they arrived, Hanne put water on to boil. She took Beatrice from Inge's arms, and wrapped her in a shawl. She mixed the boiled water with honey, and gently fed it to her with a spoon. At first, she only wet the child's lips with it. Within an hour, tasting the sweetness, Beatrice called for more. Frieda and Inge looked at each other. It was the first time in two days they had heard her speak. Hanne smiled, and coaxed her to take a little more.

Under Hanne's watchful eye, Beatrice recovered quickly. Within two days, she was sitting up, and eating the soup Hanne made for her; by the end of a week, she was eating semolina pudding; within three, she had gained back the weight she had lost, and was running around with the neighbour's children. Every other day, Hanne baked Inge a *Sandkuchen* – the German equivalent of a pound cake – for breakfast and insisted she eat it.

Hanne treated the Wiegandts like family, and as the months passed they grew to love her as if they had known each other for years. Every evening, she and Frieda sat together and chatted as they did the household mending, laughing at Inge, who hated sewing. Their conversation was of domestic matters, of the street and of its people, the kind Inge had found tedious in peacetime, but now she relished it. Routine and normality had become luxuries. She enjoyed the rhythms of this quiet life and the respite it brought after the fear and anxiety of their flight. Her daughter Beatrice was now fully recovered. Her face was round again, dimpling when she smiled. Her light blonde hair shone as if it had been touched by the sun. She played with the neighbours' children every afternoon, running, skipping and playing tag, and was soon chattering away in Danish. Hanne knitted her a blue jumper, which she insisted on wearing every day.

A few weeks after their arrival, Inge was talking to their neighbour as they watched Beatrice playing in the garden, when the sound of shouting in the street distracted them. They hurried to the gate. A flustered girl, red-cheeked, her eyes glowing, was running down the street.

'It's over!' she said. 'The war. Germany has surrendered.'

Inge and the neighbour laughed and cried with relief. Inge had dreamt of peace for so long, it had seemed it would never come. She ran into the house to tell Hanne and her parents the news. Frieda hugged Hanne tightly. But the glance she cast at Inge held a relief tinged with a new anxiety. She knew that they were aliens, bound to a nation towards whom the world felt nothing but hatred, a nation whose crimes would now be fully exposed.

Inge felt it during the days that followed, in the glances of the neighbours, in the occasional taunts of small boys in the street as she walked past. A quiet, simmering tension was building; there was an as-yet unspoken need to expunge the injustices and hardships of the occupation years. Only Beatrice was oblivious, chattering in her toddler's Danish to the neighbour's daughter.

Hanne reassured them, saying that her house was large enough for all of them. She begged them to stay with her for as long as they wanted. Inge had made friends in that quiet community and Frieda and Albert had been warmly welcomed. But they knew this hiatus could not last long. One morning in late summer, a Danish friend of Inge's cycled over to tell her that the authorities had taken a German mother and child from a house just a few streets away.

Word was that all German refugees were being sent to camps and that Danish citizens would no longer be allowed to shelter them. The police had started checking all the houses and rounding up any German citizens they found. Inge's friend told her that she and her parents must leave very soon, or they too would be interned. Inge had heard of the camps, where conditions were meant to be harsh. Once interned, there was no way of getting out. Inge looked at her daughter, fit and well again, and remembered her unnatural quiet of just a few months before, her pale, painfully thin face, dull hair and fixed stare, the look of a child slipping away from life. She felt a knot tighten in her stomach and rise to her throat in a sob. She could not allow her daughter to get so close to death ever again. She knew that they must leave Denmark. Her parents needed no convincing. Almost frantically, Inge started to pack, throwing in the jumper Hanne had knitted and the things she had been given by this community that had been so kind to them, but which she knew could be about to turn.

But leaving was no straightforward matter. The British forces that controlled Schleswig-Holstein, the German province just across the border, were refusing entry to German refugees from the eastern territories as dwindling food supplies had reached crisis point. In desperation, Inge turned to her Danish friend, who had a boyfriend in the British Army. He agreed to smuggle them to mainland Germany onboard a minesweeper, which was bound the next morning for the port of Kiel. Her friend brought bicycles for the Wiegandts to ride to the port. Inge rode with Beatrice balanced on the handlebars, while Frieda weaved all over the road; she had only ridden a bike once before in her life. Hanne cried bitterly as she watched them leave. It was a hard parting. In those few months of tranquillity, they had lost the urge to run, had thought that here, at last, they could try to belong. But no one, including Germany, wanted them now.

For people like myself, who have not lived through a war, it is hard to grasp how much survival depends on chance. I grew up with the stories of my grandparents' generation, of hardship, of conflict, of horror, but these belonged to the distant past. I had seen war close up in Afghanistan, in my work as a journalist. I had felt interest and compassion, but always with a degree of professional detachment. War had elicited no personal connection, until I started finding out more about my family's story. I had never thought about how narrow the Wiegandts' escape was, how, but for a fortunate chain of circumstances, they might never have left Königsberg at all. Inge might not have met the neighbour on the stairs that day, or never been given the number that allowed them to get a place on board the ship that took them to safety. The Wiegandts might not have avoided a Russian torpedo. They might never have met Hanne, whose care saved my mother's life. But for these tiny things that make up a chain of circumstance, Albert, Frieda, Inge and my mother could so easily have died. The generations that followed her – me, my brother and my nieces – might never have existed at all.

As I learnt in the years after Inge shared these memories with me, my family was extremely fortunate to escape Denmark when they did. Five years of German occupation had turned all Germans, even displaced women and children, into objects of hatred for most Danes. The introduction by the Germans of martial law in August 1943 to tighten their control over Denmark subjected the population to the full weight of occupation. Reprisals for those who resisted were brutal; they faced arrest and likely execution. As a result, desire for reckoning drove the immediate post-war mood across Europe, and Denmark was no exception.

Before I began investigating my family's story, I had always had an image of Denmark as one of the only countries that could hold its head high in the knowledge that it had always done right. It had saved most of its Jewish population, even while under Nazi occupation. More than 7,000 people were hidden or taken to the safety of Sweden by boat; thanks to this action, 98 per cent of Danish Jews survived the Holocaust.[1] Still, closer scrutiny nearly always brings nuance. I was about to find out that even the Danes, in those few months after the war ended, gave in to a darker side.

The fate of the East Prussians who arrived in Denmark is a story that is little known, and which remains sparsely documented. Not much is left of the camps that once housed these German refugees, though the period of occupation that preceded the camps remains one of the most researched in Denmark. One powerful marker survives in the south-western corner of Copenhagen's Vestre Kirkegård, a vast cemetery that spans fifty-four hectares. Away from the wide alleys lined with elegant oaks and well-kept flower beds, there's a forgotten corner dotted with hundreds of identical grey stone crosses, small and starkly simple. Each bears a cluster of names. It's a mass grave of East Prussia's displaced.

A tram and a bus journey took me to the park that houses the cemetery in Copenhagen's Kongens Enghave district. I knew what I was looking for, but not exactly where to find it. I had been walking around the cemetery for more than an hour and the light was starting to fade when I finally found the place where Denmark had buried some of the German dead. There was still snow on the ground and I was worried that it would get dark before I could find my way back out. A tall iron cross dominated the area, its sole inscription a date that required no further explanation, 1939–1945. At its base lay a large wreath, still green, that seemed to have been laid there during an official ceremony, adorned with a ribbon in the colours of the German flag. An effort at remembrance had been made, though the starkness of the crosses contrasts with the splendid monuments of neighbouring plots.

I first read about Copenhagen's German cemetery by chance, in an article in a German magazine. I was by then no stranger to the story of East Prussia's refugees. After my grandmother's account of their flight, I had looked for every detail I could find about the *Gustloff*, about the other ships that had sunk, and about the plight of the thousands who died before they even reached the shoreline, from exposure on the roads. I had assumed that if they survived the journey, the worst for these refugees had been over. I was wrong. I wondered why so many ended up dying in Denmark, in the safe haven they had hoped to reach.

About 10,000 Germans are buried at Vestre Kirkegård. Some were soldiers fallen in the last weeks of the war, most of them very young, sixteen or seventeen perhaps. But more than half of the dead were refugees from East Prussia, mainly women and children who had sought refuge in Denmark. Most had been weakened by a journey made in the dead of winter, with little food and almost no shelter, under constant threat of attack.

The cold was bitter. I stamped my feet to warm up and rubbed my hands together to keep my fingers from going numb. I brushed away the snow from one of the crosses and from a large plaque on the ground, to read the names engraved there: Peter, Adelheid, Christa, Gisela, a few, unnamed, marked only as *'Kind'*, the German word for child. A few crosses were dated February or March 1945, shortly before Germany's surrender, but it's from April that the deaths started coming in scores. Most of those buried here were less than three years old, children whose names were written in clusters, their exact date of birth unknown. The German corner, as the locals call it, is really a children's graveyard.

I stopped at another shared grave, that of 'an unknown German refugee' and just below it, the name of a little girl, Elsbeth Damaschke, born on 10 May 1943, died 27 July 1945. Aged just two, only two months younger than my own mother when she had come to this country. I knelt down in the snow by that cross, feeling the cold and wet seep through my clothing. I wished I'd brought something to lay beside it, to remember this small child, buried alone without her mother, beside a refugee whose name will never be known. I tried and failed to hold back my tears. I'm still not sure what moved me most, this sudden grief or the fact that I was ashamed of it; that it felt wrong, even after so many years, to cry for any German, even a child, in a Second World War graveyard. I could not bear to leave her without a mark of notice, so I wrote the words *'in Erinnerung'*, in remembrance, in the snow that covered her.

The Danes had the decency to bury the offspring of their enemies in consecrated ground, but I later learnt that it was the German community who had raised the money to put up the crosses sometime in the 1960s. Further research into the fate of East Prussia's displaced children brought up statistics that make for stark reading. More than a fifth of those children who reached Danish shores in 1945 had died within the year, perishing in their thousands within months of their arrival. They had survived

VESTRE KIRKEGÅRD.

journeys of often several days, in which many froze to death in temperatures of -20°C or lower. They had avoided the Red Army, dodged its air bombardments and torpedoes. What killed them, in the end, was starvation and simple lack of care.

These were no mere casualties of flight. A simple statement made in March 1945 by the Danish medical association goes some way to providing an explanation: 'Due to prevailing circumstances, we are of the opinion that we are not able to provide any form of medical help to German civilians.' The edict was not repeated after Germany's capitulation in May, but with the memory of years of persecution under occupation still raw, the majority of Danish doctors stuck to it and continued to withhold treatment. Even the Red Cross did not provide East Prussia's displaced with medical assistance until 1949, though in that first year of arrival, 7,000 children are estimated to have died. It's a number that remained hidden until it was made public by Kirsten Lylloff, a retired immunologist who worked out the number while undertaking academic research into the fate of German refugees in Denmark.

I had arranged to meet Kirsten after reading about her research into East Prussian refugees in Denmark. I explained my connection to their story, and she agreed to meet with me while I was in Copenhagen. Kirsten is a friendly, grey-haired Danish woman in her seventies, whose idea of retirement was to complete a PhD in history. She stumbled upon the story of Denmark's handling of the East Prussian refugee crisis by chance. A childhood spent listening to stories of the hardship of life under the occupation had initially put her off the Second World War as a subject; she felt she had heard enough. But her historian's curiosity and scientist's regard for evidence led to a remarkable discovery. Over a cup of coffee in Copenhagen's Royal Library, she explained how she had noticed the graves of German children in the town of Aalborg in northern Jutland, where she lived and worked for a number of years. She decided to search church records to find out the exact numbers and to look for the death certificates stating the causes of death. What she found horrified her.

By the sheer number of child deaths she counted, Kirsten had assumed that the cause may have been an undiagnosed epidemic, but the death certificates told her a different story. They listed causes of death such as measles, diarrhoea, pneumonia and, for the children under the age of one, mostly malnutrition. These were all treatable diseases. Furthermore, as she explained, Denmark had never suffered from a shortage of food, not even during the war years. The issue lay in the rations the refugees were allocated. Each adult refugee was given food adding up to 2,000 calories per day, enough for one person only. But children under eight – who comprised a large proportion of the displaced – only received a third of that. This amounts to about 665 calories a day on average, much too little for a child of that age. Then there was the food itself: rye bread, potatoes and twenty grams of butter and cheese. It lacked the nutrients and variation needed by the children. Infants were allocated just half a litre of milk.

'If that's all you give to a baby, it will die,' Kirsten said simply.

Refugees under the age of five were particularly at risk. Undernourished children living in overcrowded conditions often fall ill within a matter of months or weeks. This is where the most shocking aspect of this story emerges. Kirsten found evidence that Danish doctors simply refused to treat the starving, ill children inside the camps. Those who dared to do so were publicly ostracised. Her findings are unequivocal: the children died from neglect.

'For many Danes, Germans were still the enemy, even the sickest, who were so often very small children,' she said.

It is this aspect of the story that Kirsten, a doctor herself, still finds difficult to come to terms with.

'After the war, Danes just wanted to forget about these 250,000 people who had come to seek refuge. No one wanted them. Then when historians wrote this story, it became better and better, until it was told as a tale of how Denmark rescued those Germans. The shame simply got written out. But the story of these children and their mothers must be told and remembered.'

The next day, I thought over what Kirsten had told me. I'd prepared myself throughout this search for unpalatable truths, for the discovery of moral failures in those of my own kin. Instead, I'd found a tale of German victimhood, a tragedy lost in the enormity of the greater crimes their country had committed. I'm not sure which is harder to process, the depth of the hatred felt towards those Germans, or the fact that, after all, it's not so hard to understand. It's what they mean, I suppose, by the sins of the fathers being visited on their children, leaving German children like my mother to bear the weight of an identity that made them pariahs at birth.

PART IV

Chapter Thirteen

YEAR ZERO

There was a gap in my grandmother's recollections, a void around the period she had referred to as the 'worst time of all', those first years after the war. When I tried to talk to her about the year or two that followed the Wiegandts' arrival in northern Germany, her replies grew sparser, even more so than when we'd talked about her time in Denmark; it was almost as if something in her was shutting down. Very few physical traces remain of that time. They were lost, I suppose, or perhaps deliberately destroyed, unwelcome reminders that she had worked hard to forget.

I came to think of them as the years she'd rather not remember. So I turned to my mother to try and build a picture of that period and piece together a few facts. The more I looked into my grandmother's story, the more questions I had. I wanted to know what it had been like for Albert, for Frieda, for my mother, young as she then was. My mother had told me a few stories of her grandparents when I was a child, especially of Frieda. But it was not childhood tales that I wanted now. I asked her if she remembered the light, the smells, what she had eaten, what she had played with. These tiny, long-buried details, so insignificant on their own but so important to me within the context of this story, came to her in flashes, often unexpectedly: when we sat having coffee; while watching her granddaughters; on the street, seeing a little girl take her grandfather's hand. Her recollections are sketchy at best, glimpses of a world seen through the eyes of early childhood – she was only three and four years old. She tried to remember what she could of the years that she had been encouraged not to dwell on.

'I remember a low building at the end of a lane,' she said. 'I remember my mother brushing my hair, and that we shared a bed. Holding my grandfather's hand as we went together to gather leaves and berries. There were some I needed for my skin – it was sore. They said it was from lack of food.

'I remember it was always cold.'

INGE AND BEATRICE.

As these details came back to her, I thought of the memories I have from that age. My first day at nursery school, looking up at my best friend as he stood on a box in a corner of the schoolroom to plot our escape, the extra height giving him a new authority. Carrying flowers at my aunt's wedding, the feel of the rose petals between my fingers, walking down an aisle so long it seemed never to end; they belong to a life of privilege and plenty. My mother's recollections told a very different story. She recalled things like the itchy, rough wool of her stockings; sharing a bed with her mother in the long, low farmhouse they lived in at the end of a lane; a game which she and Frieda liked to play, which they called 'Grand Hotel'.

I pictured the scene as my mother described it to me. In a dark room, Frieda is leaning over a small blonde child who sits solemnly before an empty plate on a plain kitchen table. Twelve pieces of mismatched cutlery are arranged around it. A handkerchief is spread underneath in lieu of a place mat. It is a game Frieda used to teach her granddaughter fine dining etiquette. The fish knife is missing; they replace it with a wooden clothes peg.

As I dug deeper into my family's story, I became, for a while, obsessed with all things East Prussian. I longed to get a sense of it beyond my grandmother's recollections, and searched for details that could help me understand the life my family had lost. When I was still at university, my mother had given me a dog-eared copy of *Doennigs Kochbuch*, the East Prussian *Hausfrau*'s bible. Thick, at 640 pages long with no pictures, it's a cookbook from long before they became glossy lifestyle bibles. The name 'Frieda Wiegandt' is inscribed in spidery writing on the flyleaf. Recipes are strange things, so strongly do they bind us to the past. Travellers and refugees alike have carried them for centuries, recreating, in their flavours, the memory of what they once called home.

It was an unremarkable edition bound in red, missing the dust jacket, and had a tendency to fall open at its most-thumbed pages, where traces of stains spoke of years of good use. The text was first written in 1899 and has never been updated. Frieda must have bought this copy long after the Wiegandts first left Königsberg, to replace the one she left behind, a reminder of the time when she had employed a cook, and could plan her meals without giving the purchase of meat and butter a second thought.

I picked it up again after those conversations with my mother, to try and get a sense of Frieda. Flicking through the pages of *Doennigs Kochbuch* brought back, for an instant, the smells and tastes of my own childhood. *Rote Grütze*, a pudding of red berries served with whipped cream; *Mohnrouladen*, buttery cake rolls stuffed with marzipan and poppy seed; *Kohlrouladen*, rolled cabbage leaves filled with onion and beef mince, the smell of which would linger around our house for days.

A recipe highlighted in pencil caught my eye, *Ragout von Hasen, Reh oder Hirsch*, hare, deer or elk ragout in a mushroom sauce, feeding up to eight people, the words '*sehr gut*' beside it in Frieda's hand. I read the ingredients, noticing that, despite Frieda's endorsement, the page was clean, seemingly untouched by a cook's greasy hand:

1 hare, or 1.5kg of venison
120g butter to brown
Salt
An onion
4 juniper berries
Vegetables for broth
Water
Red wine

For the sauce:
50g butter

90g flour
Lemon juice
10 champignons
6–8 morels
Cayenne pepper
125g ground meat for meatballs
Half moon puff pastry

They were typical *Doennig* ingredients, designed for a diet of indulgence in which the cost of red meat, sugar, butter, cream, wine and brandy was never counted. But in those post-war years, at least until mid-1948, when the introduction of a new currency put paid to the black market and brought a semblance of normality back to Germany's shops, meat and cream were rare luxuries. Even as the Wiegandts' hardship eased over the years, I knew with some certainty that a dish of hare with wild mushrooms, for eight people, would have been unlikely to feature in their mealtimes. Had Frieda, as she annotated this copy in the austerity of the post-war years, indulged in memories of happier times in the land and the life she had lost?

And then I remembered another story of my mother's, from the post-war years when she was not yet four. She had a beloved pet rabbit; it was brown with long floppy ears and large, liquid, dark eyes, and lived at the bottom of the garden. The rabbit, which she had named Peter, would follow her round the garden like a dog. Every day she and Albert would go foraging for berries to supplement their meagre rations and, on the way home, she would pick dandelion leaves for the rabbit. One day, she and Albert had been out picking special leaves that would help cure the scurvy she'd developed, common among children suffering from malnutrition.

She gathered all the dandelions she could find alongside them, but when she arrived home she couldn't find the rabbit, and no one would tell her what had happened to him. Only when dinner was served that evening did she understand the rabbit's fate.

Though their material circumstances had changed drastically, the Wiegandts were relatively fortunate as, unlike many other displaced families during this time, they had not been separated from each other. As I later learnt, they were renting two rooms in a farmhouse in Blumenthal, a small town near Kiel. It was all they could afford, after selling all the jewellery they had smuggled over from Königsberg in their turbans. Albert was trying to find work, but there was very little work to be had, and no one wanted to employ an elderly man with a limp.

Judging from my mother's memories, there was still great love despite their new poverty. But over the course of our many conversations, I noticed that it was always Frieda, rather than Inge, who took centre stage in her memories. It was resolutely cheerful Frieda, always able to see the positive side of any situation, who told her the stories of their life before the flight, and Frieda who taught her the manners that belonged to a more prosperous life. This contrasted with my grandmother's many stories of their days in Königsberg, when she was a young mother, doting on her child. Her stories of my mother's endearing habits, her first steps, and anecdotes such as the game she played with the keys from Albert's cabinet, suggested a close bond. I thought of Inge's fear for her daughter as she lay close to death in the school auditorium in Denmark, of her determination not to be interned in a Danish camp because of it. And I could not help but wonder what had caused Inge to fade into the background of her daughter's life. I tried to find a practical explanation. Inge was younger, fitter and more streetwise. Like many women in her situation, she must have become the main provider in the family. She would naturally have been out of the house a great deal, bartering for food to supplement their meagre rations. The raising of my mother would have been given over to Frieda, who became the dominant presence in my mother's earliest memories. Yet, I was sure there was more to it than that and to answer that question, I needed to understand more of the world they found themselves in, when they first returned from Denmark.

The Germany the Wiegandts were smuggled into during the autumn of 1945 was not a place that fostered dreams of a better future. It was a no man's land of the hungry, the orphaned and the displaced. The large-scale bombing of German cities during the war had left millions homeless and hundreds of thousands of children without parents to care for them. Much of the country's infrastructure and supply chains had been destroyed, laying bare problems in the supply of food that soon reached crisis point. Even before the war, Western Germany had only produced about 40 per cent of the food it needed; in wartime, Nazi mismanagement had made the country almost entirely reliant on imports from occupied countries such as Belgium, Denmark, the Netherlands and France. Now, in peacetime, there was nothing to rely on but what the Allies could bring in; hunger soon set in, and the black market flourished.

Germany was divided into four zones: British, American, Soviet and French. The minesweeper which the Wiegandts boarded in Denmark took them to Kiel, which was in the British zone. A friend of Frieda's from Königsberg, now settled in the city's suburbs with a cousin, offered to take them in for a few weeks. A busy harbour, Kiel was still visibly damaged, the charred facades of buildings showing uneven gaps where bombs had almost destroyed them. Much of the old centre had been obliterated and piles of rubble lined the streets. At dawn and at dusk, when they were least likely to be arrested for looting, people picked through the ruins for fragments of windowsills, lead piping and bits of clothing. Everything has its value when people have nothing.

Most families lived in extreme poverty, having lost their homes and often also the men who had been the main breadwinners. Lack of food was the biggest problem, and shortages persisted until 1948. While rationing was common across Europe, the average intake for a German civilian in the autumn of 1945 was only 1,200 calories a day, less than half the average in Britain.[1] The harsh winter of 1946 brought rations in the British zone down to starvation levels. Heating was another issue. The destruction of the country's infrastructure and its labour force had led to a severe shortage of coal, so people burned whatever they could get their hands on. Albert developed a cough that he couldn't seem to shake. My mother remembered having to walk slowly beside him because he couldn't keep up with her three-year-old legs. Compensation of sorts was available for those who had lost homes and businesses, but documentation was needed, and Albert's had been snatched on the quayside in Königsberg when his leather pouch had been stolen. In the absence of papers, witnesses were needed. Perhaps he could have found some, but he had lost the will to fight.

Hunger and lack of basic necessities were not their greatest hardship, however. They faced a more insidious obstacle, harder to define, which they thought they'd left behind when they decided to leave Denmark. The Wiegandts were German by ethnicity and nationality, but they were also East Prussian, and at a time when poverty meant people could barely look after their immediate family, they were refugees from a place that they could never return to, in a land that didn't want them. The influx of displaced people to Germany from the east had brought a difficult situation close to breaking point and their presence bred resentment. Their culture and accent were only subtly different from those of their fellow Germans, but that was enough to set them apart.

Germany was suffering an identity crisis of its own. The reality of the Holocaust and the horrors of the camps had now been laid bare for the world to see. It's hard to date the exact moment when the Holocaust, the extermination of the Jews and the Roma, the disabled, homosexuals and other groups that fell foul of Nazi ideology, ceased to become an open secret. From 1945 to 1946, ten films, based on documentary footage taken from the camps, were shown to civilian audiences in all four occupation zones. The most frequently shown was an American documentary, *Die Todesmühlen*, or *The Death Mills*. Polling conducted afterwards suggests these films did not lead to the overnight mass contrition some had hoped for. Many hid behind the phrase, 'I did not know.'

Historian Ulrike Weckel argues that shame got in the way. Those polls, she says, allow only one firm conclusion to be drawn: no one suggested the horrors shown in the films weren't true. This, Weckel says, suggests that Germans had either already suspected, or at least considered the regime capable of these crimes.[2]

I don't know whether Albert, Frieda or Inge ever saw those films. The first documentary on the camps that my mother watched was the one she had told me about Dachau, shown on French television sixteen years later. For days after, she couldn't sleep.

In the eyes of the world, Germany was a pariah state whose people had lost their claim to humanity. Peace, enforced by Allied forces on a bewildered and brainwashed population, may have come to many as a relief, but it still did not sit easily. The hardship of daily life in a population that had been brainwashed over more than a decade was seen by Allied authorities as a potential breeding ground for the resurgence of extremism, something they sought to avoid at all costs. Meanwhile, relations between the US and the Soviet Union, already strained in the war, were quickly deteriorating. At the heart of the tension lay opposing ideologies: Stalin saw American intervention in Europe as a bid to expand its capitalist markets, while the US thought Soviet ambitions to expand communism into the rest of Europe were a threat to democracy. By the end of 1945, the focus, at least in the American and British zones, had shifted to reconstruction. For the British this meant 'winning the peace', for the Americans, stopping the spread of communism.

German society was now dominated by women, on whom a family's day-to-day survival mostly depended. Theirs was a role driven by necessity. The population, depleted by war, was at that time predominantly female; in 1946, women between twenty and twenty-nine outnumbered men in the same age category almost two to one.[3] The same shift in dependence was true in the Wiegandts' household. Albert's health was failing, so obtaining food, accommodation and heating fell to Frieda and Inge. Those men who had survived the war often returned with physical and psychological wounds which meant they struggled with ordinary life. Those who had been taken prisoner by the Soviet Union still remained in captivity. A number of these soldiers returned in 1946 but almost 10,000 would not be released until the end of 1955.[4]

But the women who formed the backbone of Germany's post-war existence carried their own trauma; it was hidden for decades, though they lived with its scars. In the course of the Russian advance through East Prussia and on to Berlin in the spring of 1945, an estimated two million German women were raped, often multiple times, regardless of their age.[5] The oldest recorded victim was reported to be eighty-five, the youngest only seven.

The number of children born of this violation, their origins hidden by shame, is hard to determine. Philipp Kuwert, a trauma expert and head of the department of psychiatry and psychotherapy at the University Hospital of Greifswald in north-eastern Germany, who carried out a study of the effects of wartime rape on German women, estimates it at about 200,000.[6] East Prussia, the first part of Germany to fall into Russian hands, experienced the most brutal wave of this revenge. It persisted as Soviet forces took Berlin and continued under its occupation. It was driven mainly by revenge for the many rapes and other atrocities committed by German troops against Soviet civilians and for the sexualised violence that occurred in the camps, or in territories under occupation. But once again it was women, and not the perpetrators, who paid the price. The women dehumanised in this way were not exclusively ethnic Germans, though they formed the vast majority. In the frenzy of violations that followed, victims even included Jewish, Polish and Russian women, mostly recently released prisoners. Sexual assault is always hard to measure. Some doctors who treated the victims estimated that as many as 10 per cent did not survive their ordeal; those who did were told to forget.[7]

Silence has always dominated women's experience of war. It claims to ensure the survival of the family and to maintain a semblance of a normal society at all costs, even one tainted by horror. In post-war Germany, the silence that bound these women for decades was not brought about by the hardships of war, but by the exigencies of peace, in which shame, social taboos and a post-war reluctance to dwell on the war's German victims, all played their part.

The rapes remained a taboo subject for decades. Kuwert, in his study, sought out some of the victims and persuaded them to share their story. Among them was Ruth Schumacher, who was only eighteen in April 1945 when a group of Russian soldiers found her sheltering in the cellar of a bombed-out building in the east German city of Halle-Bruckdorf, and repeatedly raped her. For decades, the only person she told was her husband.[8]

More than sixty years later, she still clearly remembered the pain, and her attackers' faces. 'The memories come back to you over and over again,' she said. 'You can never forget something like that. Sometimes, when I talk about it, I wake up in the night, crying, screaming. You can never, ever forget.'

The attack left Ruth unable to bear children. Many of her friends were also raped. But in the months and years that followed, they never spoke of it. She described it as a 'code of silence', a price that German women felt obliged to pay for the crimes of their nation.

'My conscience was heavy enough,' she said. 'I did not want to make it worse.'

Nothing illustrates this better than German journalist Marta Hillers' s diary of her life under Soviet occupation, *A Woman in Berlin*, and the public reaction that met its publication. Her decision to publish it anonymously in 1953 was one she regretted for the rest of her life. The diary is an account of a woman's survival of the sexual violence that marked Berlin in spring 1945, and was first published in English translation; it was only released in German by a Swiss publisher in 1959. It describes the multiple rapes the author witnessed and those she survived herself in the immediacy of the victorious Soviet advance. Without resorting to stereotypes, it paints a very human picture of both perpetrator and victim. Out of necessity, the narrator forges a relationship with a Russian major, trading her body for food and a protection of sorts. The major, though he accepts the trade, is still portrayed as a decent man, in contrast with many of his comrades.

Hillers described how during these months of crisis, women handled rape as a common experience, a trauma they talked about and tried to overcome by helping each other.[9] But when peace came, and soldiers returned from war, all talking ceased, and women's suffering was relegated to oblivion. In 1959 Germany, the diary was reviled as besmirching the honour of German women; the unnamed author was accused by critics of being shameful and immoral, and Hillers asked that it never be printed again in her lifetime. The book was only released again two years after her death in 2003, this time to great acclaim, and Hillers's identity as the author was finally revealed. While some have questioned whether the diary was true to her personal experience, or whether it was fictionalised in places, the veracity of its subject matter has never been in doubt.

Though the rapes stopped as the situation in Germany stabilised, sexual exploitation did not, as necessity replaced violence. In a thriving black market, without means to purchase food to sustain themselves or their loved ones, women's bodies often became their only currency. It was a society in which people lived by their wits and survived through sheer grit. With no support system to turn to, silence became a survival strategy.

Chapter Fourteen

FALSE FRIENDS

The Wiegandts' new life in Germany was punctuated by want. The streets of Kiel and Hamburg, the two cities nearest to where the Wiegandts were lodging, were lined with neatly stacked boulders of rubble, an order of sorts that tempered the destruction. They were a reminder of the wartime air raids that had rained down like a judgement, but also of a new routine that had emerged from the rubble. Poverty and displacement were part of the narrative of daily life; schoolchildren were taught to forage for food, pieces of coal were carefully hoarded and the makeshift was made permanent. Hunger was a constant companion, gnawing away at people as they went about their daily tasks, never leaving them even in sleep, when they dreamt of meals from before the war.

Adapting to this new life was a struggle, and one that the Wiegandts might have survived only with difficulty, had it not been for the help that came to them entirely unexpectedly. A few weeks after their arrival in Germany in the autumn of 1945, a letter from Dorothea reached them through the Red Cross. It was addressed to Inge. Dorothea had tried to find out what had become of them ever since she'd received the letter Inge had sent from Denmark, the only one to reach her. It was a welcome reminder that they were not quite friendless, but also offered help of a more practical kind, enclosing the sum of 10,000 marks.

'Give this money to your father,' the letter read. 'It will help him to rebuild.'

For the Wiegandts, who were facing absolute penury, Dorothea's gift was a lifeline. They did not know that it was almost all the money she had left.

Albert, Frieda, Inge and Beatrice had not spent a single day apart since Inge had returned to her parents from Berlin, almost four years before. So it was somewhat ironic that the same piece of good fortune – the unexpected gift of money from Dorothea – would turn out to be the cause of a separation that started the most difficult chapter of Inge's life.

Dorothea's generosity offered Albert a chance to try and rebuild some of the status and fortune that the family had left behind. An old friend of Albert's was thinking of opening a new liquor factory in the south of Germany. He wrote to Albert offering him the post of director in return for investment, a chance that had been out of his reach. Now, with Dorothea's money, Albert saw his chance and wrote to his friend again. He received a reply a few days later, inviting him and Frieda to visit potential premises in the Rhine region and in Frankfurt, on a journey that would take them away for over four months. The Wiegandts could not afford to turn down this opportunity and, with new optimism, they left Inge and her child behind in the rooms they had rented in the Blumenthal farmhouse.

Those months were hard for Inge, alone in a village with only her small daughter and the farmer's wife for company. People went to bed early to defeat the cold, making the dark winter evenings particularly lonely. With no friends to turn to for support, she struggled with the demands of raising a young child on such meagre resources, made worse by the increasing shortage of food. Inge often thought of Dorothea. The letter she had sent the Wiegandts through the Red Cross had enclosed an address in Ahrensburg, which Inge knew was the small town adjacent to the von Schimmelmanns ancestral seat, and where Dorothea herself had lived in the early years of her first marriage. Like Blumenthal, it was in the British zone, though on the other side of Hamburg and three hours' journey away. Inge read the letter again and again, overcome by a desire to see her old friend. In the weeks leading up to Christmas 1945, she wrote to Dorothea to say how much she longed to come and see her. Within three days of sending her letter, she received Dorothea's eager reply: 'My dearest child, come as soon as you can. Your Mütterchen.'

The second marriage Dorothea had risked so much for had not survived the war. And devastatingly, Dorothea's worries about Wolfgang had been well founded. Sometime after the German defeat at Stalingrad – there are no records surviving to indicate exactly when – he was reported missing in action. At first, she thought her son must be dead, until word reached her that he was being held captive in Russia. The news had brought relief – at least her son was alive – but it had made Dorothea more vocal that ever in her criticism of the government. While Kurt had successfully ignored Nazism's brutality, his wife's indiscreet and increasingly public statements embarrassed him. They became the subject of office gossip and colleagues in the government quietly cautioned him, saying that his wife should hold her tongue.

Dorothea's bouts of depression became more frequent as her loneliness increased. She was a woman of intense feelings who needed something to love. Her eldest son was dead, Wolfgang was a prisoner in Russia and her daughter Gisela was far away, having been sent to live with her father in Munich soon after Inge's departure, to avoid air raids. Separated from her children and with Kurt ever more distant, Dorothea focused all her affection on her dogs, two Great Danes that followed her everywhere, and growled at Kurt whenever he approached.

Kurt and Dorothea's relationship collapsed irrevocably in March 1945, a few weeks before the end of the war. By then, all those in government had privately accepted that Berlin was doomed to fall, though Hitler remained defiant. Their only hope was that the Americans, whose retribution they feared less than the Russians', would reach the German capital before the Red Army, but Soviet command was determined not to let this happen. The odds of the Russians winning were increasing by the hour. As had happened in Königsberg, civilians weren't allowed to leave, but essential administrative staff, including Kurt, were being relocated to Munich to avoid falling into Russian hands.

One evening, Kurt told Dorothea to pack their bags for their departure the next morning. Knowing that, as the aristocratic wife of a Nazi official, she would be shown no mercy if she stayed in Berlin, Dorothea prepared to leave. But Kurt told her she could, under no circumstances, take the dogs. Faced with the choice between the Great Danes and the man she no longer loved, she flatly refused to go with him. It was the final straw in the marriage. In early April, without a backward glance at his wife, Kurt headed south to Munich, leaving Dorothea in Dahlem. The next morning, she put on her most expensive fur coat, bundled the dogs into the back of their state-owned Mercedes and set off northwest towards Ahrensburg.

Her destination was puzzling for a woman who had left her former home in a cloud of scandal, though her reasons were simple enough. The collapse of her relationship with Kurt had made Dorothea think of the early years of her marriage to Carl-Otto with nostalgia. She forgot about his gambling and debts, the suffocating rules and the judgements that had made her feel so trapped, and remembered only the happy aspects of the past. With the selective memory of regret, she thought of those years as a simpler time, with a kind husband, long rides on horseback and a close group of friends. Carl-Otto had remarried long ago and was living in Munich with his new wife and Gisela, but their old circles remained as they always had been, in the country estates and grand houses they had inhabited for generations.

It was perhaps natural that Dorothea chose to seek out old friends in her hour of need. What she hadn't anticipated was that the same ties and traditions that had bound her to them in the past were what would now serve to keep them apart. She drove on triumphantly at first – by some miracle, no official stopped her to question the purpose of her journey – but the people whom she had hoped would help her offered only scorn. She had expected to find shelter in one of her old friends' houses, in Schleswig-Holstein, the province where she had lived with Carl-Otto, and far enough west, she thought, to be safe from the Red Army. One woman, once a close friend, told her she couldn't stay because they were about to leave, but Dorothea saw no signs of packing in the house. One elderly cousin was kinder, agreeing to take her in for a night, but she insisted that Dorothea leave the next morning.

Life in a city as large and varied as Berlin had allowed Dorothea to put the scandal of the divorce behind her, but in the narrow circles she now sought to return to, it was still the thing that defined her. It seems extraordinary now to think that a woman fleeing alone in a nation on the brink of collapse would meet with so little compassion, because of a social offence committed fifteen years before, but this was the reality that Dorothea encountered. As she made her way westwards, her friends' doors remained shut. When the Mercedes ran out of petrol, Dorothea continued her journey on foot, wearing the heavy fur coat, her faithful dogs on either side. She had decided to go on to Ahrensburg itself. She could think of nowhere else to go. In Ahrensburg, at least Wolfgang would be able to find her, should he ever return.

Dorothea arrived in Ahrensburg at dawn, after walking through the night. And there, finally, she found kindness, not among rich acquaintances, but in the townspeople who remembered her. The old doctor's daughter, a widow who had returned during the war, offered her a room. Dorothea lived out the last weeks of the war there, and watched the British forces settle in the town as Berlin fell to the Russians. She heard that Kurt had given himself up to the Americans in Munich. He was held along with other Nazi officials for several weeks, but he did not contact her. Wolfgang remained in captivity. She wrote letters to the British forces who controlled the zone she was living in, to the Red Cross and to friends who might once have been able to help, begging for news of his release, but they went unanswered. Meanwhile, she was forced to sell the dogs to a farmer, as she could no longer afford to feed them. While she had faced up to the scorn of her former friends with her head held high, losing those faithful companions almost broke her heart.

Inge found Dorothea much diminished when she came to see her in the winter of 1945. It had been a long journey, requiring her to change buses several times; she had left very early that morning. As she kissed the older woman's hands, she noticed how swollen they were from the frequent bouts of arthritis that almost crippled her at times. Though Dorothea was only forty-seven, she was a ghost of the beautiful and vital woman Inge had known in Berlin. The reunion reminded both women of all they had lost. But it also brought back their old intimacy, which they found again almost instantly, despite their long separation. Inge had brought Beatrice with her, the granddaughter Dorothea had never met. She watched

Dorothea lean down to stroke Beatrice's light blonde hair, so like her own, though she struggled with the pain crouching down caused her.

Inge made the journey to see Dorothea every week during the bitterly cold winter, over frozen roads still barely passable with war damage. Dorothea would wait at her window for Inge's arrival, watching for the moment she would turn the corner and walk down the cobbled street. The doctor's daughter told Inge that Dorothea sometimes woke at dawn to watch for her. The visits were mostly joyful, especially when her granddaughter's laughter brought a glimpse of the old Dorothea back to life. But sometimes it was this new, lonelier soul whom Inge found, plagued again by the depression she had always been prone to. Gisela, Inge learnt, was still in Munich, having decided to stay with Carl-Otto, who had bought her a nice flat. After that, Gisela saw very little of her mother, a decision Inge could not understand.

Dorothea, meanwhile, welcomed Inge back into her life as a long-lost daughter. Seeing Dorothea's greatly reduced circumstances, Inge offered to return some of the money she had sent the Wiegandts, but Dorothea refused. Inge learnt later, from the doctor's daughter, that the sum had come from the sale of Dorothea's fur coat. In her more positive moods, Dorothea talked of land she still owned, which had been hers from childhood. Her marriage to Carl-Otto meant the ownership of the land had been transferred to her husband, though it was hers by right; she had written to the von Schimmelmanns' lawyer to claim it back, and talked of building a house on it where she, Inge, Beatrice, Albert and Frieda could live together as a family.

But while Dorothea built houses in her dreams, Inge could see that she was far from well. She tried to make Dorothea as comfortable as she could, but she knew a new bout of depression could strike at any time, often in the aftermath of an attack of arthritis. Pain relief was what Dorothea needed most. The old doctor told Inge that, before times had got hard, he would have recommended morphine. These days, he might as well prescribe the moon, for morphine was impossible to come by on the open market. Of course, he told Inge, there were always other ways.

She understood at once what he meant. Like most ordinary Germans in those post-war years, Inge used the black market to supplement the drastically reduced food rations which, if strictly adhered to, would have left her and her child close to starvation. The dairy farmer she lodged with had shown her what to do, whom to trade with, whom to avoid. He knew the market well, having done well out of it himself, as butter was a prized commodity and cheese a luxury. The system was mostly one of barter, as Reichsmarks were only used for trading at a heavy discount. Cigarettes were in high demand both as a narcotic and for their ability to stave off pangs of hunger, and had become the currency of choice; they were non-perishable and easy to carry around. German brands such as Nordland or Bosco bought you fewer goods than American ones, which were particularly prized.* Inge had been given a packet of Lucky Strike by a British soldier, which had bought her a small piece of bacon and a whole kilo of flour.[1]

The farmer's wife, who felt sorry for Inge, sometimes gave her some butter in exchange for her carrying out household tasks. Inge would usually trade butter for a few grams of coffee. Hair clips, scarves and stockings also had their worth, though they often had to be sold through an intermediary who would always take a cut in return for taking them to Hamburg, where the market for such

---

* The blend of tobacco used in American cigarettes made them more effective at fighting off hunger.

goods was higher. Medicine, especially morphine, fell into a different category altogether. With so many men suffering from old war wounds, demand for pain relief was high and neither Blumenthal's nor Ahrensburg's quiet trade of butter and the odd pair of stockings would be able to supply Dorothea.

One day, Inge, exhausted by a particularly hard journey back from Ahrensburg, wept as she told the farmer's wife of Dorothea's suffering. The woman told Inge she knew of a man who might be able to help her; she described him as a man who was 'in the know'. Inge had heard him spoken of before. He was the owner of the grocery store in the neighbouring town and the most powerful black marketeer in the district. The farmer's wife took Inge to his store. From the manner of their greeting, Inge suspected she'd carried out business here many times before.

A short and thickset man more than twenty years her senior, he was known for his contacts among the British forces, whose wives he helped to source furs and other luxury goods. In exchange, their husbands ignored the trade that took place in the back room of his store. Business was flourishing.

Inge expected him to be brusque or even menacing, but instead found him kind and understanding. He even gave her a cup of coffee, a luxury, and listened patiently to what she was trying to buy and why. He patted her hand, called her a good girl and asked her how old her daughter was. His manner was so gentle that he reminded her for a moment of her father, who was still away in the south.

He took the silver-backed hairbrush of Dorothea which Inge had brought with her. The next day, he came to the farmhouse to look at a few more things Dorothea had given her to barter with: a few pairs of silk stockings, a scarf, a brooch – the trappings of her old life. As he left, he pressed a pair of nylon stockings into Inge's hand with a wink, saying they were a little gift from him to a good girl.

He had brought enough morphine to get Dorothea through a month of attacks, along with a lotion of herbs to soothe her stiffened joints. But though Inge had hoped to help her old friend, she had not anticipated the drug's side effects. Dorothea soon became dependent on it, so that Inge no longer knew which was worse, her yearning for the drug or the pain of her arthritic attacks. Some days, these were so bad that Dorothea begged Inge to put an end to her life. Every other week, Inge went back to the grocer's shop with things Dorothea had given her to exchange for morphine. One day it was a pendant, another a few loose pearls.

The grocer started dropping by unannounced with little gifts, a small bag of sugar or half a tin of coffee. One evening, after a long journey back from Ahrensburg, Inge arrived home cold and hungry to find her daughter playing with a wooden toy. The farmer's wife, beaming, told her that the grocer had come by that afternoon and brought them a bar of soap each. Inge tried to return the gifts once or twice, but he pressed her so eagerly to keep them that she didn't have the heart to give them back. Inge was far from naive, she had noticed the way he looked at her. But she had also started to trust him. Life was hard for Inge, a single mother, alone, hungry and almost destitute. Exhausted by looking after Dorothea and the burden of caring for a small child, she decided to accept the gifts for what she thought they were, a sign of friendship.

There was never enough food. The hunger and the strain wore Inge's nerves to shreds, and every day seemed a fresh struggle. At nights, she dreamt of life as it had once been. The dreams were so real that the shock of waking felt like losing that life all over again. One night, she dreamt she was dancing in Berlin wearing her pretty blue dress, with Wolfgang holding her tight. But mostly she dreamt of the meals they used to have, and woke with hunger gnawing at her stomach. She had no one to talk to. The worry and tension built up inside her, so that some days she wanted to start screaming and never stop.

It was on such a day that she walked past the grocer's shop, face flushed. That day's butter had turned sour. She needed to find something else for her child to eat. But where? And how? He saw her, came to the door and called out her name. She stopped and he smiled at her. It was a kind smile, she thought.

'Child,' he said, 'you look hungry. Eat first, we can talk later.'

He went to his storeroom at the back of the shop and came back with a glass of wine. She was so thirsty, she almost gulped it down. He laughed, and fetched her another. 'Plenty more where that came from,' he said, as he filled her glass again. And then her world went blank.

Chapter Fifteen

DOROTHEA'S LAST LETTER

Inge, like so many women of her time, found silence both a torment and a refuge. She chose it from the moment she picked herself up from the floor of the storeroom, as she rearranged her clothing and tidied her hair. It persisted on her return to the farmhouse, when she told the farmer's wife that she had stayed the night with an old friend. It oppressed her at first. She felt its weight when the farmer's wife's eyes lingered on the tear in her stocking, as she helped with the household chores that morning, without their usual chatter.

Why did she not say: *Look at what he did to me, that man whom you told me to befriend, that man whose kindness you always praise?* She opened her mouth to shout it, but no sound came out.

'You drank his wine,' said the voice in her head. 'You were seen speaking to him. Sometimes you even went for walks together. What did you think would happen? Nothing is free in this world.' She pressed her lips together tightly, swallowed the scream in her throat. She filled a pot of water and put it on the hob to boil, scorching her skin with the match when she lit the flame beneath it. She filled the iron bathtub with water and scrubbed her skin till it was raw. She would never speak of it. Silence, she thought, silence is safest. She did not know that the trauma of that single evening would set off a chain of events that would haunt her for the rest of her life

That night, she walked into her room to see her clothes washed and neatly folded at the foot of her bed, the torn stocking darned.

She knew the farmer's wife had done it. The gentleness of the gesture, that quiet show of support, finally broke her. Taking her daughter in her arms, she lay on the bed, and wept.

'He must have put something in the wine,' my grandmother told me. 'My head felt heavy. My legs and arms felt numb. He kept filling my glass. I remember my head spinning before I passed out. I don't remember what happened next. I woke up in the storeroom, on my back. I knew what he had done.

'I was such easy prey.'

She didn't have to use the word rape. It lay heavy between us in the silence that followed, blocking out everything else. It felt as if the whole room was holding its breath; even the old kitchen clock seemed to have stopped ticking. Her fingers were clasped so tightly together that her knuckles had gone white. I gently placed both my hands on hers, feeling them shake at my touch. I did not want to know any more details; I never even asked his name. I couldn't bear to think of him as a person.

When I first began asking about the past, I had hoped for anecdotes of making do, of triumph over hardship. I had feared I might find proof of actions or beliefs that I would struggle to forgive. I had not bargained for this uglier truth. I now knew the reason she had built the shield she always hid behind. By dint of perseverance, I had broken through her silence, but in that moment, doing so brought me nothing but guilt. In my dogged search for answers, I had forgotten to ask myself whether some truths were best left alone.

She never told me exactly when the rape occurred. I have deduced that it was in 1946 while her parents were away in the south. She didn't tell anyone about it, neither on the night it happened, nor on the next day, finding herself, as time passed, slipping into silence as so many women before her had. There was no use in speaking out. Her life was hard enough as it was without the added weight of judgement and disbelief.

It was a while before she spoke again, looking into the distance, words that I would only fully understand much later: 'It all seemed to happen at once. The storeroom. Mütterchen. Knowing that he wasn't dead. That he would be coming back.'

'Wolfgang?' I asked. 'Is that when he came back?'

She didn't look at me. I wasn't sure she'd even heard me. I didn't really understand what she said next.

'Things didn't turn out the way that Mütterchen had hoped. The letter she wrote broke my heart.'

There was no point in asking more; it was clear that those months had blended together into a single terrible void, that time she had called the worst of all. So that, I thought, was when Wolfgang, whom she had so long believed lost, finally came back from the dead.

I asked her again when exactly that had been, but she would not, or could not, answer. It's hard to remember the exact dates of a period one has spent a lifetime forgetting. But from our conversations, from the scattered memories, anecdotes and recollections of others around her, I figured out enough to piece together a chain of events and try to make sense of what had happened between them.

In the weeks when Dorothea lived between the fevered states the morphine brought her and the pain of her arthritic seizures, fate had, for once, been kind. Her youngest son was given back to her. I'm not sure of the exact date of his release – sometime in the early months of 1946. This made Wolfgang one of the luckier ones among the 3 million German soldiers held in Soviet camps. Only a third would ever come home alive, and many not for years; some were held until as late as 1956. I don't know if Dorothea found out he was on his way home – or if she only found out when he arrived at her doorstep. Some families received a letter from the Red Cross, but those relatives who had been displaced, like Dorothea, were harder to trace. Had he followed his mother's trail from the house in Berlin, now given over to the use of the US forces, to the Ahrensburg of his childhood? She would have known him at once, run her inflamed hands over her boy's face, found him terribly stooped, so thin his features had lost any trace of youth. He would have seen death and suffering, been beaten and starved, watched friends die before him, on a ground too frozen to bury them in. He would have found his mother greatly aged, a woman abandoned by her old world and unable to cope with the new. Had he taken her swollen hands in his, and wept with her for the past they had both lost?

How had Inge, already so buffeted about by life, reacted to the return of her lost sweetheart, the boy who had loved and then betrayed her, the father of her daughter, whom she had learnt to live without? I pictured the note arriving, written by Dorothea, the writing blotted and crossed with excitement, or a telegram perhaps, telling her that Wolfgang was back. I can almost see her holding it, her hand shaking, reading Dorothea's words: 'Come, my child, my son has come home!'

I imagined her opening the note at the farmhouse, her face frozen in shock, one hand on the rough kitchen table to steady herself and stop her knees from buckling underneath her. Had she sat down then, believing in Dorothea's dreams of a happy ever after, of a life together in the house she had built for them in her morphine-fuelled dreams? Had it been before or after her rape? Was she by then already too traumatised to go back to a love that belonged to the past? What had really happened, when they finally met again?

And I thought about the other thing my grandmother had said, about things not turning out the way Mütterchen had hoped. About the letter she had written. Could they hold a clue to what had happened with Wolfgang?

Much later, after my grandmother's death, once I knew about her rape, and how it had intersected with Wolfgang's return, I tried to piece together a clearer picture of what exactly had happened between them. It had not been something I felt I could ask in the days that followed the revelation; her pain had been too raw, too visible. There would be other conversations between us, which would reveal more of her life. But what exactly had happened to him eluded me still.

My mother had told me a few things about him over the years, though she didn't know much. She had made contact with him a few years before his death, first through letters, then in a few meetings; he had died in 2004, before my brother and I could meet him. He had been absent from her life for decades; she had waited many years before contacting him, from fear of wounding her stepfather, Vati. She had met him a few times towards the end of his life, though for decades he had been absent from her life. She had been close to her aunt Gisela, who sometimes told her small things about Wolfgang before her death in her mid-forties. Gisela had spoken of her brother as someone who had retired from the world; for a time he barely spoke. Wolfgang's time in Ahrensburg with Dorothea had been short. His wasted lungs forced him to seek treatment in hospital for a few weeks.

It was the period that immediately followed Wolfgang's return that was still difficult to pinpoint. I knew they'd met during that time, and that the encounter had ended in their parting. What I still didn't know was how Dorothea had reacted. Had she tried to support Inge? Or had Inge not confided in her? After my grandmother told me about the rape, all mention of Dorothea, the woman whom my grandmother regarded as her soulmate, ceased; her story became a blank. I knew, of course, that she had died, though I did not know when. In an earlier conversation, my grandmother had told me about a letter from Dorothea that had broken her heart. She had, she said, given the letter to my mother. I had not pushed for further details then; the significance of the timing of Dorothea's death, her absence from that crucial part of my grandmother's narrative, had eluded me until it was too late to ask.

Shortly after my return from Denmark, the year following my grandmother's death, I looked through files, family albums, old papers, scoured archives for traces of the woman my grandmother had loved. I turned over photographs, hoping for a scribbled date. I found a handsome profile portrait of Gisela. But of Dorothea, there was no further trace. My mother could not remember her at all.

'Surely you have one memory of her?' I said.

'No,' she said, thinking hard. 'I only ever knew her through her photograph.'

I told her about the letter my grandmother had mentioned. She paused, searching through her memory.

'My mother did give me a few things Dorothea had given to her. A diamond brooch. A couple of letters. I remember them because I couldn't read one of them. It was in old German script.'

'Where is it now?' I asked. The answer made my heart sink.

'Somewhere in the attic.'

My mother did not know what the letter said, but she thought it had been written after the war. The timing made me hopeful. I

GISELA AS AN ADULT.

hoped it would contain some answers to my questions. But organisation is not my mother's strong point. She remembered putting it in a green box but, try as she might, she could not remember where she had put it.

Finding the box was no small matter. The attic of our family home is something of a black hole. It holds the clutter of decades, a repository for hoards of memories and keepsakes that no one has ever bothered to throw out. I climbed up the steep staircase to the landing and over a pile of discarded outdoor cushions to get to the door. I had to crouch to go through it. My eyes adjusted to the surroundings, as the one lamp in the room cast only a dim light. Mine and my brother's entire childhood, hobbies passionately followed then discarded, was condensed into this single space. It had once been our playroom; in a corner, I spotted the Lego air-traffic-control tower my brother and I had built together, the remote-controlled plane he had convinced me to help him buy. Now trunks and old suitcases were piled up along the walls. Plastic wardrobes full of old clothes, the remains of my brother's model aeroplane workshop and large baskets stuffed with toys filled the middle of the room.

I searched for hours on my hands and knees through the mementoes of my own past: old filing cabinets, bags and papers, endless photograph albums of childhood holidays. The room was airless and smelt of mothballs. The little porthole window told me night had fallen. I was close to giving up. But then I saw it – a small green shoebox, which had slipped behind one of the trunks.

WOLFGANG AS A SOLDIER.

Inside the box were two letters and two photographs, both black and white and more than a little faded. One was clearly of Wolfgang in his army uniform. I guessed that it had been taken early on in his army life, possibly on the day of his enlistment, for the roundness in his jaw was not that of a man who had suffered in war. The second was of a handsome blonde woman in early middle age, taken in profile. It made me catch my breath, for the forehead, eyes and nose could have been my mother's. On the back a faint caption was written in pencil, which read simply, 'Dorothea, February 1946'.

DOROTHEA TOWARDS THE END OF HER LIFE.

The letters were in a single blank envelope. The first was written on thick, smart white paper, embossed at the top with the name 'Gisela, Gräfin Schimmelmann'. It contained a lock of blonde hair streaked with grey and was dated 5 April 1946. 'Dear Pünktchen,' it read, the von Schimmelmanns' nickname for my grandmother. 'Two days ago Mütterchen left us.' But grief shines through the letter in other ways, in the round and slightly childish handwriting, in the blots and crossed-out words that dot its pages. Time and many upheavals had changed the friendship between my grandmother and Gisela but, in her sadness, Gisela remembered the old closeness they had shared in their Berlin days. Her letter did not say how Dorothea had died. Instead, it told my grandmother that the note she had enclosed would make everything clear. Of Wolfgang, there was no mention at all.

The second note was written on yellowed paper of a thinner and less expensive kind, its bottom edge ragged from where it had been torn from its pad. There was no address, just a date, 2 April 1946. The writing was ornate and barely legible. I knew at once that this was the letter I had been seeking. It was written in *Sütterlin*, the old script once used by educated Germans. All I could make out was the first line, 'My beloved, good child', and the signature, 'Mütterchen'. There was a sentence, underlined, which I could not read at all. It had lain in this box, unread, for decades and I guessed from its date that it was the last letter Dorothea ever wrote.

I turned to an old friend, a historian and a German speaker, for help. He told me to send him a copy. His reply, an hour later, was discouraging; he could not make head nor tail of it. Try an antique dealer, he suggested. A directory of experts in old manuscripts in Germany directed me to a lady living near Rostock. I sent her an email with a scan of the letter attached, and received a reply the next morning. She could transcribe it, she said, for a sum. I replied at once to go ahead; I didn't even ask how much. Within hours, she had sent me a transcript in modern German and her bill. I printed it out and placed it on a table beside the original, the invoice on top. Unlocking its secrets had cost me fifteen euros and thirty-six cents.

My beloved, good child

Let me once again thank you with my whole, whole heart for all the great love that you have given me, in the saddest time of my life.

A love that you have given, despite it being undeserved, because I, like all the others, did not treat you, my poor dear, as kindly as I should have.

Your worries and your efforts for me, the tender, childish and great love that you have given me are the last glimpses of light in my life, its last rays of sunshine.

May God grant you in your own children the good that you have given me, abandoned as I have been.

And He will grant it you, my heart, because He is righteous and wise, and I see, now I must depart, the wrong I did to Him when I left Carl-Otto, who had only ever been good to me. This step brought upon me all the terrible consequences that led to my being so lonely, which I could not endure.

If my beloved Buschi should ever be this lonely, I ask you with my whole heart to look after him. He has far too soft, good and great a heart, one he can hide so brilliantly with brusqueness.

I thank you again, send my love to your kind parents, the little one I kiss and hug and I kiss you with loving gratitude.

Your so terribly lonely Mütterchen

The letter that had lain forgotten in a shoebox was Dorothea's suicide note.

*

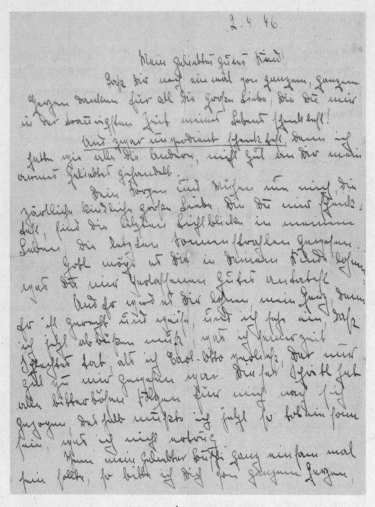

DOROTHEA'S SUICIDE NOTE.

The feeling of intrusion I had experienced when my grandmother told me about her rape all those years before surged up again as I read Dorothea's final letter. I felt guilty for my curiosity, and for assuming I had a claim to a past that was not mine. Reading the

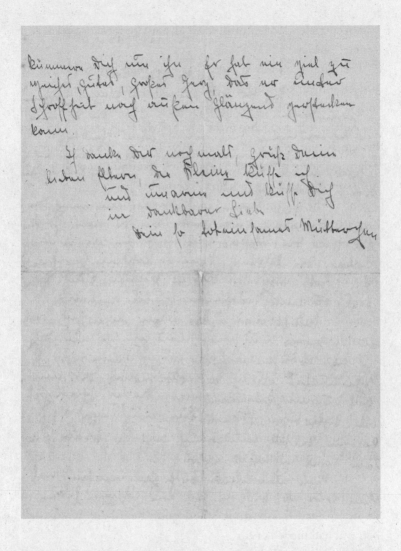

despair in her lines, I felt like a voyeur spying on a private fare-well, prying into another woman's heart. What right did I have to intrude upon this private grief, to reveal and prise apart another woman's story? She had written this for my grandmother, who had been a friend to her until the end, and not for me to read, two generations later.

The letter itself raised more questions than it answered. Why had Dorothea, knowing her son had returned to her, still chosen to take her own life? In writing of her 'Buschi', as she called him, his 'far too soft, good and great a heart' which he knew to hide so brusquely, she seemed to acknowledge that her son had returned a damaged man. But she also begged my grandmother to look after him; so why had my grandparents chosen to part?

For all the discomfort and soul-searching it caused me, Dorothea's final note had brought her to life. I grieved for the woman who had ended her days living in the shadow of the youth she had left behind, perpetually reminded of the choices she had made, which she felt had caused her downfall. A phrase of my grandmother's, when she'd first described Dorothea's beauty, stuck in my mind: 'She loved men, fatally. That was her greatest weakness.'

Then that line, in Dorothea's note: '_A love that you have given, despite it being undeserved, because I, like all the others, did not treat you, my poor dear, as kindly as I should._'

I thought about Inge's pregnancy and about Wolfgang's failure to live up to his promises. About his mother's sadness at it, her inability to stand up to the control her ex-husband still wielded over his son. I think I understood what she had tried to tell Inge. Dorothea in her final hours, had wanted my grandmother to know she had finally understood quite how hard Wolfgang's betrayal had made her life.

They had both lived through brutal times, when to love had been a weakness. But it was the judgement of others, and not love, that made Dorothea, at the age of forty-seven, think life no longer worth living. In a society that had lost its capacity for compassion, a broken world which still clung to moral absolutes, Dorothea and my grandmother, like many other women, had paid a price for loving. The guilt I had felt turned into wrath, bringing with it angry tears, and I wept for them both.

Chapter Sixteen

INGE'S SECRET

It was my mother, after I showed her Dorothea's letter, who told me about the time her parents had met again, when she was a little girl of about three or four – she did not know exactly when. My grandmother, whom she had occasionally asked about it as a child, had never spoken of it to her in detail. She had told my mother that she had worn a blue dress and no lipstick. That he had been thin and drawn. That he had not been well.

In a drawer, as I continued my search for missing pieces, I found a stack of photographs of an elderly couple which Wolfgang had sent to his daughter after their second meeting in 2001, almost sixty years later, along with a letter he wrote to my mother. In it, he remembered her refusal to eat her vegetables in white sauce. It had made him laugh. It was a small detail, but one he had remembered all his life.

This is how I imagine the reunion between Inge and Wolfgang:

They meet at lunchtime, in a restaurant in Hamburg, one that he can't quite afford. He has been given a quiet table in a corner, at the back; he can't see the entrance from where he is sitting. At the next table, a waiter drops a fork and the clatter of metal on tiles makes him jump. He cannot bear loud noises.

Inge stands outside the restaurant, holding her child by the hand, checking her reflection in her pocket mirror. There is a crack across one corner, so she has to strain to see. She had put on lipstick that morning, before rubbing it off again, thinking it aged her, though she is only twenty-two. There is still a smudge of red by the right corner of her mouth. She wipes it off.

She is wearing her only good dress, a blue one. The material has been darned too often, and is visibly frayed under one arm, but she hopes he won't notice. Beatrice's hair is tightly plaited – to look nice, Inge had told her, for the father she had never met. Inge had wondered for a moment whether she ought to bring the girl. Now, in her nervousness, she hopes the presence of his daughter might help break the ice.

She sees him as soon as she walks into the restaurant, though she has to look twice to be sure. Can it be him, that gaunt, taciturn man who is sitting in the corner, nervously rubbing a piece of the tablecloth between his thumb and forefinger? She remembered a boy of twenty-three. Here sits a man who looks at least ten years older. Yes, those are his features, or rather, their dulled, distorted shadow. Those are his blue eyes, but they are now sunken. The skin is stretched taut over his cheekbones, the softness of his face gone. His hair, which she remembered being long, as he used to wear it in defiance of the close-crops of the *Hitlerjugend* boys, is cut short.

Lost in his thoughts, he does not notice her at first, and she is glad; he does not hear her gasp at his appearance. When he sees her, he stands up with a start; his suit jacket hangs loosely on his shoulders and he carries himself with a stoop. They greet each other with a laugh, hers nervous and thin, his rasping, his breathing still shallow from damage to his lungs. He crouches down to greet his daughter, who holds back shyly. Gravely, he holds out his hand and she shakes it with a face so solemn it makes him smile. They sit down and order their meal, trying to talk of old times. She cannot help but see how much the war has altered him, and is worried that her expression shows her shock. She misses his easy laugh; the Wolfgang who had left her had been quick to joke, but the one who has returned is barely able to smile. He'd come home from a Soviet camp, a broken man returning to a broken country, a family in turmoil and a world radically changed from the one he had left behind.

They speak briefly of his mother's funeral, which only he and Gisela had attended at his request. He had refused his father's offer of financial help, though he had almost no money to pay for it. With a voice full of remorse, he describes the coffin of cheap pine they had buried her in. She sees he is close to tears, and tentatively touches his hand. He jumps a little and, though he does not pull it away, nor does he return the pressure. After a brief moment, she withdraws her hand from his. He is staring at his plate as though he doesn't want to look at her. They both fall into a silence, every minute widening the gulf between them. A wail from their daughter breaks it; she is pushing her plate away in disgust, refusing to eat her vegetables in white sauce.

I'll never know exactly how this meeting was arranged, or what really took place. Had Wolfgang written to suggest it, or had Inge? Had he chosen the time and the place? What I do know is that there was no cinematic ending in which the two lovers embrace after a long time apart. Reality is more brutal than fiction, and love stories rarely withstand the changes these two had endured. The boy and girl who'd fallen in love four years before were no more. In their place were a man and a woman who had survived against the odds, hardened by experience, whose old world had all but disappeared, taking their love with it.

That he had seen his mother before her death was apparent from Dorothea's final note. She too had seen the great changes in him. By writing that final plea to my grandmother to look after her son, and describing the brusqueness that hid his sensitive heart, it was almost as if she'd intended to prepare Inge for the difficult meeting to come. Perhaps seeing the damage war had wrought on her son had contributed to her final act.

What could a love so rooted in another life have been to him then? Some may have seen it as a chance to rediscover the memories of past happiness, or a way to build something new through fatherhood. For Wolfgang, the sight of his lost sweetheart was a tangible reminder of his old betrayal, and of a past that he could never salvage. His own daughter was shy of him, and though she charmed him, for him she belonged to a world that might have been if the war had never happened, and which seemed impossible now.

How had Inge felt, seeing him again that day? Bitterness, perhaps, towards the man who had promised so much, whom she had loved and who had betrayed her, leaving her to face the shame of unmarried pregnancy, of motherhood, and to fend for herself during the hardships of flight. It would have taken a great deal to forgive him, even if she hadn't already developed something of the detachment that would define her in later life. Or had she simply felt pity as she looked at his changed face? I wonder what would have been harder for them both to bear – her compassion, or her wrath? This alone would have been enough for my grandparents to decide to go their separate ways, he to his father in the south, she back to her parents. Of the various family explanations my family had given me over the years, this was the one that fitted best, that of an infatuation that faded, of lovers too traumatised by what they had survived to try again, one of many romances turned casualty of war. I knew they never met again. And yet, now that I knew more, this explanation did not suffice. They had a child to bind them together, or at least to encourage them to try. My grandmother had very little to live on. Besides, I knew from the way she spoke of Wolfgang in later years that she had still loved him. I remembered her words when she told me of his betrayal, 'I still don't understand.' It was the bafflement of someone who yearned for that old feeling still.

Every account of Wolfgang described a quiet, kind man who spent most of his later life alone. That line in Dorothea's last letter, begging my grandmother to look after her son, struck me as an appeal to make allowances, to give her son a chance. So why had my grandmother not fought harder to win him back?

It was she, in the end, who provided me with what I believe to be the missing piece of the puzzle. It brought no triumph of discovery, bursting out, as revelations of this kind often do, on the eve of a family wedding and threatening, for a while, to damage my family so deeply it led me to question why I had ever set out to uncover it. It was a secret long withheld, which Inge had carried with her for more than six decades, buried by trauma and shame.

On the day before my cousin's wedding in May of 2013, I decided to skip the rehearsal dinner to finish making her wedding cake. My grandmother, who had again travelled over from Germany, thought the outing would tire her too much for the ceremony the next day and joined me in the kitchen of our house in France, sitting at the table as I stood at its end trying to finish the task at hand. It was a few months after our conversation in which she had revealed her rape. I had only arrived that morning, and had not yet had a chance to see her alone. She wore a blue cashmere cardigan buttoned up to the neck, though it was an unusually warm evening for late May and the heat from the oven made the room stiflingly hot. Her hands, with their trademark red nails, rested on the table, folded on top of each other, her make-up and hair immaculate. The smell of vanilla sponge, strawberries and buttercream filled the air with an almost sickly intensity.

Beads of sweat formed on my forehead as I worked. My cousin, masking a mounting anxiety with an air of forced cheer, had already called twice to enquire how the cake was getting along. My enthusiastic offer to make it when she had got engaged a year before was starting to feel like a mistake. I was trying not to panic as I carefully stacked the layers of cream and sponge together, positioning the dowels and praying the heat of the room wouldn't make the cream run.

'Mütterchen died before she could find out.'

My grandmother's words came without preamble. I did not take them in at first, for once not focusing too closely on what she was saying, my mind too occupied with the cake. I wasn't even looking at her as I listened to her speak of the months before Dorothea's death, then about how much she had missed her in the time that had followed. I'd started to knead the icing, feeling the egg white and sugar become pliant in my hands.

'Maybe it was better so.'

I glanced at her then. She was staring into the distance.

'I could never talk about it, what had happened to me with that man, about his child, this child who cried all the time. The child I could not love.'

The icing stuck to my hands, the sticky mass working its way between my fingers as they clenched in shock. I'd picked away at her reserve until that last wall crumbled and the full weight of her secret came bursting out. Her voice started shaking as I went to sit beside her, my hands full of fondant; there'd been no time to wipe it off. I told her that we all loved her, that she could tell us anything, thinking all the time, *Dear God, this is my doing*, knowing, as I tried to comfort her, that no words could ever be enough.

In the months that followed, she revealed further details to me. In the first weeks of her pregnancy, she went to confront her rapist. Her father had returned from Frankfurt exhausted. His investment in the liquor factory had failed, and this additional piece of bad luck proved too much for his already weakened heart. His health was failing fast. Frieda walked her to the door of the shop, holding her hand all the way for reassurance. I don't think Inge would ever have told her if the pregnancy had not forced her to reveal something of what had happened. Frieda, I imagine, had guessed the rest. She was wearing her most practical clothes, so her visit would not look out of the ordinary. Frieda squeezed Inge's fingers before she entered, and said that she would be waiting just outside the door. Inge wanted to talk to him alone.

It was almost time for him to close up shop. He was polite, talking as if she were a customer, pulling up a chair for her to sit on. He leant forward with his arms on the counter, asking how he could help. She took a deep breath and blurted it out.

She told him she was carrying his child. She wasn't able to speak the word 'rape', though she had always known what it was.

He was silent, and then he laughed, a low, brief chuckle. He knew she liked a drink, he said. He had heard that she had seen her former lover, the man who had been in Russia.

'How can I know,' he said, looking up at her, 'that you're not trying to pass off his child as mine?'

She returned his stare without a word, though to look at his face took all the strength she had. Then she stood up without a word, turned and left. She had nothing to fight him with, as her own shame and the weight of the judgement of others gave him all the power, leaving her with none at all.

When I looked back, all these years later, to try to piece together those last details of my grandparents' story, I thought of the strength of mind the confrontation must have demanded of her. I remembered the words of Ruth Schumacher, another victim of sexual violence: 'You can never, ever forget.' Did my grandmother think of it in the months and years that followed? Did she remember his face? Did she enter a shop, accept a drink, walk the street alone, followed by the shadow of fear and shame? I thought of how much it must have taken her to look that man in the eye, to tell him that he owed her some form of reparation, to demand he took responsibility for what he had done. I thought how, throughout my childhood, I had only seen the difficult side of my grandmother's single-mindedness. Now all I saw was courage.

After that confrontation, my grandmother went home to nurse her dying father. It was then that her mind had shut down, her will to fight spent. For a while she thought of getting an abortion, but she had my mother to think of, and the risks of the procedure seemed too great. She never told any of this to Wolfgang; she did not have the strength.

She gave birth to a daughter, keeping her for a few months until an adoption could be arranged. She never told me this daughter's name in the conversations that followed, nor did I ask her for it. But she revealed, in that one sentence, the thing that lay behind her years of silence. The child cried constantly, and she turned away from it, unable to love a baby in whom she saw her rapist's face. She could have borne the stigma of unmarried motherhood. The failure to love on demand, to conform to what was expected of her as a mother, she could not.

After she gave her child up, she carried her secret for decades, built another life and a loving marriage, and had another child, my aunt Conny. And still she hid the existence of that other daughter. I have since found out something of her story, and it is not an easy one to hear. Her life, by all accounts, was a hard one. She came to find her biological mother many years later, full of resentment and anger. Their meeting was not happy and my grandmother, once again, chose to keep her secret. But this lost daughter's story is not mine to write.

I wish I had found better words than I did to tell my grandmother that what had happened to her was not her fault, that she was a victim herself. That traumatic experiences shrouded in silence must find a way of coming out, as many women before and after her have found to their cost. That her feelings of detachment were her mind's way of coping, the only way it knew how. That few today would ever judge her. That I admired her and loved her more than I had ever done before. But all I could do then was hold her and tell her that I loved her, my hands still full of icing, in an awkward embrace, while she stiffened, still lost in a time far away. One so rarely finds the words just when we need them most. All I can do now, is write them.

Chapter Seventeen

TRUTH AND ITS REPERCUSSIONS

The past, once it has been disturbed, will not be left alone. It had broken through the wall of silence that bound my grandmother to her secret for decades. Though her speaking it would lighten its weight over time, the impact reverberated through our family in the weeks and months that followed. I watched the aftermath shake the truths we had grown up with, full of guilt for what I had unthinkingly unleashed, but it was too late to turn back.

Life has its own way of dealing with events that would otherwise shatter us. After telling me her story, my grandmother went to bed. I finished making my cousin's wedding cake. The cream didn't run, the tiers held fast, the icing set. The wedding proceeded as though nothing had happened, while I tried as best I could to put the knowledge of her secret child out of my mind.

The storm I feared broke a few weeks later, when my mother and my aunt Conny went to visit my grandmother in Kiel. The evening before they returned, she told them about the sister whose existence they had never suspected. My mother's reaction was muted. She tried hard not to judge her mother and was careful with her words. She had known the hardship of the post-war years, though she had been too young to remember anything about her mother's second pregnancy or the presence of a baby. Psychologists say that most of our childhood memories aren't fully formed until about the age of four. What she found harder to process was the secret's relationship to herself. Such was her equanimity that I wondered whether she had taken it all in: the whens, the whys, and how they all fit into her own parents' story. I think the only way she knew to react without jumping to conclusions, without judging her mother, was to stay calm. Perhaps she felt guilty, too, for she had been a child of love, kept through the hardship, in contrast with the unknown sister. After talking to me about it on the night of her return, she hardly mentioned it again. She seemed to put the story out of her mind, almost as if it had happened to somebody else.

Conny's reaction was more violent, taking the form of angry tears. She internalised nothing and spoke to friends about it at length. Though I found her wrath excessive, I understood it better; it was closer to the way I think I would have dealt with it myself, had I been in her position. It was the lack of honesty that hurt her most, from a mother who had always emphasised the value of truth.

As I watched my mother and aunt's world turn inside out, I realised I had never stopped to think of the repercussions of my single-minded search for answers, nor considered how it might affect the people I loved. From the comfort of the next generation, I had thought the past too distant to still hold the power to wound. I had stirred, questioned, muddied the markers that made us who we were as a family, shaking my mother and my aunt to their core. They had seen themselves as a team of two. This was no longer really true. When you discover something as fundamental as that to be untrue, the very foundations of your childhood start to shift. The truth, far from setting them free, had shattered and disturbed, and I wondered for a while whether it ought to have been spoken at all.

My grandmother's reactions were harder to measure. Her talent for aloofness made her emotions less visible on the surface. She continued to dress as immaculately as before, and though age was making her increasingly frail, we resumed our conversations as if we had never shared the moment when I had held her shaking hands at the kitchen table. We never mentioned her secret child again. But somewhere inside her, I could see a burden had been lifted. In the months that followed, she confided, for the first time, in the lady who came to clean for her, who had, over the years, become a friend. She used the word 'rape', which she would not have done before, and she spoke openly and without reserve of how hard those times had been and the dilemma she had faced. She had reclaimed her own story. The code of silence had been broken for ever, and she was free. And so, while my family struggled to come to terms with this new knowledge, my grandmother simply turned the page. She was not one for dwelling, and so she did what she had always done before, and moved on. This time, it was in rather a dramatic fashion, by leaving her home of almost seventy years and returning to the east, at the age of ninety-two.

Her decision, extraordinary as it seems, was both an emotional and a practical one. She had not wanted to leave her home, so we had found a succession of carers who could look after her. Her relationship with them had been mixed, often distant, professional at best. It was then that Christina came into her life. A middle-aged Polish former teacher, tall and thin with a soft voice, large glasses and long flowing skirts, Christina was no match for her at first. Her shaky grasp of German made my grandmother inclined to bully her a little. But Christina was gentle and patient, and their relationship soon turned to a mutual respect and affection.

In 2016, a year after Christina's arrival, my grandmother told us she was going to Poland to spend Christmas with Christina and her family at their farm in a small village a couple of hours' drive from Warsaw. She was happy and animated. When we spoke on

Christmas Eve, she told me Christina's husband and three children spent the winter evenings by the fire, singing and playing the guitar. It was, she told me, 'just like the old times'. She was so taken by this rural Polish life that, once the festivities were over, she decided that she did not want to go back to Kiel at all.

She returned to her flat in Kiel just once, to pack. She focused on packing clothing and make-up, taking with her a smart fur hat, her red nail varnish and her favourite dresses. She wanted very few mementoes: a book or two and, apart from one album, very few photographs. She would have left behind the silver-framed photograph of Vati, which had stood on her bedside table, if my mother and Conny had not put it in her suitcase.

After she left Germany, we spoke on the phone from time to time, but it was becoming hard for her to recognise people by their voice alone, and every time I called I felt she had drifted a little further away.

I was on holiday in France, at the beginning of September 2017, when the call I had both dreaded and expected came. I heard my mother's voice, full of tears. 'She is gone,' she told me. 'She died in her sleep.' I had been folding a shirt when I'd picked up the phone. As I hung up, I looked out of the window at the courtyard with the lime tree, under whose branches my grandmother and I had so often sheltered from the sun and talked. The sadness I felt was tinged with guilt. I had meant to visit her, but work, a busy life, had meant that I had kept putting my plans off. Now, it was too late.

Hers was what they call a good death, one that comes gently after months of increased frailty. It felt, in a way, like a passing that had taken place months before. She had, aged ninety-three, been waiting for death without fear, but it was more than that. I knew that on the day she moved to Poland she had already left us behind, bidding farewell to her old life and our world, to embark on a journey of her own for a few months. I stood there for a long time, the shirt still in my hand, looking at the lime tree. It had grown, undisturbed, through the changes, deaths, heartbreaks and joys I had known throughout my life, and I found something soothing in its permanence. I walked outside and lay down on the ground beneath it, looking up at its leaves, at the sun flashing in glimpses through the dark canopy of green, the branches, grown long and low with age, blocking out all else in a comforting embrace.

Part V

Chapter Eighteen

A POLISH FARMHOUSE

The forest was a vast and impenetrable mass that started at the bottom of the garden. The village we had driven through to get here was little more than a cluster of houses, dwarfed by an enormous red-brick church, unremarkable except for its size. Now all I could see was the top of the spire, as the darkness of the trees had all but swallowed it up.

I was standing on the porch of the Polish farmhouse that my grandmother had lived in for the last few months of her life. The wooden railing, with its peeling pale-green paint, creaked gently as I leant over it. It was a small, out-of-the-way place that few travellers would know. I had come here with my family to attend my grandmother's funeral that morning, and Christina and her husband had invited us back to their home for lunch.

It was a small, simple house of beige concrete with an ancient thatched stone barn across a courtyard, where a couple of stray hens pecked at the ground. I could just make out the sound of my family's voices as they talked, crowding round the dining-room table. I had excused myself by claiming the need for fresh air, wanting to be on my own for a while. I looked around at this unfamiliar place and thought of the people I had just been eating with; although kindly and interesting, ultimately, they were strangers. I wondered what had really driven my grandmother to move here.

Christina's family had welcomed my grandmother as one of their own. Her bedroom had been the best one in the house, overlooking the neat front garden. Though it was the end of September and the wind already had the bite of autumn, the garden was still bright with the last of the summer's lupins, flashing pink and purple in the fading flower borders. I imagined how it would look in winter, the narrow road cut off by snow, the skyline lost in the top of the trees as the vast expanse of white brought with it months of unrelenting cold. This was nature without mercy. It felt foreign and intimidating to me, this eastern land, flat and austere, with its endless horizon. There was nothing here of the gentleness of the west, of the sun-warmed hills of my family's home in France, or of the comfortable urban neatness of Kiel. It was a wildness as uncompromising as it had been hundreds of years ago, yet it had somehow brought her comfort. For a brief moment, I saw the forest through her eyes. This was the landscape of her childhood.

Christina's son had driven us to the town crematorium that morning, a large building designed along utilitarian lines, low ceilinged and harshly lit. Immediately upon our arrival, an unsmiling clerk gave us some paperwork to fill out. The space was so impersonal that it felt inappropriately like a wedding in a busy town hall, a formality to get through when all anyone is waiting for is the party later. Christina's family had organised it all and we followed their lead, quiet and bewildered, like travellers on a guided tour. In this unfamiliar place, the effects of my grandmother's self-imposed distance suddenly hit home. I could almost have been mourning a stranger.

She was lying in an open casket, in a room where everything was made of pine. Chairs had been set out in neat rows and smelt strongly of furniture polish. We sat in the front while Christina and her family stood on the other side, next to the priest, an oddity in his black robes in this modern, functional room. My grandmother looked tiny and frail in her bed of white satin; they'd made her coffin a foot or so too long. She was dressed smartly, in a black velvet frock with a white collar. Someone had carefully done her make-up. We walked up to the coffin in turn to pay our respects. Hesitantly, as though trying not to wake her, I placed my hand on hers and felt a shock of cold. For a few seconds, my mind carried me back to my father's deathbed more than ten years before. His hand had still felt warm and with this memory, a sense of loss almost overwhelmed me.

Back at my seat, I waited for the priest to finish a prayer in Polish. My mother was staring ahead of her, her usually transparent thoughts now impenetrable. I felt an urge to speak, to reclaim my grandmother as one of our own. I put a hand in my pocket, reaching for the folded piece of paper I had put there earlier, on which I'd written a few lines. I took a step forwards, but then Christina's eldest daughter walked up to the coffin, carrying a long eulogy that she'd prepared, printed out and carefully laminated. She and the rest of her family were openly weeping; our quiet sadness must have looked so cold by contrast. I sat down again, my words unspoken, and the ceremony drew to a close. The jealousy I felt was ungracious, but I let it sweep over me like a wave.

Another clerk, gentler than the first, came into the room to shepherd us out, explaining the cremation would take place without the family present. I glanced at my watch. It had all been over in twenty-five minutes.

The others were still indoors having lunch, and the sound of exclamations told me that someone had brought out more vodka. There was enough food for about fifty people; Christina must have been cooking for days. As I had walked into the house through the small hall, the first thing I'd seen was a modern depiction of the Virgin

Mary, brought back from Rome by the eldest daughter. In the dining room at the back of the house, a table was set with candles and their best china on a lace tablecloth. A large wooden crucifix adorned the back wall, beneath which a large framed colour photograph of my grandmother stood on a table. An array of dishes had followed: chicken soup with noodles, two different kinds of *pierogi*, roast pork knuckle with boiled wheat and mashed potato. As I'd stepped back outside through the kitchen, I'd spotted dessert, a large cheesecake, a Black Forest gateau and a platter of Polish doughnuts filled with jam.

The children, two daughters and a son, still mostly lived at home despite being in their early twenties. They were charming, intelligent, well-read, spoke perfect English, and were a source of understandable pride to their parents. Theirs was a kind, close-knit Polish family, a little old-fashioned, deeply Catholic, leading a simple life; the very last people I would have expected Inge, an atheist, to have been drawn to.

Christina's daughter had spoken in her eulogy of how much my grandmother had enjoyed their family life, from their meals together to their musical evenings by the fire in the winter. Looking out at the garden, I spotted a white wrought-iron bench with thick, flowered chintz cushions, the garden seat she'd said my grandmother had been so fond of. At the sight of that bench came a new sadness, the thought that my grandmother had found in this family something ours could never give her. I thought of our long conversations, and of the secrets she had revealed to me. But I knew, deep down, that part of her had always belonged in Europe's east, to a past that was hers only, and which could never be mine.

It felt as if I'd been standing on the porch for an hour, though it could only have been fifteen minutes. I lingered to look at the forest a while longer. It smelt of pine needles and reddening oak leaves turning musty as they died. It was a landscape that spoke of another time, one where travel took an entire day, of fields that stretched as far as the eye could see, of cities whose buildings held the familiarity of centuries. It spoke of my grandmother's youth, as she had revealed it to me.

My aunt came out to join me, lighting a cigarette. I don't smoke, but I shared it with her, and we stood together for a moment in silent companionship. I thought of how my grandmother had weathered heartbreak, flight, displacement, violence and loss, and yet found the strength to rebuild her life. She had started again, finding new love with a man six years her junior, undamaged by the war that had destroyed others. It may not have been the life she and Wolfgang had mapped out for themselves as young lovers in Berlin, but it had been a happy one on the whole. Perhaps this move to Poland was her way to finally close the circle of her life, to live her last months in a home whose landscape reminded her of the lost land of her childhood, which she still carried in her heart. And I could not begrudge her that.

Had Wolfgang, the boy she had loved, the grandfather I had never met, found the same ability to rebuild his life? I had kept him at arm's length, always on the periphery of my search, seeing him only through my grandmother's eyes. But his story was a part of mine too. The ties we shared, now I had pieced the past together, were stronger than just those of blood. I had made my peace with my grandmother's choices; it was time for me to discover who he really was.

Chapter Nineteen

A MEETING

A tall old man, bald, his shoulders slightly stooped, approaches two women in late middle age at a cafe in Stuttgart in the summer of 2000. The blonde one looks slightly nervous; the other puts a hand on her arm in support.

He is late; the place was hard to find. He lives in a village in the outskirts, he explains, was delayed by traffic and briefly lost his way. They shake hands before embracing, a little awkwardly.

'So, you are Beatrice,' he says to the blonde woman.

They eat cake, then order another slice, which they share. They talk for a long time. Laughter occasionally punctuates their conversation. She has brought photographs of her children, which he lingers over. He shows her a picture of his fiancée. He is eighty, and the bride-to-be a couple of years younger.

The light is low when they decide to part, with promises of further visits.

As he leaves, he takes her hand again.

'The journey here was long, and difficult. But it has been worth it.'

She squeezes it in return. She knows he does not mean the one he undertook that afternoon; his lateness is one of many decades.

That day in June was the first time Wolfgang had seen his only daughter after a separation of more than fifty years, since the lunch in Hamburg at which she had refused to eat her vegetables. He remembered how her hair had been tightly plaited, and her poise, though she had been a little child then.

His life had been uneventful and solitary. After his return from Russia, he lived alone in the Black Forest region for most of his life. But he found contentment again too, in his last years. His wife, Ingrid, a distant cousin with whom he moved to the remote region of Telemark in her native Norway, taught him how to love again. She had encouraged him to see his daughter. He had written to Inge at her old address in Kiel, asking her to forward a letter to their daughter, and the letter had eventually reached her. She had sent my mother the letter, and replied to him that she had done so, enclosing a photo of his childhood home at Ahrensburg, which she had visited with her husband the year before. It was a courteous, impersonal, unremarkable exchange between two former lovers who had not spoken a word to each other in decades.

Despite his natural reticence, the long-estranged father and daughter found themselves drawn to each other. With Ingrid's encouragement, a relationship grew. My brother and I made plans to go and see him, but his death, in November 2004, cut them short. Ingrid, unable to reach my mother, called me instead. She cried as she told me that he was gone, from a heart attack, as he had been tending their garden. As I comforted her, I thought, *I shall never meet him now.*

But I did get to know him years later, through the photographs and emails he had exchanged with my mother. After my grandmother's funeral, wanting to find out more about Wolfgang, I asked my mother if I could read them. She had showed them to me willingly; there were only a dozen, which she had printed out and kept. It was hard to see in this old man the boy my grand-mother had passionately loved for so long. There was so much I would have wanted to ask him. A line in an email, complaining of his bronchitis, mentions a weakness in his lungs, a legacy of his time in a Russian camp. I wanted to know more, but that is where the reference ended.

I would have asked him about the mother he had loved and lost. Where he had learnt his expertise in Morse code, a language that required no words, the study of which he enthusiastically pursued. What had happened, during that war he never spoke of, to make him withdraw into silence for so long. Whether he had ever thought, in the years that followed that first meeting, of getting in touch with his daughter.

I had come to know him through my grandmother's eyes as a gentle, unconventional boy, a jazz-lover who hated rules, lacking courage, perhaps, but not kindness. He had been forced to fight those he did not hate and defend a creed he despised. I spoke to his much younger half-sister, the child of Carl-Otto and his English wife, and to his old friends, who described a quiet soul who hated conflict, a somewhat withdrawn man of extreme discretion. His half-sister told me, 'He was a gentle soul. He wasn't a fighter, he was an idealist who loved all things British. To be a soldier ... he just was not that kind of man.'

I went back to Berlin one more time, to conduct another search through archives and through records, hoping to find more information about the trauma that had marked him as a young man. Ingrid had told my mother that Wolfgang had still blamed his father, all those decades later, for having him sent to the Eastern Front. He had seen it as a punishment for his love affair with Inge, one whose consequences scarred him for life.

WOLFGANG IN LATER LIFE.

I am, as a rule, suspicious of silence: it so often implies the existence of something to hide. I wondered for a long time whether Wolfgang, out of fear, or out of weakness, had done something in the war he was ashamed to admit. Had he, as a soldier, succumbed to the brutality of his peers? Nazism found some of its strongest adherents in the young; had he finally joined the party he had claimed to hate? So many young men, whose families described them as good and kind boys, had proved to be capable of the worst atrocities. Pressure to conform is a powerful force. Had Wolfgang, too, I wondered, come to defend the indefensible?

I had accepted that the Wiegandts had done no more than try and get by. But now, I was delving into the past of a soldier. Fear, brainwashing and peer pressure have a great impact on boys too young to really know themselves. And then, he would have been forced to follow orders. It would have been impossible for him to have just been a bystander. Could I reconcile myself to that?

Of his captivity, I knew very little. An old HR file of my grandmother's, found among her papers, hints at it briefly. 'March 1943: Birth of daughter, Beatrice. Fiancé missing in Stalingrad.' In the archives in Berlin, I searched for documents bearing Wolfgang's name, and found none. I knew next to nothing of his military life: no regiment, no medals, just that old photograph taken, I believed, on the day he had enlisted. A search of military records proved inconclusive. Any documents that had existed were probably lost, and further knowledge of his wartime years remained a blank.

Instead, I turned to the voices of others who had served on the Eastern Front. I read of kind sons and loving fathers who used Nazism to justify the horrors they committed at the front. I read of looting, of rapes, of arson and of civilian executions. I read letters from young soldiers who described a world without humanity. Some found the strength to stay true to themselves, and see clearly the horror of their army's actions. Others sought to justify them.

I read of the conditions in Soviet camps like the one he had been imprisoned in, where death and hardship were the norm, and of the lice-infested men who survived to return home to find their families did not recognise them. If he had indeed been captured at Stalingrad, he would have endured at least three years as a prisoner, and watched friends die terrible deaths.

I had stayed in touch with Kirsten Lylloff, who had shared her work with me in Denmark. I mentioned my search of Wolfgang's war records, and she offered to help, suggesting the archives in Copenhagen might yield some results given Wolfgang's Danish connections. She did so gently; on the Danish side of Wolfgang's family there were those who had indeed been committed Nazis, and any records on him might reveal unpalatable truths. Kirsten's findings arrived a few weeks later. There were dozens of pages, mostly in Danish, largely relating to Wolfgang's attempts to claim back some money that his brother had left him on his death in 1935, which had been held in a savings account in Aalborg, in Northern Jutland. It was a substantial, but not life-changing, sum, and Wolfgang's repeated endeavours to claim it, over the space of about ten years, indicated a life far removed from the wealth he had enjoyed in his youth.

The files built a paper trail that started in 1948, by which time Wolfgang had moved to a farm near Lautzkirchen in the French zone. It finished in 1957, when the Danish state sent its final rejection of Wolfgang's request. Among them was a letter by Wolfgang written in blue ink in a small, compact hand, betraying both frustration and resignation, as if he knew by then that he'd never get the money back. I carefully read through all the files until, buried among the Danish papers, one page in English caught my eye. It was a document stamped by the US military, dated 15 October 1956, from the Berlin Document Center. I'd come across the BDC on a number of occasions in works I'd read about Nazism; it was the organisation that collected and classified all documents related to Nazism, where the evidence of war crimes was collated for the Nuremberg trials and where, on a smaller scale, all individual files on German citizens were prepared to prove or disprove any Nazi Party links.

J.-nr. 6.X.185

The Danish Military Mission

Berlin W.35, Tiergartenstrasse 48
(Name and address of requesting agency)

Date: 15th October 1956

TO: Berlin Document Center, APO 742 U, S. Army, Berlin, Germany.

Request NSDAP Records be Checked for:

1) Name: Wolfgang Hasso Elard Graf Schimmelmann
Place of birth: Ahrensburg, Holstein, Germany
Date of birth: 2.4.1921
Occupation: not given
Present address: Bornbacher Hof, Lautzkirchen, Saar
Other information:

It is understood that the requested information will be supplied at cost to this organization, and that payment will be made when billing is received. Estimated cost is: _____ (Not applicable to US Army organizations in USAREUR.)

Telephone: 24-8595

Signed _____
V.C. Hammershaimb
Lt/Col.

2) ITEM: Neg.   Pos.   Checked by:
a) NSDAP Master File
b) Partei Kanzlei Correspondence
c) RuSHA and other SS Records
d) SS Officers
e) SA
f) OPG
g) NS-Lehrerbund
h) Rückwandererzentrale
i) EWZ
j)
k)

3) Remarks

Date Request Received: _____   Date Answer Transmitted: _____

OCT 16 1956

AGO, (1) 4-56-58038-38130

US MILITARY DOCUMENT FROM BERLIN DOCUMENT CENTER.

This investigation of my grandfather's past comprised four columns. The first, to the left, listed possible Nazi affiliations: Nazi party (NSDAP) membership, traces of official correspondence, branches or affiliates of the SS, membership of the Nazi teachers' union, or further organisations under the Nazi Party umbrella. The two columns in the middle had space for either 'yes' or 'no'. My eye travelled down the line of 'no's; there was not a single 'yes'. To the right, the last column provided the final verdict. The official stamp in blue ink, 'Berlin Document Center: negative' gave me the answer I thought I'd always searched for, the proof that Wolfgang had not been a Nazi after all.

Of course, this paper did not tell me whether Wolfgang, the soldier, had shown himself capable of looting, of violence, of killing. What it did was to officially exculpate him from party membership. And for someone whose stepfather was the vice president of the Reichsbank, to avoid this would have required some degree of willpower. Many men of power and influence had sought to have similar pieces of paper produced, for a clean bill of health, so that Germans called them *Persilschein*, or whitewash. But the Wolfgang who first wrote to the Danish government in 1947 was poor. His father no longer had any influence. I felt reasonably certain that what the certificate showed was true.

The small things I had learnt about him flitted through my head. His reluctance to reveal his wealth while a student engineer, working on the factory floor. His defiance as he declared to a young Inge that he didn't kiss gloved hands. His love of jazz and its celebration of the unconventional. The years he had spent alone. His quiet, gentle acknowledgement to my mother of his failings as a father, but also of his pleasure in having found her again, after so many years.

Because he had betrayed my grandmother, I had been looking for proof of moral fallibility. I had prepared myself for anger and instead felt only pity. I would never discover exactly what had happened in his war. But while Wolfgang had not been the hero my childish self had longed for, neither had he been a villain. I had discovered an ordinary man, flawed and weak perhaps, but kind and sensitive. I am sure he, like many others, had done things in war he had regretted. But I no longer felt the need to judge him for it.

I showed the certificate to my brother. He read it, quietly, and was silent for a while, almost as if he was about to cry. To him, it was a seal of a clean past, something to show to others, to validate the things we had been told as children. 'We must frame this,' he said.

I printed out a copy for him, and put mine away in a drawer. When I started this journey, more than ten years before, I would probably have wanted to frame it, too. But now, I thought of it as just a piece of paper. I had come to realise, before I'd even read it, that my grandfather was a good man.

LINDENBORG CASTLE.

On a snowy day in late March 2018 I set off for Denmark's northern shore. The drive to northern Jutland from Copenhagen is long, through a landscape of gentle, snowy hills and pine forests. I went to Lindenborg Castle first, where Wolfgang had spent many childhood summers and where Carl, his brother, had lived his last years. It emerged, fairy-tale-like, from behind a copse of trees, its lines marked by a red-tiled roof, the white stone of its turrets hardly distinguishable from the snow. I imagined the two brothers walking among the woods: boisterous Carl, and Wolfgang, three years his junior, a quieter soul, following his brother's every lead. I pictured Dorothea, arriving here too late to say goodbye to the son whose death she never recovered from. The gate was open, but not a soul was in sight; the castle was only inhabited when rented out for hunting trips, and no family lived there now. It was hauntingly beautiful, deserted, a place asleep, a vestige of another time long

WOLFGANG'S GRAVE.

past. At the foot of a tree, I saw a clump of hellebore, the flowers known as winter roses, their creamy blooms gleaming on the harsher, luminous white of the snow.

The churchyard was hard to find in the gathering dusk, a tiny, neatly kept graveyard beside the simple stone church. A large rock marked the place where the von Schimmelmanns lay, the inscription resembling the runes Norsemen used to carve in jutting stones to honour the deeds of their dead. At its foot lay a simple unshaped stone, with a single word inscribed in bronze letters: 'Buschi'. Wolfgang's grave. Beside it lay a marble plaque covered in ivy. I brushed away the snow: Carl von Schimmelmann, born 31 July 1918, died 4 December 1935. Between the two, I placed the posy of hellebore I'd gathered in the gardens at Lindenborg, and left the two brothers at peace.

Chapter Twenty

THE PAST IS ANOTHER COUNTRY

The phone call I made to my grandmother the first time I went to Kaliningrad set me on a decade of discoveries, unravelling secrets and uncovering a past that gradually came back to life. But of the city itself, I remembered very little. I had not known then what I was seeking. Now, in the map of my mind, I walked through the places the Wiegandts held dear, strolled around the park facing their block of flats, walked along the Pregel, took a train to the coast as they had done every summer. The outlines of a landscape lovingly remembered all formed a past I had learnt almost by heart.

It had been cold and grey when I'd last come here, but it was now the height of summer and the icy winds of early spring had given way to a sweltering heat. It was as if I'd come to a different place. Even in the arrivals hall, there was evidence that money had been spent. Shiny new signs were still on display for the football World Cup Kaliningrad had hosted a few weeks before. I was not the only one to have come here in search of a family past. From the mid-1990s, as tourism to the region started to be encouraged, some of the *Vertriebene*, as the East Prussians called themselves, started to come back to look at the land they had lost. Now, this tourism is geared to their children, curious to see what's left of the old places. In the airport, the souvenir shops offer a selection of memorabilia, from amber figures of the cathedral to tea towels with the name 'Königsberg' emblazoned on the edge. At the news-stand, I bought a map of the city as it had been in 1928. The summer light dispelled much of the drabness I remembered.

For a few hours that evening, I was almost seduced. After dropping my bag at the hotel, I went for a walk along the banks of the River Pregel,* to the point where it divided into old and new. There was something of an old, Mittel-European feel to this small pocket of Kaliningrad, with its odour of fried fish drifting along the quayside. I sat at a restaurant terrace and dined on pike perch, admiring the prosperous-looking waterfront, with its clean pedestrian promenades, and watching the families that strolled along its banks, some local, others Russians from farther afield, breaking their journey on their way to the coast. Over the water, in the shadow of the trees, I spied the red-brick spire of an old Gothic cathedral, delighting in such a rare, tangible sign of its pre-war past. In the glow of the sunset, I could almost pretend those few blocks along the river's edge, which housed most of the city's hotels, were the original buildings, rather than Russian rebuilds in the old German style. The next morning, daylight revealed a harsher reality.

The House of the Soviets, built on the castle ruins, was fully visible in daytime. It enjoys a notoriety of sorts for being one of the ugliest buildings in the history of communist architecture: a concrete box, one its own architect was said to think of with shame. Though it was beset by structural problems making it unsafe for use, the asbestos in its walls meant no official had yet dared to have the building torn down. Even the cathedral's German-style facades looked garish in the sunlight and the church spire turned out to be that of Königsberg's main cathedral and the site of Kant's tomb, which had been entirely rebuilt in the early 1990s.†

---

* Now known by its Russian name, Pregolya.
† Germany funded the rebuilding of the old Könrigbserg cathedral.

I knew the original had dated back to the fourteenth century; a photograph from 1961 revealed its wartime fate: a roofless, blackened ruin, a tower without a spire, a facade without windows or supporting walls. But though the city lacks the charm of the old, there was certainly renewal here. The foundations of Königsberg's old synagogue, burned down during Kristallnacht in 1938, now showed a busy building site, soon to be a new place of worship for Kaliningrad's Jewish community, now 2,000-strong and hailing mainly from the former Soviet Union.[1]

Armed with my old map and hoping to recognise some of the city's topography, I began my walk through the echoes of the past. There were almost no reliable signs of the old Königsberg, save for the river and some venerable old trees, but I told myself that seven centuries of German life, the foundation and being of an entire city, could not have been entirely erased. A lengthy and painstaking search revealed only the faintest of traces: three feet of rails buried in the grass of a central reservation in the middle of a busy six-lane road, once the tracks for Königsberg's trams; the old stock exchange on the New Pregel, ostentatious by its age in a city where almost nothing pre-dates the war. The ruined brick facade of the old children's hospital, its broken windows gaping, like missing teeth.

My first stop was the Paradeplatz, where the Wiegandts once lived. I searched for their home with my grandmother's description in mind: a tall white apartment building on one side of the King's Gardens, with pointed gables and a turret, from whose windows you could see all the way across the square to the Albertina University, which, in the summer, was filled with flowers. I looked for the Cafe Berlin, where Alfred used to take Inge for hot chocolate, and the bakery in the next block which sold the best marzipan in the city. But all I found was a *Khrushchyovka*, a concrete apartment block of the uglier kind found in Soviet urban planning, its small, boxy windows dotting the facade like measles. Where the statue of King Friedrich Wilhelm III on horseback once stood, only a fragment of garden remained. In front of the campus of the Kaliningrad Immanuel Kant Baltic University, built on the wreckage of the Albertina University, stood a statue of Kant, the one German in Königsberg who was still allowed to be remembered.

'THE MONSTER', KALININGRAD.

Much of the Paradeplatz was destroyed in the RAF bombings of August 1944. I knew the Wiegandts' apartment block had survived the raid, but that turned out to be a short reprieve. The square holds the old bunker built by German general Otto Lasch in 1939, now a museum of Russia's victory. In it I found a model of the Paradeplatz on the day the city fell in April 1945. It showed the Wiegandts' building in flames, recognisable by the awning of the Cafe

Berlin three doors down. But in the gardens by the Oberteich, a narrow tree-lined lake a short walk away, I gained a sense of the city as it had been. The light, shimmering on the water, softened the edges of the buildings mirrored in its surface, and the path running alongside it was framed by huge, ancient oaks. On the banks of the lower pond, I paused next to a large statue of a Soviet hero in a submarine capsule, aiming a torpedo. His name, Alexander Marinesko, was familiar to me. He was the man who'd sunk the *Wilhelm Gustloff*, standing next to the torpedo that killed so many passengers, an act of destruction immortalised in bronze, the experience of which had led my grandmother to lose her faith in God.

In Amalienau, once the city's western suburb, where Albert had often driven my grandmother as child, old houses remained that had been spared the intensity of the British raids that obliterated the city centre. Most of the surviving streets were built in the 1930s; the signs of age are so sparse in Kaliningrad that I delighted in an old water pump and a manhole cover, both of which still bore the old German traces. But tangible as they were, I still hoped to find something that would tell me of the old city's people.

There is remembrance of Königsberg's darker past in its Holocaust memorial and in the few remaining graves of the old Jewish cemetery, mostly desecrated by the Nazis. There is even commemoration of the German war dead, both soldiers and civilians, in a dedicated cemetery established by the German War Graves Commission in 2000. But what I was after were the resting places of those who had lived before Hitler brought about the region's obliteration, and I set off to look for them. On the map of the old city, I counted at least seven cemeteries within an hour's walk. But the Soviet zeal for urban development and creating a new history viewed these as a waste of space, a reminder of a past that no longer existed. Where the grounds of the Altstadt Friedhof, the old town

KÖNIGSBERG MANHOLE COVER.

cemetery, should have been, I now found tangled woodland. Only fragments of black granite, scattered among the undergrowth, hinted at the land's past purpose, before nature reclaimed it for its own. Another Jewish cemetery, once the biggest in the city, was desecrated by the Nazis before vanishing forever under more *Khrushchyovka* residential blocks. After another hour of searching, I reached the Old Queen Louise Friedhof, Kaliningrad's main cemetery, a vast and sprawling expanse just off Prospect Mira, once called the Hammerweg.

Here, rows of graves lay among the oaks and pines, the plots mostly overgrown, their carefully planted flowers lost in a tangle of nettles and ivy. Most of the black granite headstones feature pictures of the dead, while other plots bore markers of blue or red metal, their colours flashing amid the darkness of the trees. But even here I drew a blank, for every grave held a Russian name, and the oldest I could find was dated 1947. In a clearing, by what looked like a caretaker's lodge, guarded by a friendly black dog, I finally found what I'd been searching for, in a pile of discarded headstones, weathered, chipped and barely legible. At my feet, part of another, the letters just visible where it had been used to pave over a hole in the road. I read the names carefully: Johanna Radtke, Aurelius Charisius, Oskar Bartsch, Lucie R—, the broken stone wouldn't let me know the rest. A pile of stones, chipped and discarded, seemed to be all that was left of the city's German dead.

GERMAN GRAVE USED AS PAVING STONE.

Though Kaliningrad's streets had shown me little but marks of destruction, I had found understanding and kindness in its habitants. The old hatred of the German past does not persist among the people to whom the city now belongs. On my ride back from the cemetery, the tram conductress took the time to show me where all the old landmarks once stood; the old man who sat beside me urged me to come again the following year, and bring my mother with me. It's a strange city, whose soul remains a pawn in Russia's power struggle with the West. A no man's land, stripped of its past and with an uncertain future, held fast in Moscow's grip.

It was with a bittersweet feeling that I left the next morning on a train bound for the coast. My destination was Svetlogorsk, once called Rauschen, in search of that strip of beach from the snapshot of the young, carefree beachgoers which I still carried with me, like a pilgrim in search of an illusory past. The rail tracks still followed the old route, through the expanses of fields and forest that sheltered Kaliningrad from the rough winds of the Baltic. It was the route Inge had first taken as a small child, then as a teenager, bound for her summer holiday and, finally, to seek refuge when she returned to East Prussia, unmarried and pregnant. The train was comfortable and modern, packed with holidaymakers off to enjoy a long weekend by the sea, and did little to feed my craving for nostalgia. But looking out of the carriage window, the eastern landscape which had once seemed so alien, seemed both comforting and familiar, far removed from the urban sprawl and its memories of hatred and war. The passing of time and people had done little to dent it. I read in its outlines, something of the old land.

The train pulled in first to Svetlogorsk-Gorod, or Rauschen-Stadt, as my grandmother had known it, before its final stop, where the dunes started. Off the main drag, the paths sloped steeply downwards, winding their way between the trees to the sea. The dunes, dotted with pines, led almost to the water's edge, acting as a buffer against both the strong winds that came in from the north and the pounding of the waves. Even on this windless August day, the Baltic was rough and only the bravest of swimmers ventured into its waters. It was as sheltered a spot as you could get on this coast, the long sandy beach framed by jutting rocks, the hills on either side covered in forest.

The promenade opened at the bottom of the path, overlooking a wide and sandy beach. Paving stones had replaced the old wooden boards, but the view, stretching far out to the horizon, was exactly as my grandmother had described. Here were the holidaymakers strolling up and down, pausing to look at the stands that sold amber figurines. East Prussia's seaside towns had fared better than its larger cities, and some of the old houses remained intact.

To the right, by some steps leading steeply down to the beach, was a jetty I recognised at once. A concrete block had replaced its wooden base to guard against erosion by the sea, but the surroundings and position were the same. A placard behind it showed the original structure with the criss-cross wooden base; it was identical to the backdrop in my grandmother's old holiday snap. I made my way down the steps, strangely elated, wading into the sea to the spot where the little group had stood, oblivious to their fate. After the destruction I had seen in Kaliningrad, I had finally found the echo I had sought, that of a place once loved, which I could now remember without tragedy. There was little of war, of exile, of parting in this spot, just the memory of a young girl, on the beach with her friends, on a summer holiday.

I continued to Cranz, and saw there the coloured houses and seaside cafes of my grandmother's recollections. Changed perhaps, bigger, uglier in places, thanks to its popularity with tourists, but still a place of happiness and laughter.

As the evening drew near, I went back to the beach to gather a handful of sand. I had not found the visible past that I had hoped for. I would never see the building my mother had been born in, or sit in what had once been the Cafe Berlin. The city was a different place today, its identity reshaped and changed. But something of East Prussia still lingered beneath the surface, in its trees, its history and in people's consciousness, and this helped me to accept its present.

I returned to France a week later, carrying the little handful of sand I had taken from the beach in Cranz. I took it to the small village cemetery where we had finally buried my grandmother's ashes, a stone's throw from the house where she had chosen to reveal her secrets to me.

As I tipped the sand out on her grave, a gust of wind caught some of it, spreading its grains across the hillside. It was a fitting epitaph, I thought, for a woman born in what was now Russia, who had lived her adult life in Germany, died in Poland and been buried in France, to share some of the land she had always kept in her heart.

She had seen Europe implode and lived to watch its pieces be put back together, imperfect, fragile and slightly misshapen, like a mended piece of china. I wonder sometimes whether I forced her into revealing her secret, and if I had a right to know all the things I had learnt. I'm still unsure. It's still an uncomfortable subject in my family, though my mother and aunt have long forgiven their mother. But I do know that in speaking her secret, she had finally set herself free from its shame.

My grandmother's life was not one of innocence or guilt. It was one of extraordinary events, of the things we do to survive, and how they shape our lives. What would I have done in wartime? Growing up in a Europe at peace, I always thought I'd known the answer, confidently imagining myself among those who would stand up and be counted. Only now do I understand what was meant by Thomas Nagel's phrase, 'moral luck', which casts doubt on whether we can judge actions influenced by events beyond an individual's control.[2]

Nothing can ever excuse the complicity of a nation's people in the crimes committed in its name. But with every war come layers of suffering, and only by acknowledging it all can we ever stop hatred from tearing people apart.

My grandmother's story taught me a lesson I will carry with me for the rest of my life. That the imperative to survive can bring with it difficult choices, which don't always come out well in their telling. That moving forward requires examining, understanding, and accepting those decisions. That memory cannot be forever buried, but must be given space to evolve with time, for the past is a moving target.

EPILOGUE

THE STORY OF AN ENDING

I returned to Berlin on a sunny week in September 2018, on a pilgrimage of sorts, not to the past, but to the present. I had reached the end of the road, the place where all searches must conclude if they are to bring peace to those who undertake them. It was time to accept the facts I had uncovered, and to let go of the things I could never know. I could lose myself forever looking for a truth that must always be imperfect in places. But I had learnt that the past can never yield its whole, and that some parts must remain forever lost. What mattered was that I now understood its essence.

I took the U-Bahn to Dahlem. The sun warmed my back as I walked down the tree-and-shrub-lined streets, their green leaves not yet turned by autumn. I knew my destination.

At the top of Vogelsang, I turned to walk through the narrow gardens that separated both sides of the wide cobbled street, between the silver birches on whose trunks lovers had triumphantly carved their names. It had been a dry September and the grass rustled beneath my feet, filling the air with the scent of hay. I reached the bench that faced the big white villa where my grandmother had lived, and sat, looking at the gate where Wolfgang had first kissed her, after an evening dancing to the music of a forbidden band.

I held a piece of paper torn from a notebook. On it were written names and dates, some overlapping, others underlined, a few crossed out, one or two with a question mark still beside them: the timeline of a love cut short. For the truth I had searched for and discovered, which I have tried to tell over these pages, is not a tale of heroism or evil, but of survival. That of women who, through the generations, have loved, endured and overcome: Dorothea, Frieda, Inge, my mother, myself.

I had pieced together the events that had led to my mother's birth and to her parents' final goodbye. Some things I would probably never know for certain: for example, how much time elapsed between Wolfgang's return from a Soviet camp and his meeting with Inge. I can only speculate that it may have been weeks, or months, whether the delay was due to his health, or to his state of mind. I did not know the exact date of Inge's rape. But I knew that it was close enough for her assailant to accuse her of trying to pass off a child that was his, as Wolfgang's. And I believed its timing dealt the final blow to a love that war had already all but condemned.

In some sense, my mother had been right: her parents' teenage love had not been strong enough to survive the war and its aftermath. It was an everyday tragedy, lived in extraordinary times. What she had not known was quite how much they had both endured.

Battered by life, neither Inge nor Wolfgang had tears left to weep. So she drifted away, and he let her go. Wolfgang would never tell her of the horrors he had seen and endured in Russia, and she would never tell him about the child she had given up. Neither ever confided their hardships to the other, for in the wasteland of war's aftermath, they had not found the words.

Silence is a treacherous friend. It had been my grandmother's armour and her torment. It had both shielded her from the judgement of others and robbed her of the chance to find the comfort of love. In the turmoil of the years that followed the war, it was the only safety she knew. Though hers was a story of violence and displacement, it was one shared by many women who became collateral damage in the wreckage of Europe's collapse.

As I sat looking at the villa, I took the bracelet she had given me all those years before out of my pocket, a small, heavy circle, the gold dulled by decades of touch. I ran my fingers round its edge. I cannot wear it on my wrist. I chose not to have its clasp repaired; it will stay shut.

Would my grandparents have stayed together in more peaceful times? I like to think so, though I can never know for certain. I had searched for the truth, and had come as close as I could. My knowledge of the past may not be perfect, but I know it in my heart to be fair. The circle of Inge and Wolfgang's story is now closed.

Prologue: Königsberg, 1932

1 Thomas Mann, 'Was Wir Verlangen Müssen', *Berliner Tageblatt*, 8 August 1932. Copy of article on display at the Thomas Mann Memorial Museum in Nida, Lithuania.
2 Antony Beevor, *Berlin: The Downfall: 1945*, Kindle edn (Viking, 2007), chapter 27.

Chapter Two: A Time of Darkness

1 Nicole M. Eaton, 'Exclave: Politics, Ideology, and Everyday Life in Königsberg–Kaliningrad, 1928–1948' (Doctoral dissertation, University of California, Berkeley, 2013), Part I.
2 Michael Wieck, *A Childhood Under Hitler and Stalin: Memoirs of a 'Certified Jew'*, trans. Penny Milbouer (University of Wisconsin Press, 2003).

Chapter Four: *'Bei Mir Bist du Schön'*

1 Nicholas Stargardt, *The German War: A Nation Under Arms, 1939–45* (Vintage, 2016), p.114.
2 Michael Kater, *Different Drummers: Jazz in the Culture of Nazi Germany* (Oxford University Press, 2003), p.73.

Chapter Five: Vogelsang

1 Richard J. Evans, 'Coercion and Consent in Nazi Germany', Raleigh Lecture on History (2006).
2 Ibid.

Chapter Six: Swing Time

1 Kater, *Different Drummers*, p.130.
2 Ibid., p.104.

Chapter Eight: An Uncertain Future

1 Stargardt, *The German War*, p.113.
2 Henry Friedlander, *The Origins of Nazi Genocide: From Euthanasia to the Final Solution* (University of North Carolina Press, 1995), p.139.
3 Peter B. Clark, *The Death of East Prussia: War and Revenge in Germany's Easternmost Province*, Kindle edn (Andover Press, 2013), chapter 2.
4 Peter Longerich, *'Davon haben wir nichts gewusst!' Die Deutschen und die Judenverfolgung 1933–1945* ['*We Didn't Know Anything About It!' The Germans and the Persecution of Jews 1933–1945*] (Siedler Verlag, 2006).
5 Evans, 'Coercion and Consent in Nazi Germany'.

Chapter Nine: Trapped

1 Graf Hans Lehndorff, *Ostpreußisches Tagebuch: Aufzeichnungen eines Arztes aus den Jahren 1945–1947* [*East Prussian Diary: A Doctor's Observations of the Years 1945–1947*] (Dtv, 1967), p.9.
2 Erna Heidusch, who emigrated to the United States, kept this map until the day she died. Her mother, Helene, fled Königsberg in April 1945 with Erna's younger brother Gustav and sister Anita. Erna's father, Peter, a lawyer, was last heard from on the Eastern front in January 1945.
3 Evans, 'Coercion and Consent in Nazi Germany'.
4 This is explored at some length in Ian Kershaw, *The End: Germany 1944–45*, Kindle edn (Penguin, 2011), chapter 1.

5   Ibid., chapter 1.

6   Ibid., chapter 6.

7   Rudolph Herzog, *Heil Hitler, das Schwein ist tot!: Lachen unter Hitler – Komik und Humor im Dritten Reich* [*Heil Hitler, the Pig is Dead!: Laughter under Hitler – Comedy and Humour in the Third Reich*], Kindle edn (Kiepenheuer & Witsch 2018), chapter 5.

8   Kershaw, *The End*, chapter 1.

9   Ibid., chapter 3.

10 Ibid., chapter 3.

11 Inge's own account of hearing of a family burned to death in their cellar adds to other accounts of people meeting similar fates, as referenced in Clark, *The Death of East Prussia*.

12 Figures taken from the official RAF report on the bombing raid, Bomber Command Campaign Diary August 1944, entry from the UK National Archives, https://webarchive.nationalarchives.gov.uk/20070706054833/http://www.raf.mod.uk/bombercommand/aug44.html.

13 Ian Kershaw and Richard Evans are among many historians who believe atrocities were certainly committed, though inflated by the Nazi propaganda machine.

14 Stargardt, *The German War*, p.471.

15 Lehndorff, *Ostpreußisches Tagebuch*, p.10.

16 Beevor, *Berlin*, chapter 4.

17 Kershaw points out that, as late as 22 January, Admiral Dönitz agreed that dwindling coal reserves for the military should be given priority over refugees. While the navy managed to ferry 679,541 refugees from Baltic harbours to the west, many more could have been saved if its highest command hadn't given priority to military demands.

Chapter Ten: The Flight

1 Heinz Schön, *Flucht über die Ostsee: 1944/45* [*Flight over the Baltic: 1944/45*] (Motorbuch Verlag Stuttgart, 1995), p.78.

Chapter Twelve: Sins of the Fathers

1 Data according to the Museum of Danish Resistance. Some put this figure at 7,500.

Chapter Thirteen: Year Zero

1 The average daily intake in Britain was 2,800 calories for an adult: Christopher Knowles, 'The British Occupation of Germany 1945–49: A Study in Post-Conflict Reconstruction', *RUSI Journal*, 158 (6) (2013).

2 Ulrike Weckel, 'Disappointed Hopes for Spontaneous Mass Conversions: German Responses to Allied Atrocity Film Screenings 1945–46', Washington, DC: German Historical Institute (2012).

3 According to the 1946 census there were 171 women to every 100 men.

4 Antony Beevor, *Stalingrad*, Kindle edn (Penguin Books, 2007), chapter 25.

5 Beevor, *Berlin*, chapter 27.

6 Philipp Kuwert, Thomas Klauer, Svenja Eichhorn, Elena Grundke, Manuela Dudeck, Georg Schomerus and Harald Freyberger, 'Trauma and Current Posttraumatic Stress Symptoms in Elderly German Women Who Experienced Wartime Rapes in 1945', *The Journal of Nervous and Mental Disease*, 198 (6) (2010), 450–51.

7 Beevor, *Berlin*, chapter 27.

8 Ruth Schumacher was interviewed by NPR after she took part in a wider study carried out by German psychiatrists, led by Philipp Kuwert, in the early 2000s.

9 The historian Atina Grossmann, in 'A Question of Silence: The Rape of German Women by Occupation Soldiers', *West Germany Under Construction: Politics, Society and Culture in the Adenauer Era*, ed. Robert G. Moeller (University of Michigan Press, 1997), concludes that during the rebuilding, or what she calls the 're-masculinization' of post-war Germany, discussion of the rapes was repressed in order to build up the confidence of German male veterans. Grossmann notes that the fact that so many women had been raped was perceived as an injury to male pride, and not a direct violation of women's bodies, in order to rebuild traditional male roles.

Chapter Fourteen: False Friends

1 Vincent Bignon, 'Cigarette Money and Black-Market Prices during the 1948 German Miracle', economix.fr (2009).

Epilogue: The Past is Another Country

1 Data taken from Jews in East Prussia, a Berlin-based organisation dedicated to preserving Jewish culture in the region.
2 Thomas Nagel, 'Moral Luck', in Nagel, *Mortal Questions* (Cambridge University Press, 1979).

Alexievich, Svetlana, *The Unwomanly Face of War*, trans. Richard Pevear and Larissa Volokhonsky (Penguin Classics, 2017)

Beevor, Antony, *Berlin: The Downfall: 1945*, Kindle edn (Viking, 2007)

—, *Stalingrad* (Penguin Books, 2007)

Bielenberg, Christabel, *The Past is Myself* (Chatto & Windus, 1968)

Clark, Peter B., *The Death of East Prussia: War and Revenge in Germany's Easternmost Province*, Kindle edn (Andover Press, 2013)

Dönhoff, Marion, Gräfin, *Kindheit in Ostpreußen* (Verlagsgruppe Random House GmbH, 1998)

Egremont, Max, *Forgotten Land: Journeys Among the Ghosts of East Prussia* (Picador, 2012)

Evans, Richard, *The Coming of the Third Reich: How the Nazis Destroyed Democracy and Seized Power in Germany* (Penguin, 2012)

—, *The Third Reich in Power, 1933–1939: How the Nazis Won Over the Hearts and Minds of a Nation* (Penguin, 2012)

—, *The Third Reich at War: How the Nazis Led Germany from Conquest to Disaster* (Penguin, 2012)

Falk, Lucy, *Ich Blieb in Königsberg: Tagebuchblätter aus Dunklen Nachkriegssjahren* [I Stayed in Konigsberg: Diary Pages of Dark Postwar Years] (Verlag Gräfe und Unzer, 1965)

Friedlander, Henry, *The Origins of Nazi Genocide: From Euthanasia to the Final Solution* (University of North Carolina Press, 1995)

Grass, Günter, *Im Krebsgang* [*Crabwalk*] (Steidl, 2002)

Grossmann, Atina, 'A Question of Silence: The Rape of German Women by Occupation Soldiers', *West Germany Under Construction: Politics, Society and Culture in the Adenauer Era*, ed. Robert G. Moeller (University of Michigan Press, 1997)

Herzog, Rudolph, *Heil Hitler, das Schwein ist tot!: Lachen unter Hitler – Komik und Humor im Dritten Reich* [*Heil Hitler, the Pig is Dead!: Laughter under Hitler – Comedy and Humour in the Third Reich*], Kindle edn (Kiepenheuer & Witsch, 2018)

Kaplan, Marion A., *Between Dignity and Despair: Jewish Life in Nazi Germany* (Oxford University Press, 1998)

Kater, Michael, *Different Drummers: Jazz in the Culture of Nazi Germany* (Oxford University Press, 2003)

Kershaw, Ian, *The End: Germany 1944–45*, Kindle edn (Penguin, 2011)

Lehndorff, Hans, Graf, *Ostpreußisches Tagebuch: Aufzeichnungen eines Arztes aus den Jahren 1945–1947* [*East Prussian Diary: A Doctor's Observations of the Years 1945–1947*] (Dtv, 1967)

—, *Menschen, Pferde, weites Land* [*Men, Horses, Vast Land*] (Beck C. H., 2001)

Longerich, Peter, *'Davon haben wir nichts gewusst!' Die Deutschen und die Judenverfolgung 1933–1945* [*'We Didn't Know Anything About It!' The Germans and the Persecution of Jews 1933–1945*] (Siedler Verlag, 2006)

Nagel, Thomas, 'Moral Luck', in Nagel, *Mortal Questions* (Cambridge University Press, 1979)

Reck-Malleczewen, Friedrich, *Diary of a Man in Despair*, trans. Paul Rubens (Audiogrove Ltd, 1995)

Satjukow, Silke and Rainer Gries, *'Bankerte!': Besatzungskinder in Deutschland nach 1945* [*Bastards: Children of the Occupation in Germany after 1945*] (Campus Verlag GmbH, 2015)

Schön, Heinz, *Flucht über die Ostsee:1944/45* [*Flight over the Baltic: 1944/45*] (Motorbuch Verlag, 1995)

Stargardt, Nicholas, *The German War: A Nation Under Arms, 1939–45* (Vintage, 2016)

Wieck, Michael, *A Childhood Under Hitler and Stalin: Memoirs of a 'Certified Jew'*, trans. Penny Milbouer (University of Wisconsin Press, 2003)

Articles

Bignon, Vincent, 'Cigarette Money and Black-Market Prices during the 1948 German Miracle', economix.fr (2009)

Eaton, Nicole M., 'Exclave: Politics, Ideology, and Everyday Life in Königsberg–Kaliningrad, 1928–1948 (Doctoral dissertation, University of California, Berkeley, 2013)

Evans, Richard J., 'Coercion and Consent in Nazi Germany', Raleigh Lecture on History (2006)

Knowles, Christopher, 'The British Occupation of Germany 1945–49: A Study in Post-Conflict Reconstruction', *RUSI Journal*, 158 (6) (2013)

Kuwert, Philipp, Thomas Klauer, Svenja Eichhorn, Elena Grundke, Manuela Dudeck, Georg Schomerus, and Harald Freyberger, 'Trauma and Current Posttraumatic Stress Symptoms in Elderly German Women Who Experienced Wartime Rapes in 1945', *The Journal of Nervous and Mental Disease*, 198 (6) (2010), 450–51

Mann, Thomas, '*Was Wir Verlangen Müssen*', *Berliner Tageblatt*, 8 August 1932

Official RAF report on the bombing raid, Bomber Command Campaign Diary August 1944, entry from the UK National Archives: https:// webarchive.nationalarchives.gov.uk/20070706054833/http://www. raf.mod.uk/bombercommand/aug44.html

Weckel, Ulrike, 'Disappointed Hopes for Spontaneous Mass Conversions: German Responses to Allied Atrocity Film Screenings 1945– 46', Washington, DC: German Historical Institute (2012)

ACKNOWLEDGEMENTS

Before I thank the many people who helped and supported me in the writing of this book, I must first of all acknowledge the debt I owe my family, especially my late grandmother Inge, for telling me her story, as well as my mother Beatchy and my aunt Conny, for allowing me to delve into a sometimes unsettling past.

This book could not have been written without the support and advice of my friend and mentor Michael Holman, advocate of the *rungu* (or 'big stick') approach to manuscript completion. Some of the best lines in this book were thought up sitting together on the veranda in Jinchini or in his East London sitting room, sustained by feline company and cups of Kenyan tea.

To the Darnton family, most especially Nina, I owe a great debt, for their advice, encouragement and critical eye.

I would also like to thank the following people who each played a part in this book's existence: my agent, Felicity Bryan, for her invaluable suggestions and for taking a chance on me in the first place. My editor at Ebury, Clare Bullock, whose guidance and sensitivity made this manuscript the best it could be, helped by the narrative flair of Lindsey Schwoeri at Viking. Poppy Trowbridge, for hours of reading and for supporting me in taking the plunge to get this project started. The 'coven', Miranda Doyle, Dominique Green, Halina Watts and Eleanor Tattersfield, for their ever-useful ideas and for keeping me going throughout the process. Kirsten Lylloff, for being kind enough to share and explain her research on East Prussian refugees in Denmark. My partner Austin Tasker for humouring the mood swings that come with getting a book completed. David McClafferty, Mats Boesen and Mitzi de Margary, for keeping me company through far-flung corners of Europe and Russia.

Many other friends supported me by providing everything from good advice, random knowledge of military ranks and troop movements, to, simply, a sympathetic ear: Alex Woolfson, Tom Coghlan, Rob Hutton, Thomas Penny, Kitty Donaldson, Charles Emmerson, Lisa Levinson, Stephanie Kuku, to name but a few.

INDEX